In Tender Consideration

In Tender Consideration

Women, Families, and the Law in Abraham Lincoln's Illinois

EDITED BY
DANIEL W. STOWELL

UNIVERSITY OF ILLINOIS PRESS
URBANA AND CHICAGO

Library of Congress Cataloging-in-Publication Data
In tender consideration : women, families, and the law in
Abraham Lincoln's Illinois / edited by Daniel W. Stowell.
p.   cm.
Includes bibliographical references and index.
ISBN 0-252-02702-7 (alk. paper)
1. Women—Legal status, laws, etc.—Illinois—History.
I. Stowell, Daniel W.
KFI1291.W6I5   2002
346.77301'34—dc21   2001002746

For Miriam, Boni, Kevin, Kathy, Tammy, and Ron

Contents

Foreword

MICHAEL GROSSBERG

In Tender Consideration is a signal contribution to American legal and social history. The authors use the unique resources of the DVD version of the Lincoln Legal Papers, *The Law Practice of Abraham Lincoln: Complete Documentary Edition* (2000) to recover and analyze family legal experiences. They do so in a series of compelling essays exploring the intersection of law, gender, and childhood in antebellum Illinois while documenting the realities of legal practice and adjudication in the state during the era. This analytical combination makes the book at once a significant analysis of nineteenth-century families and the law and an illuminating primer on the analytical possibilities of archival collections.

The essays in this collection resurrect the full range of family woes that antebellum Americans took to the law. From divorce suits and filial inheritance claims to rape prosecutions and demands by wives for family property, the volume documents the fissures in families of the era. Focusing on the legal travails of women and children, the book not only chronicles such legal problems as household struggles over alienated affections, estate planning, and parental responsibility but presents them in a way that highlights their implications for our understanding of legal, family, women's, and social history in the era. Indeed, the primacy of property as an individual and household resource, and as a source of family conflict, runs like a fault line through all the chapters, as does the persistence of gender and age as defining issues in legal rules and practice. And both realities enable the authors to demonstrate the connections between the cases and various realms of historical experience.

Chapter after chapter also records the lure of legal resolutions to those ensnared in family problems. And the chapters document the accessibility of the legal process to all warring family members, including women and children. Significantly, because most cases presented in these pages began and ended in the lower courts, the essays document the role of trial courts as the primary resolvers of antebellum family disputes. Although litigation was the dominant family legal experience, the chapters include instructive analyses of appellate opinions, the major staple of U.S. legal history. However, instead of presenting these pronouncements simply as judicial interpretations of legal rules, the authors place them in context by explaining how the rulings were applied to the resolution of particular cases in trial courts and law offices. Equally notable, as the analytical focus shifts through the volume from one legal subject to another and from one courtroom to another, the authors suggest that paternalism and regionalism were foundational realities in the organization and experience of families and the law in antebellum Illinois. Through such assertions they make a compelling case for exploring the distinctive ideological and spatial realities of nineteenth-century American law more fully.

In addition to recounting family litigation in antebellum Illinois, the essays illuminate the practice of law in that time and place. Each chapter highlights the powerful role that lawyers played as they struggled to serve their clients by tackling heart-wrenching family problems as negotiators and advocates. The strategic role of lawyers in the social order becomes clear as the authors narrate particular contests about legal rules, evidence, jurisdiction, and the other variables of advice to clients, performance in the courtroom, and advocacy before the appellate courts. The chapters also reveal the problematic nature of winning family law cases because legal resolutions rarely healed the breaches in homes that had sent wives and husbands or fathers and daughters to the law in the first place. Instead, the legal stories in this book underscore the difficulties that lawyers experienced when they took on household conflicts. Thrust into the middle of disintegrating families, lawyers found these disputes to be some of the most personally troubling and emotionally draining cases they had to handle. The chapters in this book suggest why family law cases were—and are—so troublesome for lawyers and thus compel speculation about the experience of practicing particular forms of law then and now.

Finally, the pages of this volume revive one life in law—Abraham Lincoln's. Lincoln grappled with family law cases throughout his legal career. The authors document the breadth of his engagement with the family problems of antebellum Illinois women, children, and men. And they offer countless examples of the various roles he performed in trying to resolve their disputes. Lincoln represented wives seeking divorces, children fighting for their inheritance, women who claimed they were slandered, and many other clients. And he handled these cases at all levels of the Illinois legal system, from the trial courts to the state supreme court. Like other lawyers, Lincoln found the cases distressing, and the authors consistently suggest that they evoked in him a particular kind of paternalism toward women and children. Their arguments about Lincoln the family lawyer thus raise intriguing questions about the influence of his legal life on his subsequent political one. Equally significant, by identifying and analyzing Lincoln's family cases, the authors offer readers an unparalleled opportunity to conduct their own forays into the legal past by turning to the recently published Lincoln Legal Papers. Readers can look at the cases themselves and make their own judgments about their meaning. In this way, the volume demonstrates how both researchers and readers can use archival collections to explore the past.

In Tender Consideration demonstrates how much we can gain by using the legal conflicts of a particular time and place to analyze American history. It provides us with a new understanding of the legal experiences of antebellum families while prodding us to think about the legal and social world in which these household conflicts erupted. The essays are thus models for a legal history rooted in the localities and regions of the American Republic.

Acknowledgments

Many individuals contributed to the successful completion of this volume. Thank you to Michael Grossberg, William Novak, and Robert Lawless for insightful comments about earlier versions of these essays as papers at various conferences. Professor James Davis offered vital early encouragement to publish a collection of essays drawn from the work of the Lincoln Legal Papers.

Richard L. Wentworth at the University of Illinois Press quickly recognized the value of such a volume and patiently shepherded the book through revisions. Two anonymous reviewers challenged both our ideas and our prose, making both better and clearer. Professors Tim Huebner and Peter Bardaglio also read the entire manuscript and offered valuable suggestions to improve the essays. Thank you to all these fine scholars for their professionalism and encouragement.

Each essay relies heavily on the discoveries of the Lincoln Legal Papers. We acknowledge with gratitude all the members of the project's staff who accomplished so much over fifteen years and all the project's supporters who made this revolutionary documentary edition possible. Both the Lincoln Legal Papers and this book relied on the assistance of many archivists and librarians. We particularly want to thank Thomas Wood of the Illinois Regional Archives Depository at the University of Illinois at Springfield for making Sangamon County records accessible, and Mary Ann Pohl of the Illinois State Historical Library for cheerfully handling numerous interlibrary loan requests.

Finally, we must express our appreciation for the support and sacrifices of our spouses, to whom this volume is dedicated, and of our children—Samuel, Joseph, Rachel, and Benjamin Stowell; Katherine, Anne, and Lauren Suttles; and Savannah and Mackenzie McDermott.

In Tender Consideration

Introduction

DANIEL W. STOWELL

For twenty-five years, from 1836 to 1861, Abraham Lincoln practiced law in the local and county circuit courts of central Illinois, in the Illinois Supreme Court, in the federal courts within Illinois, and on a few occasions in the U.S. Supreme Court. He and his three successive partners—John Todd Stuart, Stephen T. Logan, and William H. Herndon—handled more than five thousand cases during the quarter century that Lincoln practiced law. Many were simple debt collections and divisions of land, while others involved complex legal and constitutional issues. For most of his adult life Lincoln followed the rhythms set by court terms—a tour of the Eighth Judicial Circuit for three months in the spring, beginning in his home county of Sangamon and extending north and east to the Indiana border and swinging south and west to return to Sangamon; another session of the Sangamon County Circuit Court in the summer; a summer session of the federal court; another tour of the Eighth Judicial Circuit for ten to twelve weeks in the autumn; and a session of the Illinois Supreme Court back in Springfield, beginning in December and lasting into the new year. Between the sessions of various courts Lincoln represented clients in inferior courts in Sangamon County and handled various other legal matters, from drawing up deeds and wills to applying for petitions and providing legal opinions.

Every two or four years political campaigns vied with the court schedule for the loyal Whig's attention and time. The practice of law allowed Lincoln to hone his rhetorical and analytical skills, communicate with a wide range of Illinois citizens, gain exposure to the larger world of developing corporations and professions, cultivate valuable political contacts, and earn a comfortable income.

Between 1985 and 1999 the staff of the Lincoln Legal Papers meticulously collected and assembled all surviving documents related to Lincoln's career as a lawyer. The result is an unprecedented collection of more than ninety-six thousand documents, including pleading documents, court orders, judges' opinions, dockets, letters, evidence, depositions, and newspaper reports. These documents come from more than fifty-one hundred cases and nearly five hundred nonlitigation matters that Abraham Lincoln and his partners handled. The staff of the Lincoln Legal Papers extracted from the documents more than two million facts about the cases, including participants, dates, subjects, venues, legal actions, authors, signers, and document types. The staff entered each piece of information into a relational database and scanned each document. In February 2000 the University of Illinois Press published *The Law Practice of Abraham Lincoln: Complete Documentary Edition* on three DVD-ROM discs.[1] This revolutionary edition makes the documents accessible through a custom-designed user interface. Users can search for documents or cases using one or several of more than a dozen indexes and can view facsimile images of each document.

The rich documentation from Lincoln's legal career offers insights both into Lincoln's own life and into many aspects of life in nineteenth-century America. This documentary evidence is an invaluable resource for social historians, legal historians, and students of Abraham Lincoln's life. The essays in this volume, each written by an experienced member of the Lincoln Legal Papers' editorial staff, draw principally upon this previously inaccessible collection of primary source material. Here are cases, issues, and people drawn from Lincoln's daily life as an attorney in central Illinois.

The two central themes of this collection of essays are the status of women and children before the courts of antebellum Illinois and the closely related issue of the experiences of women and children before those courts. These concerns shed additional light on the social history questions of how antebellum Americans viewed women and children and what their lives were like. In this manner legal history can illuminate women's history, family history, and social history. The collection of materials developed by the Lincoln Legal Papers offers extensive documentary evidence on a variety of issues. When properly interpreted, these cases and other materials will open new vistas on many questions central to a better understanding of antebellum America.

Most cases involving women and children originated and concluded in the circuit courts and other inferior courts. Few women and children—indeed, few litigants—appealed their cases to the state supreme court. Of the fifty-one hundred cases in Lincoln's legal practice, only about four hundred (8 percent) are Illinois Supreme Court cases—the typical resource that legal historians have used.[2] In contrast, these essays draw heavily on the circuit court cases that comprised the vast majority of Lincoln's legal practice and of legal activity in general. In some cases lower courts even ignored earlier decisions of the state supreme court and decided cases according to their own local sense of justice. Even when examining Illinois Supreme Court cases, the analyses that follow rely on the entire case files from both the supreme court and the lower courts in which the cases originated, rather than simply the printed opinions that have supported so much legal history. By doing so, these historians have learned much about the experiences, rights, disabilities, and fates of women, children, and families before the courts of antebellum Illinois.

Circuit courts were the primary forums for civil and criminal disputes in nineteenth-century Illinois. Each county in the state had one circuit court, which usually met two times each year—once in the spring and again in the fall—at the courthouse in the county seat. A few larger counties had a third term in the summer if necessary. Court sessions lasted from three or four days to two weeks, depending on the size of the county and the number of cases on the docket. A circuit court judge convened court in each of several contiguous counties seriatim, as he, the state's attorney, and a handful of other attorneys traveled from county seat to county seat. The Eighth Judicial Circuit, which Lincoln traveled, stretched eastward from his home county of Sangamon in the center of the state to the Indiana border. Before 1848 the circuit court judge was often also a justice of the Illinois Supreme Court; the state's 1848 constitution provided for elected circuit court judges who did not sit on the state's highest tribunal. Circuit courts tried criminal, common law, and chancery (or equity) cases. Juries usually decided criminal cases, but the judge or a jury might decide cases in the common law and chancery divisions. The court drew jury members from the surrounding community, and in some cases a single jury sat for the entire term and decided a variety of cases. The records these courts have left behind offer us a broad window into antebellum Illinois society.

For more than twenty years students of women's history have recognized the value of legal documents for understanding women's lives in the past. In 1979 Joan Hoff Wilson called attention to the "hidden riches" in county court records for the study of women's societal and legal status. However, such hidden riches abounded in legal records only "for those historians who want to take the time to do such painstaking research and to develop legal and quantitative skills for analyzing the riches." Perhaps because of these challenges, much of the new legal history of the 1970s "ignored women," and most women's history "dealt with law tangentially at best." By the mid-1980s, however, Norma Basch could note that "a considerable amount of scholarship on women and the law has emerged." Basch called for scholars to abandon the "women-as-victim theme" and to integrate the insights of legal history and women's history. Like many recent studies of women's legal history, several of the essays that follow have women's experiences with the law as their interpretive focus.[3]

Both family history and legal history have burgeoned as areas of historical inquiry, but Michael Grossberg in the mid-1980s expressed concern that these fields "have developed in isolation from each other." The result, Grossberg lamented, was that "a history of the law of the family does not exist." Too often, legal historians "have tended to discount the study and appreciation of social values and cultural practices that were not clearly commercial in nature." While some scholars have since addressed this interdisciplinary gap, much remains to be done. With their attention to "the law of domestic relations," the authors of the essays here offer perspectives that address the interests of both family and legal historians.[4]

In addition to providing new views of the legal history of women and families, these essays address an important regional gap in the historical literature. Many scholars have examined the lives of women in the New England and mid-Atlantic states during the colonial period and the nineteenth century; fewer studies, though still a substantial number, explore the history of southern women, both black and white. In marked contrast to the historical attention devoted to women and families in these regions, the West and especially the Midwest have long been neglected. Glenda Riley's pioneering work on the "female frontier" suggests that women experienced frontier conditions differently than did men and that married women on many frontiers shared a "domestic focus" on child care and home production regardless of the prevailing economic system of the region. While their husbands' lives varied considerably from region to region on the frontier, Riley argues, women's lives had "a high degree of similarity from one frontier to another." Therefore, "frontierswomen's responsibilities, life styles, and sensibilities were shaped more by gender considerations than by region."[5]

Some students of the trans-Mississippi West insist that women's experiences varied significantly in different portions of the West. A collection of essays that explored the lives of women settlers on the mining and ranching frontiers found considerable "diversity of the female pioneer experience" and simultaneously discovered "themes common to all western frontier women." While women settlers held a similar status and shared common hardships on various frontiers, they "necessarily developed their own specific methods of coping and adapting."[6]

Because of the focus on New England and the Atlantic seaboard, few studies in legal history have focused on the influence of regionalism, with some notable exceptions. James W. Ely Jr. and David J. Bodenhamer have chided scholars for their failure to explore regional differences in attitudes toward law or in legal practice. They challenge those historians who through a heavy emphasis on Wisconsin or New England (especially Massachusetts) have overemphasized "the degree of uniformity present in American law during the late eighteenth and nineteenth centuries." Ely and Bodenhamer argue that from the colonial era through the nineteenth century, law was "essentially local in focus and effect," although several developments paved the way for national legal norms by the end of the nineteenth century.[7] In women's history Wendy Hamand Venet and Lucy Eldersveld Murphy have challenged historians to "reconsider the Midwest as an area with particular regional experiences, to integrate women more fully into midwestern history, and to develop more thoroughly concepts of the midwestern 'female experience.'" To do so would require rethinking old questions and asking new ones.[8]

This collection of essays responds in part to these calls for fresh regional perspectives on the law. By providing a wealth of details for a prominent midwestern state, it both addresses a lacuna in the scholarship and supplies material for interregional comparison. It is an important building block in the study of regional variations in the experiences of women and families and in laws relating to women and children.[9] This volume details women's legal experiences on a part of Riley's "female frontier."

Some historians have described the attitude of nineteenth-century courts toward women as judicial patriarchy.[10] Other scholars view U.S. society in the late eighteenth and early nineteenth centuries as adopting a more compassionate paternalistic attitude toward women and children.[11] Gerda Lerner defines patriarchy as "the manifestation and institutionalization of male dominance over women and children in the family and the extension of male dominance over women in society in general." Although the antebellum Illinois legal system had features that merit the term *patriarchal,* such as the ideal of female sexual purity, *paternalism* better defines the attitudes of Illinois jurists. Lerner defines *paternalism* as "the relationship of a dominant group, considered superior, to a subordinate group, considered inferior, in which the dominance is mitigated by mutual obligations and reciprocal rights." It is this paternalistic variant of patriarchy that best characterizes how antebellum Illinois legislators and judges viewed women.[12]

The mitigation of dominance by mutual obligations and reciprocal rights is central to understanding this distinction. No one would argue that the courts treated women in Illinois or elsewhere in antebellum America as the equals of men. Paternalism does not suggest equality. In fact, it implies the opposite. However, to argue that all of nineteenth-century America, at all times and places, was unrelievedly patriarchal renders both terms useless for this period and obscures rather than illuminates the lived historical experience of women and children in a variety of contexts. Were women in Illinois disadvantaged relative to men? Yes. Were women in Illinois disadvantaged relative to women in other, particularly eastern, states? The essays in this volume suggest that perhaps they were not. In that sense these essays contribute to a larger reconsideration of both absolute male dominance and the doctrine of separate spheres. Scholars are beginning to question whether eighteenth- and nineteenth-century American men held complete dominance over women either in supposed male arenas like politics and the law or in family life.[13]

The paternalistic attitudes of Illinois courts reflect a "jurisprudence of the heart" in litigation involving women similar to that which Peter Karsten finds in antebellum economic litigation: decisions based on Judeo-Christian motives that served the needs of the poor and powerless, including women and children. Judges and legislators, Karsten argues, "were not cut off from the egalitarian reform impulses, the child-centered culture, or the 'christian civilization' around them." Just as Karsten found judges who mitigated the harshest aspects of the common law as it applied to workers and other less powerful elements in society, so the authors of this volume found Illinois legislators and jurists who responded to the social dilemmas of women and children by seeking to protect their interests.[14]

Karsten also finds regional variations in the application of a "jurisprudence of the heart." Such decisions were strongest in the Midwest and the West, where elected judges felt less bound by precedent and were more responsive to the religious and humanitarian impulses of antebellum America. Similarly, Norma Basch finds that "regional variations in divorce law were more pronounced on an east-west axis than a north-south one." Legislatures and courts in "western" states like Illinois and Indiana were more willing to grant divorces than were those bodies in older eastern states.[15]

· · ·

Like *The Law Practice of Abraham Lincoln,* this volume illuminates an important context of Abraham Lincoln's life—that of his quarter-century legal career. Much as a Renaissance artist might enhance the portrait of an individual, painted by another, by painting in the background scenes from the subject's life, these authors have filled in vital details of Lincoln's environment. Far from minor or insignificant, such contextual scholarship yields a bolder, more striking portrait of Lincoln himself. People, places, and ideas from Lincoln's Illinois emerge sharper and clearer from these essays. By examining the social conflicts and legal issues with which Lincoln grappled on a daily basis, readers gain a better understanding of what his life and the lives of those around him were like in central Illinois in the midnineteenth century.

Abraham Lincoln, forty-nine, Beardstown, Illinois, May 7, 1858. Courtesy of the Illinois State Historical Library, Springfield.

By placing Lincoln more clearly within the context of the legal culture in which he lived, these essays help readers understand him more fully. After his election to the presidency but before he assumed office, Abraham Lincoln quoted a biblical proverb to explain his understanding of the interrelationship of the principles of the Declaration of Independence and those of the

Constitution and the Union. The proverb declares, "A word fitly spoken is like apples of gold in pictures of silver." For Lincoln the Declaration was the "apple of gold," whereas the Union and the Constitution were the "picture of silver, subsequently framed around it." The picture was designed "not to conceal, or destroy the apple; but to adorn, and preserve it." Lincoln urged his countrymen to act so that "neither picture, or apple shall ever be blurred, or bruised or broken." To act thus, Lincoln continued, "we must study."[16] These studies of the picture of silver that framed Lincoln's life illuminate his world.

. . .

The essays that follow are arranged in three parts. In the first part Dennis E. Suttles and I offer overviews of the attitudes of courts toward children and women, respectively, and their particular experiences within the court system. I show that although married women theoretically had no legal personality, in Illinois, as elsewhere, they often participated in the legal process. Single and widowed women also appeared in courts to seek justice or to defend their interests.[17] Nearly one-fifth of Lincoln's cases involved women as litigants. Hundreds more women were involved in trials as witnesses and deponents, while male judges and jurors listened to their testimony. Other women entered the courtrooms of central Illinois as spectators, thus participating in one of the local community's primary educational, social, and entertainment opportunities. I also posit that the attitudes of legislators and judges can be characterized as paternal rather than patriarchal. Simultaneously subordinating women and providing safeguards for their legal interests, many of these men showed genuine concern (within their time and place) for deserted wives, destitute widows, jilted brides with illegitimate children, and slandered women.

Suttles explores how courts viewed children and the types of cases that brought children or their interests before Illinois courts. While children appeared only rarely in antebellum courtrooms, sometimes to offer testimony, their interests were represented in a variety of cases, especially those involving inheritance and custody. Across the nineteenth century, Suttles asserts, U.S. society began to view children as individuals who required an investment of nurturing and education rather than being regarded solely as economic assets and laborers within the household. Courts responded to the changing status of children by asserting, through the English common law doctrine of *parens patriae*, the parental authority of the state to protect the interests of children. Faced with difficult choices in custody and guardianship cases, Illinois courts likewise applied the "tender years" and "best-interests-of-the-child" doctrines to fulfill their roles as social guardians. Upholding parents' rights to the property and labor of their children while intervening to appoint guardians when children's interests were vulnerable, antebellum Illinois courts exerted paternal care over the state's children as a public trust.

In the second part of the volume Stacy Pratt McDermott, John A. Lupton, and Christopher A. Schnell offer in-depth analyses of specific areas of the law that particularly concerned women and children. McDermott focuses attention on divorce and what it meant for the hundreds of Illinois women who obtained divorces in this period. McDermott finds that divorce was "a viable legal option" for women in antebellum America and that courts exhibited a paternalistic rather than patriarchal attitude toward women seeking to end their marriages. Most women who filed for a divorce in Illinois obtained one. They also often obtained custody of their children, especially their daughters, and they rarely had to pay the court costs. Reflecting the economic realities of the nineteenth century, husbands, win or lose, as plaintiffs or as defendants, paid the court costs. Antebellum Illinois laws were relatively liberal among the states in the number of grounds that the courts accepted for a divorce, although the Illinois Supreme Court allowed the circuit courts little latitude in expanding the definition of permissible grounds. Courts also accommodated women seeking a divorce by allowing them to sue as paupers or by providing them with temporary alimony *pendente lite* (pending litigation) from their husbands, while the women pursued a legal dissolution of their marriage.

While explaining the avenues for divorce that were open to women, McDermott also highlights the economic and social challenges divorced women faced. Most chose to remarry, perhaps as much out of economic necessity as for other reasons. Despite these difficulties, Illinois courts, unlike contemporary courts in some other states, opened the divorce process to women and generally lent a sympathetic ear to their petitions for divorce.

Lupton surveys inheritance laws and the inheritance process in antebellum Illinois. Although based on English inheritance laws, U.S. law abolished primogeniture for the benefit of both younger sons and daughters. In land-rich antebellum Illinois daughters inherited equal portions with their brothers, and the laws provided widows with important economic protections. Lupton finds that women and children were active participants in inheritance cases in the courts. Widows frequently administered their husbands' estates, and they claimed their dower rights in estate property. Children also had particular interests in the orderly and equitable transfer of land from one generation to the next. They challenged inequitable wills, and court-appointed guardians protected the interests of minor heirs in the division of estates. Although Lupton concludes that courts were quite reluctant to overturn wills or challenge established patterns of succession, they were sympathetic to the interests of all involved. Demanding strict adherence to a widow's dower rights and her right to administer the estate, the notification of all interested heirs, and the protection of children's interests by a guardian, courts oversaw every detail of the inheritance process. In doing so, they contributed to the social and economic security of local communities and their residents.

Schnell examines the property rights of married women and widows in antebellum Illinois. Focusing on dower rights and women's role as managers of property that they often did not own, Schnell finds that widows were able to carve out an economic niche for themselves and their dependent children by using the legal provisions for dower. His examination of women's wills in Sangamon County offers revealing glimpses of widows' material culture and their role as producers in the expanding frontier market economy. Women's property rights changed most dramatically in 1861, when the Illinois legislature provided the legal avenue for married women to own their own property separate from their husbands.

In the third part of the book Stacy Pratt McDermott, Susan Krause, and I examine three fascinating individual cases that illuminate larger themes of the interaction of women and children with the legal system. McDermott carefully chronicles one couple's persistent pursuit of the wife's inheritance, taken from her by her stepfather. Although she possessed no legal standing, first as a minor and then as a married woman, Nancy Robinson Dorman repeatedly pressed her legal and equitable claim to the land she should have inherited from her father. The case drew on a wide array of legal talent, involved complicated legal maneuvers in several different courts, and went three times to the Illinois Supreme Court before it reached a resolution near the time of Nancy Dorman's death. This engaging story of one woman's encounter with the courts simultaneously demonstrates both the disabilities that women and children faced in antebellum law and the paternal care with which attorneys like Samuel Marshall and Abraham Lincoln and courts like the Illinois Supreme Court approached such issues.

Krause relates the horrible tale of the rape of a seven-year-old girl and the disturbing aftermath of the crime. Outraged, the citizens of Pekin, Illinois, quickly seized Thomas Delny, an Irish miner and a recent immigrant to the United States, and nearly lynched him before he could stand trial. Anti-immigrant sentiment, class bias, anti-Catholicism, community paternalism, sexual fears, and temperance sentiment converged on the defendant as he stood trial without an attorney on the charge of raping the young girl. Krause places Delny's trial in these multiple contexts while also exploring the issue of rape trials generally in antebellum Illinois. This case also presents an opportunity to examine executive clemency—Delny received a pardon from the governor after serving only six years of his eighteen-year sentence. Although rare in antebellum Illinois, rape trials reveal much about the differing attitudes of courts toward adult and child victims of rape. Prosecuting attorneys, judges, and juries tended to view women's charges of rape with skepticism and often initiated sharp inquiries into the victim's reputation, seeking evidence of unchaste behavior. However, when the victim was a child, consent was not an issue, and the courts or sometimes the communities dispensed swift justice to avenge the wronged girl.

Although antebellum Illinois courts provided married women with legal access to divorce, these same courts also upheld an ideal of female sexual purity against fornicators, adulterers, and those who would slander others with such charges. When a woman had committed adultery, she could not expect a hospitable reception in the courts of the day. These attitudes are precisely what make *Wren v. Moss et al.* such an intriguing case. I provide a detailed account of the process by which a jury granted Aquilla Wren a divorce from his adulterous wife, Clarissa Wren. Undaunted, she insisted on obtaining an alimony payment from him, and although he died during the course of the litigation, the Illinois Supreme Court effectively reversed the lower court's decision. By judicial decree the divorced adulteress became once again a wife (widow) with her dower rights restored.

• • •

The phrase "in tender consideration" that begins the formulaic conclusion to a bill of complaint in an equity case captures the paternalistic attitude of courts toward women and children. Male legislators, judges, and jurors considered women and children inferior, dependent, and in need of protection, and they created and maintained a legal edifice that reflected these cultural attitudes. Such a perspective was far from either modern egalitarianism or historically stereotypical patriarchy.

Notes

1. Martha L. Benner and Cullom Davis et al., eds., *The Law Practice of Abraham Lincoln: Complete Documentary Edition* (DVD; Urbana: University of Illinois Press, 2000), hereafter cited as *LPAL*.

2. For the limitations of appellate decisions as historical sources, see G. Edward White, "The Appellate Opinion as Historical Source Material," *Journal of Interdisciplinary History* 1 (1971): 491–509. Of 411 Illinois Supreme Court cases in Lincoln's practice, 67 (16 percent) included female litigants and 47 (11 percent) involved children.

3. Joan Hoff Wilson, "Hidden Riches: Legal Records and Women, 1750–1825," in *Woman's Being, Woman's Place: Female Identity and Vocation in American History*, ed. Mary

Kelley (Boston: G. K. Hall, 1979), 8, 19; Norma Basch, "The Emerging Legal History of Women in the United States: Property, Divorce, and the Constitution," *Signs: Journal of Women in Culture and Society* 12 (Autumn 1986): 98, 116.

4. Michael Grossberg, "Crossing Boundaries: Nineteenth-Century Domestic Relations Law and the Merger of Family and Legal History," *American Bar Foundation Research Journal* (Fall 1985): 799, 801.

5. Glenda Riley, foreword to *Midwestern Women: Work, Community, and Leadership at the Crossroads*, ed. Lucy Eldersveld Murphy and Wendy Hamand Venet (Bloomington: Indiana University Press, 1997), x; Glenda Riley, "The 'Female Frontier' in Early Illinois," *Mid-America* 67 (April–July 1985): 71–72; Glenda Riley, *The Female Frontier: A Comparative View of Women on the Prairie and the Plains* (Lawrence: University Press of Kansas, 1988), 2. See also Julie Roy Jeffrey, *Frontier Women: "Civilizing" the West? 1840–1880*, rev. ed. (New York: Hill and Wang, 1998).

6. Ruth P. Moynihan, Susan Armitage, and Christiane Fischer Dichamp, eds., *So Much to Be Done: Women Settlers on the Mining and Ranching Frontier* (Lincoln: University of Nebraska Press, 1990), xi. See also Susan Armitage and Elizabeth Jameson, eds., *The Women's West* (Norman: University of Oklahoma Press, 1987); Sandra Myres, *Westering Women and the Frontier Experience, 1800–1915* (Albuquerque: University of New Mexico Press, 1982).

7. James W. Ely Jr. and David J. Bodenhamer, "Regionalism and American Legal History: The Southern Experience," *Vanderbilt Law Review* 29 (1986): 539–40, 545–47, quotations are on 545. For an exception to this trend see Marylynn Salmon, *Women and the Law of Property in Early America* (Chapel Hill: University of North Carolina Press, 1986).

8. Wendy Hamand Venet and Lucy Eldersveld Murphy, "Introduction: The Strange Career of Madame Dubuque and Midwestern Women's History," in *Midwestern Women, 2.*

9. See Riley's call for scholars to "reconstitute and evaluate the history of women in each of the regions" (Foreword, xi).

10. Michael Grossberg, "Who Gets the Child? Custody, Guardianship, and the Rise of a Judicial Patriarchy in Nineteenth-Century America," *Feminist Studies* 9 (Summer 1983): 236–38.

John Mack Faragher views antebellum Illinois as a patriarchal society of "male domination" and "female exploitation." Although women in the antebellum Midwest "did not mount much sustained criticism, nor much evident resistance to male rule . . . within the structures of patriarchy women created a strong place for themselves and demanded that these places be preserved if not acknowledged" ("History from the Inside-Out: Writing the History of Women in Rural America," *American Quarterly* 33 [Winter 1981]: 550–51, quotation on 555). See also John Mack Faragher, *Sugar Creek: Life on the Illinois Prairie* (New Haven, Conn.: Yale University Press, 1986), 115–18.

Grossberg asserts that "as the major arbiters of nineteenth-century family governance, judges took the lead in framing and applying the growing body of American domestic relations law. Family law became their patriarchal domain." He also insists that "patriarchy best explains the way judges themselves viewed their role in domestic relations law" (*Governing the Hearth: Law and the Family in Nineteenth-Century America* [Chapel Hill: University of North Carolina Press, 1985], 290–91). Judges did take the lead in applying domestic relations laws, but their vision was paternalistic rather than patriarchal.

11. Rhys Isaac, *The Transformation of Virginia, 1740–1790* (Chapel Hill: University of North Carolina Press, 1982), 309, 320; Elizabeth Fox-Genovese, *Within the Plantation*

Household: Black and White Women of the Old South (Chapel Hill: University of North Carolina Press, 1988), 63–64, 132. Like this volume, Peter W. Bardaglio's examination of family law in the nineteenth-century South adopts Gerda Lerner's definitions of patriarchy and paternalism. Bardaglio finds that "state paternalism," rather than judicial patriarchy, characterized the legal system of the southern states. Although slavery hindered the development of state paternalism in the South during the 1840s and 1850s, it did begin to emerge in this period. Largely free of the influence of slavery, such judicial paternalism could emerge in Illinois earlier and more rapidly. See Bardaglio, *Reconstructing the Household: Families, Sex, and the Law in the Nineteenth-Century South* (Chapel Hill: University of North Carolina Press, 1995), 3–36, 241–42 n. 70.

12. In an absolute patriarchy, such as ancient Roman society, a male head of household could kill his wife, children, or slaves at will. Clearly, this strict definition did not apply to American society at any time. However, Lerner rejects this "narrow meaning" of the term as "troublesome because it distorts historical reality" (*The Creation of Patriarchy* [New York: Oxford University Press, 1986], 238–39). See also Andrew J. King, "Constructing Gender: Sexual Slander in Nineteenth-Century America," *Law and History Review* 13 (Spring 1995): 65–66.

13. Laura McCall and Donald Yacovone, eds., *A Shared Experience: Men, Women, and the History of Gender* (New York: New York University Press, 1998), 2–8, 141–75.

In his nuanced reevaluation of women and litigation in Elizabethan England, Tim Stretton finds that on average, one-third of the cases before the Court of Requests involved a female plaintiff or defendant. "Women went to law in England, not in their hundreds, but in their thousands," and produced "a steady stream of women participating in civil litigation in a variety of different courts" (*Women Waging Law in Elizabethan England* [Cambridge: Cambridge University Press, 1998], 7–8, quotations on 42).

14. Peter Karsten, *Heart versus Head: Judge-Made Law in Nineteenth-Century America* (Chapel Hill: University of North Carolina Press, 1997), 4–6, quotation on 5.

15. Ibid., 305–18; Norma Basch, *Framing American Divorce: From the Revolutionary Generation to the Victorians* (Berkeley: University of California Press, 1999), 9–10; Norma Basch, "Relief in the Premises: Divorce as a Woman's Remedy in New York and Indiana, 1815–1870," *Law and History Review* 8 (Spring 1990): 1–24; Hendrik Hartog, *Man and Wife in America: A History* (Cambridge, Mass.: Harvard University Press, 2000). In *Heart versus Head* Karsten finds Illinois the most innovative of midwestern states, and nearly all midwestern states more innovative than older, eastern states.

16. Roy P. Basler, ed., *The Collected Works of Abraham Lincoln*, 8 vols. (New Brunswick, N.J.: Rutgers University Press, 1953), 4:169. The scriptural reference is to Proverbs 25:11.

17. This finding conforms to patterns present in other times and places in eighteenth- and nineteenth-century America. See Cornelia Hughes Dayton, *Women before the Bar: Gender, Law, and Society in Connecticut, 1639–1789* (Chapel Hill: University of North Carolina Press, 1995); Deborah A. Rosen, *Courts and Commerce: Gender, Law, and the Market Economy in Colonial New York* (Columbus: Ohio State University Press, 1997), 96–100.

PART 1

Considering Gender and Age in the Courts

1

Femes *Un*Covert: *Women's Encounters with the Law*

DANIEL W. STOWELL

Tabitha Ann Edwards sued Maria Patterson for slandering her by spreading malicious gossip. Nancy Jane Dunn sued Albert Carle for breaking his promise to marry her and for fathering her illegitimate child. Caroline Beerup petitioned for a divorce from her husband, Stephen Beerup. The county sheriff brought Isabella Hill before the court for disturbing the peace. After the death of her husband, Sarah Lucas petitioned the court for her dower. At the same time, Sarah Lucas's four oldest daughters sued the other family members to break their father's will. Another widow, Sarah Carrico, guided the administration of her husband's estate through the courts after he died without a will. Each of these women had encounters with the law in central Illinois during the midnineteenth century. Initiating lawsuits or responding to those initiated by others, these women took an active role in the antebellum Illinois legal system.

Mirroring Illinois society as a whole, the legal system permitted, and in some cases required, participation by women. Thousands of women appeared in Illinois courts—as litigants, criminal defendants, deponents, and spectators—in a wide variety of cases. Thousands more were litigants or deponents in cases in which they did not personally appear in the courtroom. Despite their absence from the courtroom, their interests and their words (through written depositions) did enter directly into the "male sphere" of law. From debt to divorce, from adultery to slander, cases with women as plaintiffs, defendants, or both appeared regularly on antebellum docket books. Courts also turned to women to provide testimony in a similarly broad array of cases. Male judges and male juries sometimes accorded women's words equal or greater weight than men's in written or oral testimony. Women also entered the "male domain" of courthouses to observe, to learn from— and sometimes to comment upon—the proceedings. Furthermore, male legislators provided special protections and provisions for women and their interests, and male court officials applied and enforced them.

Like other states, Illinois initially adopted English common law rules regarding women. The very first law passed by the First General Assembly of Illinois in 1819 declared that "the common law of England . . . of a general nature . . . shall be the rule of decision, and shall be considered as of full force, until repealed by legislative authority." In theory, single women older than eighteen and widowed women, known as *femes sole* (women alone), had the same legal standing before the courts as did men—they could sue and be sued, they could enter into contracts, and they could dispose of their property as they saw fit. However, married women—and most antebellum Illinois women were married—could take none of these actions without the consent and cooperation of their husbands. In his widely influential commentaries on the English common law, William Blackstone wrote in 1765, "The very being or legal existence of the woman is suspended during the marriage, or at least is incorporated and consolidated into that of the husband: under whose wing, protection, and *cover,* she performs every thing."[1] In this condition, called coverture, the law referred to the woman as a *feme covert.* However, coverture was never as complete as this statement implies, as a variety of cases makes clear.[2]

Walking, riding horses, or riding in wagons, each traveled from several yards to many miles to the county courthouse to receive justice. Each county held at least two terms of its circuit court each year, one in the spring and another in the fall. More populous counties added a third—summer—term during the 1850s. Terms typically lasted from three days to a week, and a court would open, continue, or close dozens of cases from all areas of law during a term. The court dispensed with some cases in one term, while others lasted for several terms and a few went on for years. While awaiting the trial of their case, men and women often sat in the courtroom and listened to other cases or gathered outside to swap news, opinions, and gossip.

In 1846 Sangamon County, Illinois, constructed a new two-story brick courthouse in Springfield, the county seat and state capital. The new building reflected the Greek Revival style of architecture with pilasters on the sides and a portico in front supported by six ionic columns. In this temple of justice officials conducted the affairs of the county and held terms of court. The courtroom occupied most of the second story and was approximately forty feet wide and fifty feet long, with a twenty-foot ceiling. At the western end of the courtroom were the judge's bench and the bar, which occupied about a third of the room. A wooden railing separated this area from the rest of the room. Within the bar were plain pine desks and common wooden chairs.

Outside the bar the room had long pine benches with backs. Rows of windows along the northern and southern walls provided air in the summer and light. A wood stove near the center of the room provided heat in the winter. It was in this room that Caroline Beerup sought a divorce from her husband in 1853 and Isabella Hill faced the criminal charges against her a year later.[3]

Other counties in central Illinois also built two-story brick or wooden courthouses in the 1830s and 1840s; many resembled Sangamon County's earlier courthouse, built in 1831. "First in both importance and influence" among a number of new buildings constructed after what was known ever after as "the deep snow" in the spring of 1831, Sangamon County's then new two-story brick courthouse boasted a hip roof with a cupola. Located in the center of the town square, it was "the most pretentious building in town." Virtually every county courthouse was located in the center of the town that served as the county seat, which was itself often near the geographical center of the county. Both their (relative) structural impressiveness and their central physical setting demonstrated the practical and symbolic importance to antebellum life of courthouses and the activities that occurred within them.[4]

Women held no positions of formal authority in antebellum Illinois courtrooms. The first woman to practice law in Illinois was Alta M. Hulett, who was admitted to the Illinois bar on her nineteenth birthday in 1873. The first woman elected as a justice of the peace was Amelia Hobbs in Jersey County in 1871. Although elected, she was not able to serve in that office under state law. A woman did not serve as an Illinois judge until 1923, when Mary Bartelme was elected to that office in Cook County. Bartelme served as judge of the juvenile court for ten years. Although Illinois women acquired limited voting rights in 1913, they could not serve on juries until 1939.[5]

Despite their exclusion from positions of authority, women made use of Illinois courtrooms in the quarter century before the Civil War, which suggests that the metaphor of separate gendered spheres of life requires some reevaluation.[6] Viewing women's domain, or "sphere," as the private world of home and family and men's as the public world of business, politics, and law, one might consider Illinois courts during the period that Abraham Lincoln practiced law to be exclusively male affairs. After studying women's lives during the Revolutionary period, Linda Kerber concluded that "the courtroom remained a male domain. . . . Women were present in the courtroom only as plaintiffs, defendants, or witnesses—as recipients, rather than dispensers, of justice." Although Kerber accurately portrays women's functional role in both the Revolutionary and the antebellum eras, these structural limitations tell only part of the story. In his study of eighteenth-century Pennsylvania, for example, G. S. Rowe concludes that although they were barred from participation as judges, lawyers, or jurors, "women played bold and visible roles" in the "legal apparatus" and participated fully in the "courtroom culture."[7]

How, then, should one understand women's encounters with the law in antebellum Illinois? Although excluded from official roles within the legal system, women nonetheless appeared frequently in courtrooms, and their interests appeared even more frequently. What reception could single, married, and widowed women expect when they appeared before nineteenth-century Illinois tribunals? An examination of hundreds of cases involving female litigants, supreme court decisions involving women's interests, and the statutes of the state suggests that legislators and courts treated women in a paternalistic fashion.

Legislative and judicial paternalists had three primary goals in legislation and litigation regarding women. First, they provided and liberally enforced a mechanism through which women (and men) could end a marriage to an abusive or absent spouse. Second, they worked to maintain an ideal of female sexual purity by punishing those who deviated from that ideal and those who falsely accused others of doing so. Third, they sought to promote economic stability by providing legal safeguards for dependent women and children.

Lawyers like Abraham Lincoln also felt an obligation to exercise paternalistic care in cases involving women and children. William H. Herndon, who as Lincoln's third law partner watched him for seventeen years, described Lincoln as "truly paternal in every sense of the word." After considering Lincoln's relationship with his wife, Mary, and with younger lawyers at the bar, the historian Michael Burlingame concludes that "Lincoln had a deep paternal streak." Lincoln expressed this attribute in his relationships both with women and with younger men and children.[8]

Additional suggestive evidence comes from Lincoln's love letter to Mary S. Owens near the beginning of his legal career. In it Lincoln used legal metaphors to communicate his feelings for the young woman. Uncertain whether she understood his feelings for her, Lincoln wrote, "I consider it *my* peculiar right to plead ignorance, and your bounden duty to allow the plea." In the midst of this romantic-legal language Lincoln declared, "I want in all cases to do right, and most particularly so, in all cases with women." Although the letter was a personal one, Lincoln here expressed his more general attitude toward women in litigation.[9]

During the course of his quarter-century legal career (1836–61), Abraham Lincoln and his partners handled approximately five thousand cases before county circuit courts, the Illinois Supreme Court, and the federal courts within Illinois. Women were litigants in nearly 20 percent of these cases.

Sometimes their role was minimal, as in friendly suits about the partition of a parent's estate or in debt cases involving their husbands. Many inheritance cases included multiple plaintiffs and/or defendants, some of whom were women. In such cases these women may have left the resolution of legal matters to husbands, brothers, sons, or attorneys and never entered the courthouse. Guardians and guardians *ad litem* performed similar functions for girls and women younger than eighteen. At other times, however, women were active participants in the legal process, as they defended themselves against criminal charges or slanderous words or as they petitioned the court for a divorce or personally asserted their property rights (see table 1.1).[10]

Illinois state courts divided litigation into three divisions—common law, chancery, and criminal. Women were far more likely to be litigants in the chancery (equity) division than in any other. While 64 percent of Lincoln's law practice was devoted to common law cases, only 20 percent of the cases involving women were in the common law division. Similarly, 6 percent of all his cases but only 2 percent of those with women litigants were in the criminal division. However, while the chancery division accounted for only 24 percent of Lincoln's practice overall, it made up 75 percent of the cases with female litigants. Furthermore, more than half (55 percent) of all of Lincoln's chancery cases had women as litigants.[11]

The common law division, with its emphasis on private injuries and specific remedies, addressed few of the issues that were specific to women or their interests as women. The chancery division arose as a body of law devoted to settling disputes when common law provided no remedy. For this

Table 1.1. Types of Litigation with Women as Litigants, 1836–61

Type of Litigation	Number of Cases	Percentage
Inheritance/estates	446	45.2
Divorce	143	14.5
Foreclosure of mortgage	120	12.2
Dower	70	7.1
Miscellaneous	69	7.0
Debt	63	6.4
Slander	23	2.3
Ejectment	22	2.2
Criminal prosecution	16	1.6
Bastardy	8	0.8
Breach of marriage contract	7	0.7
	987	100.0%

Source: Martha L. Benner and Cullom Davis et al., eds., *The Law Practice of Abraham Lincoln: Complete Documentary Edition* (DVD; Urbana: University of Illinois Press, 2000).

reason it was also called equity jurisdiction. It was within this more flexible division of the law that jurists most often addressed the needs and interests of women. Legal actions such as divorce and petitions for dower, which by definition involved women, were all part of the chancery division of the law. Students of eighteenth-century American law have concluded that while the common law provided women with some protections, "equity procedures could further mitigate the limitations of coverture." Mary Beard, in her *Woman as Force in History,* likewise concluded that chancery courts offered the greatest benefit to women in nineteenth-century America by mitigating the rigidities of the common law.[12]

In 1836 the Massachusetts jurist and legal scholar Joseph Story reflected upon the activities of "Courts of Equity, in regard to married women, for their protection, support, and relief; in some of which they are merely auxiliary to the Common Law; and in others, again, they proceed upon principles wholly independent, if not in contravention, of that system." Story concluded that "we cannot fail to observe the parental solicitude, with which Courts of Equity administer to the wants, and guard the interests, and succor the weakness of those, who are left without any other protectors, in a manner, which the Common Law was too rigid to consider, or too indifferent to provide for." In antebellum Illinois women were clearly involved more frequently in cases in the chancery division. This tendency does not imply, however, that women avoided the common law, as they sued and were sued over debts, contracts, and property rights in more than two hundred cases in Lincoln's practice alone.[13]

Marital discord was one of the most common motives for women to enter the courthouse as a litigant. There they brought suit against husbands who were adulterous, bigamous, cruel, habitually drunken, criminal, impotent, or, most commonly, deserters. Women who acted in a similar manner often found themselves as defendants in divorce cases. As many as one-sixth of Lincoln's cases with women as litigants were divorce cases.

In this area of law nineteenth-century Illinois courts came closest to treating men and women as equals. The common law of England provided that only an act of Parliament could dissolve the marriage contract. However, a law giving authority to circuit courts, sitting as courts of chancery, to grant divorces for some offenses was among the first pieces of legislation passed by the legislature after Illinois became a state in 1818.[14] During the next three decades legislators liberalized the divorce laws to include more grounds for divorce and even allowed courts to grant divorces for grounds not enumerated.[15] These changes primarily addressed the needs of Illinois women, who brought two-thirds of the suits for divorce in the antebellum era. Where the common law held marriage as inviolable, paternalistic legislators and jurists in Illinois altered the law to provide women with a mechanism for obtaining a divorce.

Two divorce cases from Sangamon County in the mid-1850s illustrate women's experience in divorce cases.[16] Caroline Beerup appeared before the Sangamon County Circuit Court in March 1853 and declared that her husband of twenty years, Stephen Beerup, was guilty of "extreme cruelty and torture, torture which can never be seen by eyes here, and such as no man whose senses of love and humanity were not crusted and hardened by baseness and infamy would do." Stephen Beerup had also "committed adultery with various persons and at various times." Furthermore, Stephen Beerup had deserted her and moved to California, leaving her with six children and "no means of support." Caroline Beerup requested that the court grant her a divorce and the children, "their care custody and control[,] education nurture and support." After examining witnesses, the court granted the divorce, gave Caroline Beerup custody of their children, and ordered Stephen Beerup to pay the court costs.[17]

The following year John Brewer appeared before the same court and declared that his wife of eight years, Nancy Brewer, was guilty of "repeated, and constant acts of adultery with sundry and divers individuals" during their marriage. From the time that he refused her "his bed and board" in February 1852, she had "continued to live as a professed, acknowledged, and notorious harlot." John Brewer requested a divorce and the custody of their three children. Nancy Brewer failed to appear before the court, and the court granted the divorce and apparently gave John Brewer custody of the children. The court ordered John Brewer to pay the court costs.[18] In each of these instances and in many other cases as well, Illinois courts proved quite willing to dissolve marriages and to grant custody of children to the offended party, regardless of gender. Only when both husband and wife were guilty of marital indiscretions did gender play a role in the courts' decisions. However, as these two cases demonstrate, courts generally charged court costs in divorce cases to men, whether plaintiff or defendant, perhaps because they were more likely to be able to pay.[19]

Although infrequently, women also appeared before judges and juries as defendants in criminal cases. Then as now women were a tiny minority of criminal defendants—less than 3 percent in Sangamon County in the 1840s and 1850s. Approximately 5 percent of the criminal cases in Lincoln's law practice had female defendants. Criminal cases, though few in number, reveal much about judicial and societal attitudes toward women. Illinois grand juries indicted women for a wide variety of offenses, including assault, larceny, and murder. However, grand juries most frequently indicted women in sexual crimes. For example, more than half (57 percent) the indictments of women in the Sangamon County Circuit Court between 1837 and 1860 involved sexual crimes such as adultery, fornication, and keeping a "second house" (or house of prostitution).[20]

The doctrine of coverture could, in theory, work to the advantage of a married woman in criminal matters. According to Illinois law, a married woman "acting under the threats, command or coercion of her husband, shall not be found guilty of any crime or misdemeanor." Instead, the court would prosecute the husband and punish him if he were found guilty. However, the defendant would have to prove that she acted under her husband's command, and none of Lincoln's cases suggests that married women avoided the consequences of their actions under this statute. When Isabella Hill, for example, violated the public peace, the state's attorney won her indictment from the grand jury but did not seek to indict her husband. The court dismissed the case, and Isabella Hill's husband, Robert Hill, paid the court costs.[21]

One of Lincoln's cases from Christian County was typical of criminal cases involving women. In December 1841 Elizabeth Berry went to Justice of the Peace Aquilla Council and swore that Catharine Babbitt had assaulted her. Council ordered the sheriff to apprehend Babbitt and bring her before the court. Babbitt pleaded not guilty, but the jury found her guilty and fined her $100 and court costs. Babbitt retained Abraham Lincoln and appealed the jury's verdict to the Christian County Circuit Court. Babbitt insisted that the judgment was "unjust and onerous" because she did not assault Berry. Instead, Babbitt declared that she came to "the necessary defense" of her eleven-year-old daughter, "whom the said Elizabeth Berry was at the time beating." Because she was "poor and a widow," Babbitt was unprepared to request an appeal immediately. The circuit judge allowed the appeal but in June 1842 dismissed the case for lack of prosecution.[22]

Antebellum Illinois law also made criminal offenses of certain breaches of the moral order, such as gambling, selling liquor without a license, and adultery and fornication. While grand juries often indicted men on the gambling and liquor offenses, the sex offenses necessarily involved male and female defendants. For example, in March 1850 the state's attorney won the indictment of Henry McHenry and Martha Graves in Sangamon County on charges of adultery. McHenry requested and received a continuance to the next term of court. In the November 1850 term McHenry promised to appear at the next term of court, and the court issued a capias, or order to bring Martha Graves before the court. In March 1851 McHenry pleaded not guilty, but the jury found him guilty. McHenry then made a motion for a new trial, but the court denied it. The court fined him $50 and court costs and ordered that he be held in jail until he paid the fine. The state's attorney then refused to prosecute the case against Graves. The decision is telling. Had McHenry and Graves been a married couple and together committed some other sort of crime, the court would likely have held the man entirely responsible, assuming that the woman had acted under the man's coercion. Perhaps in this case as well, even though McHenry and Graves were not married to each other, the court found the man more responsible. After the conviction of McHenry the state's attorney had no interest in continuing the prosecution of the less culpable Martha Graves.[23] As the experiences of Isabella Hill, Catharine Babbitt, and Martha Graves illustrate, antebellum Illinois courts dismissed many criminal indictments against women for lack of prosecution.[24]

Perhaps one of the most revealing criminal cases involving a woman as a defendant was *People v. House*. In June 1856 a deputy sheriff arrested Maria House, a twenty-five-year-old widow who lived in Chatham, just south of Springfield, and charged her with murdering her baby. Maria House's husband had died in September 1854. During the November 1856 term of the Sangamon County Circuit Court, the grand jury indicted Maria House in the death of her illegitimate baby. Later in the term House pleaded not guilty. On the motion of her attorneys, the court continued the case until the next term and placed House in the custody of the sheriff.[25]

When the case came to trial on Wednesday, April 29, 1857, the court called seventy potential jurors. After the attorneys dismissed twenty-five potential jurors through peremptory challenges and thirty-three others for cause, the court finally obtained a jury of twelve men to try the case. The court allowed the jury to disperse for the night and to reassemble the next morning. State's Attorney James B. White and his cocounsel presented their witnesses first. John and Elizabeth Broeckel testified that they took in Maria House in November 1855 and that she remained in their home for five months until she delivered a baby boy in March 1856. Maria House continued to live with the Broeckels until the child was about six weeks old. Elizabeth Broeckel declared on cross-examination that Maria House "appeared to take good care of child, was fond of her child as women generally are." A Mrs. McMullan testified that Maria House came to work for her after leaving the Broeckels' home; House remained at the McMullan home for six or seven weeks. Under cross-examination McMullan acknowledged that Maria House "always exhibited fondness for child." Dr. John R. Lewis, a physician who lived in Chatham, examined the child's body after it was found beside a fence on the town square in Chatham. He declared that the child had died of strangulation and suffocation. After examining more witnesses, the prosecution presented testimony from Dr. Alexander S. Halbert, who had known Maria House for fifteen years. Halbert insisted that Mr. House had been dead for several years and that she had lived at the home of Hiram Alexander and his wife for a year before the child was born. According to John T. Jones, the deputy sheriff who arrested her, Maria House declared after her arrest that Alexander was the father of the child. Halbert also stated that he did not consider Maria House to be "very bright" and that she had taken a large quantity of camphor on one occasion when he visited her at the Alexanders' home.[26]

Late on Thursday afternoon the defense attorneys presented their witnesses, working to establish a defense of diminished capacity or insanity. Among the witnesses were Maria House's father and older sister. They testified that Maria House had had a fever ten or twelve years before during a trip to Iowa with her parents. Since that time she had experienced "spells," was "feeble-minded," and occasionally had "wild looks." On Friday morning the defense called one more witness, before both sides called their rebuttal witnesses. The deputy sheriff who arrested House suspected that she "acted possum" at the time of her arrest but said that "there was nothing unusual in her conduct." The jailer said he "never judged this woman crazy." The prosecutors recalled two doctors to discuss issues of insanity. Based on the testimony of other witnesses, Dr. E. S. Fowler concluded that "the prisoner is a fitter subject for an insane hospital than a jail." He did not believe that "she is morally an accountable being." He said he believed that she suffered from the "melancholy class of insanity." Dr. Charles Ryan said he concluded from the testimony that House "was weak in mind" but that she "would be able to judge of right and wrong." House did not appear to Ryan to be a person "who is subject to attacks of insanity," though "pregnancy is sometimes accompanied by insanity, more frequently after delivery." The case went to the jury at 6 P.M., and two hours later the jurors returned with a verdict of not guilty. The court immediately released House from custody.[27]

The testimony in this case suggests much about legal attitudes toward women. First, it is significant that of the twenty-five witnesses, six were women. The testimony of prosecution witnesses Elizabeth Broeckel and Mrs. McMullan that House was "fond" of her child perhaps assured jurors that House had normal maternal feelings for the child and would not have harmed him unless temporarily insane. Four physicians testified for the prosecution regarding the body of the child and on matters of insanity. Fowler's conclusion that House should be sent to a mental hospital and that she was not morally responsible for her actions likely carried much weight with the jury. Even Ryan, who was skeptical of claims that House was insane, declared the prevailing medical wisdom that "pregnancy is sometimes accompanied by insanity." The testimony of these witnesses, together with Maria House's behavior before and after the death of her child, reassured the jury that she was not the worst possible female fiend—a mother who killed her own child—but rather a "weak-minded" woman who deserved pity rather than punishment. Extensive reporting of the testimony in local newspapers allowed the community to accept the jury's verdict as a reasoned response to the particular facts of the case. The jury was not condoning infanticide; rather, it was extending mercy to a "deranged" woman.

Even some respectable women found themselves in court when their actions violated the law. Agitation to limit the manufacture, sale, and consumption of alcohol in Illinois reached a climax in the mid-1850s. After earlier efforts at moral suasion had accomplished all that they could, social reformers turned to legislation to control "Demon Rum." However, immigrants, southerners, Catholics, and other groups united to oppose legal prohibitions against alcohol. After Maine passed the first statewide prohibition law in 1851, temperance legislation spread quickly across the northern states. During the next four years twelve northern states and territories passed prohibition statutes. Between 1851 and 1855 the Illinois legislature passed several bills regulating and restricting the manufacture and sale of alcohol as a beverage. State legislators tightened licensing laws and even prohibited the public sale of liquor by the glass. In 1855 the legislature passed a statewide prohibition ordinance, subject to approval by referendum. In a deeply divisive and hotly contested campaign opponents of prohibition narrowly triumphed in June 1855, and the campaign to prohibit alcohol at the state level subsided.[28]

But in the spring of 1854 at least nine women in Marion in De Witt County, Illinois, had defied virtually every notion of proper female behavior when they entered the grocery (saloon) of George Tanner and destroyed the liquor in his store by opening several whiskey barrels and dumping the contents on the ground. The state's attorney won the indictment of the women on a charge of riot. The women retained Abraham Lincoln to represent them, perhaps in part because one of the defendants was Rowena Herndon, the sister-in-law of Lincoln's junior law partner, William H. Herndon. At the spring term of the De Witt County Circuit Court, Lincoln defended the women.[29] According to a reminiscence recorded fifteen years later, Lincoln addressed the jurors before they retired. Lincoln reportedly said that he would change the order of the indictment to "The State against Mr. Whiskey" instead of "The State against the Ladies." Drawing a parallel between the women's actions and those of the men who threw tea overboard into Boston harbor in 1774, Lincoln insisted that the saloon keeper, Tanner, "neither feared

God nor regarded man." The jury found the defendants guilty, and the judge fined the women $18 ($2 each) and court costs, which totaled $68. According to the criminal statute governing riot, the maximum punishment was $200 or imprisonment for six months. Whether the minimal fines reflected the court's attitude toward these defendants as women or toward their cause remains unclear, but the paternalistic judge merely chastised rather than punished them.[30]

Just as many criminal indictments of women addressed sexual misconduct, slander cases involving women as litigants almost always involved accusations of sexual impropriety. In twelve of thirteen slander cases involving female plaintiffs where the nature of the slander is known, the slanderous words involved accusations of adultery, fornication, or prostitution.[31] Such accusations could seriously damage an unmarried woman's reputation in a community and endanger her marriage prospects, concerns that were prominent in the minds of paternalistic judges and juries.[32] Slanderous words could also diminish the reputation of a married woman. In contrast, slander cases with male plaintiffs "typically involved accusations of false swearing or larceny."[33] The Illinois legislature in 1821 had made slander a criminal offense punishable by a fine of up to $1,000. Dissatisfied with strict common law rules for punishing slander, the legislature a year later also deemed certain words "actionable" in civil suits. Such words included false accusations of adultery or fornication and accusations of swearing falsely. All the slander cases from Lincoln's practice were civil suits in which a victim of slanderous words sued the person alleged to have said them.[34]

The case of *Edwards et ux. v. Patterson et ux.* illustrates the contest about the meaning of certain words typical of a slander case. In October 1843 Tabitha Ann Edwards complained to the Mason County Circuit Court that Maria Patterson had "wickedly, maliciously & falsely" injured Edwards's "good name fame & credit" by accusing her of "having raised a family of illegitimate children by a Negro, and of having criminal sexual intercourse by & with said negro." Before Patterson's slanderous words, Tabitha Ann Edwards avowed, she "bore a good character & was known & reputed to be a virtuous honest & worthy citizen and stood high in the estimation of the community in which she lived & had deservedly acquired the good opinion of all her neighbours for chastity & virtue."[35]

Because both Tabitha Ann Edwards and Maria Patterson were married women, they could neither sue nor be sued apart from their husbands. As William Blackstone wrote in his *Commentaries,* "If the wife be injured in her person or her property, she can bring no action for redress without her husband's concurrence, and in his name, as well as her own: neither can she be sued, without making the husband a defendant." Under the doctrine of coverture the law required Tabitha Ann Edwards to sue—with her husband, Ambrose P. Edwards—both Maria Patterson and her husband, William Patterson. The Edwardses insisted that Maria Patterson had said, "Mrs. Edwards has raised a family of children by a negro, and I can prove it," and that these words meant that Tabitha Ann Edwards was guilty of the crimes of fornication and adultery. They requested $2,000 in damages. The Pattersons responded with a plea of not guilty.[36]

The case came to trial in the June 1844 term of the Mason County Circuit Court. After hearing the evidence, a jury of twelve men reached a verdict: "We the jury find the defendants guilty in manner and form as set forth in the plaintifs declaration and assess the damages at Two Hundred and Twenty dollars." The Pattersons made a motion for a new trial, but the court denied it. The court also rejected a motion for an arrest of judgment, and the Pattersons appealed to the Illinois Supreme Court. The Edwardses retained Abraham Lincoln and Murray McConnell to represent them before that court.[37]

In December 1845 the attorney for the Pattersons insisted that the Mason County Circuit Court had made three errors. First, it had refused to allow the introduction of evidence that suggested that Maria Patterson was referring to Ambrose Edwards's mother rather than his wife. Second, the court refused to allow a new trial, and third, it refused to arrest judgment in the case. The attorney for the Pattersons argued that the evidence did not support the Edwardses' allegations and that the statement "Mrs. Edwards has raised a family of children by a negro" did not necessarily imply fornication or adultery. Lincoln and McConnell countered that the words spoken must be understood in the context in which the community understood them. Because Tabitha Ann Edwards was a white woman, saying that she had children by an African American implied miscegenation and therefore adultery or fornication because interracial marriage was illegal in Illinois. The supreme court rejected Lincoln and McConnell's argument.

Finding the Edwardses' declaration defective, the court insisted that the words spoken—"Mrs. Edwards has raised a family by a negro"—"do not in their plain and popular sense, or in common acceptation, necessarily amount to a charge of fornication and adultery, unconnected with other circumstances." The supreme court remained unconvinced by the record from the lower court that the words spoken necessarily meant that "the defendant thereby meant to charge plaintiff's wife with fornication and adultery" or that the words "must have been necessarily slanderous in their character." The court reversed the circuit court's judgment and remanded the case but allowed the Edwardses to amend their complaint. Lincoln immediately requested a rehearing, but the court denied the request. Unfortunately, there is no record of the remanded case.[38]

Like most other slander cases in which the plaintiffs were women, *Patterson et ux. v. Edwards et ux.* revolved around charges that a woman had crossed the boundaries of sexual propriety. However, in this case, perhaps because the plaintiff was a married woman, the Illinois Supreme Court interpreted the spoken words in an extremely narrow manner, though the court did offer the plaintiffs the opportunity to amend and clarify their initial charges.[39]

Cases involving the support of illegitimate children lay at the intersection of the two primary legislative and judicial concerns of maintaining an ideal of female sexual purity and of promoting economic stability. When these two goals clashed, as they did in bastardy cases, the law favored economic stability over the maintenance of an ideal of female virtue. Rather than proclaim the mother or the father of an illegitimate child as guilty of adultery or fornication, Illinois legislators and judges established a paternal mechanism by which the mother could obtain economic support from the father for the support of the child.

Bastardy cases also placed women in a unique situation in antebellum Illinois courts. Classified as a criminal case, a bastardy case was a curious mixture of criminal and civil proceedings. As in a normal criminal case, the state's attorney would seek a grand jury's indictment of the man alleged to be the father but only upon the complaint of the mother of the illegitimate child. The mother had to bring the suit within two years of the birth of the child. In the trial itself "the mother shall be admitted as a competent witness, and her credibility shall be left to the jury." If the defendant confessed or the jury found him guilty, the court would require that he pay as much as $50 annually for seven years for the "support, maintenance and education" of the child. However, after the child reached three years of age, the father had the statutory right to custody.[40]

The oldest of Zephaniah and Lavinia Dunn's nine children, Nancy Jane Dunn, was twenty-one in 1849. The Dunns had migrated from Kentucky to Illinois around 1834, and by 1850 Zephaniah Dunn was a substantial farmer, the owner of 320 acres of land worth $2,000 and numerous livestock.[41] The birth of a child to unmarried Nancy Jane Dunn in December 1849 produced three separate lawsuits. She insisted that twenty-seven-year-old Albert J. Carle was the father of her child and that he had promised to marry her.[42] In the May 1850 term of the Champaign County Circuit Court, Nancy Jane Dunn sued Carle, claiming he had breached his promise to marry her. She also informed the state's attorney of her situation, and he won the indictment of Carle on a charge of bastardy.

Illinois law also provided Zephaniah Dunn with a legal remedy. He sued Carle for seducing his daughter and requested compensation for his loss of her services while she was pregnant. By the time Zephaniah Dunn sued Carle, however, the courts had virtually abandoned the legal fiction of "loss of services" in seduction cases in favor of direct punitive action against men who seduced and abandoned young women. In the 1842 case of *Grable v. Margrave* Abraham Lincoln represented Thomas Margrave in his case alleging that William G. Grable had seduced Margrave's daughter. In the appeal the Illinois Supreme Court accepted Lincoln's reasoning that compensation in such cases served "the double purpose of setting an example, and of punishing the wrongdoer." In 1846 Lincoln became the victim of his own earlier success when he represented a man accused of seduction, Elias Anderson, in a case brought by Michael Ryan. In this case the Illinois Supreme Court rejected Lincoln's argument that Ryan had to demonstrate that he suffered financial loss because of his daughter's inability to perform labor. The court declared that the "loss of character and happiness of the unfortunate female, and the consequent injury inflicted upon the heart of the parent" were sufficient to award damages in such cases. Seduction cases brought by a parent were no longer designed to recover damages for loss of services but to punish the seducer.[43]

Lincoln represented Nancy Jane Dunn and her father in each of the three cases against Albert Carle. The Champaign County Circuit Court settled the breach of marriage contract case quickly in May 1850. The court called a jury, which heard the evidence, but then Dunn either agreed to a dismissal or decided not to pursue her case further. The court ordered her to pay the costs of the case. In the other two cases Carle asked for and received a continuance until the next term of court. In October 1850 Carle once again obtained continuances in both cases.[44]

In the April 1851 term of the Champaign County Circuit Court, Carle pleaded not guilty both to the bastardy and the seduction charges. On May 1 Judge David Davis called a jury to hear the case. The cases had excited "a great deal of interest" in the county. As the lawyers argued the case before him, Davis composed a letter to his wife. Lincoln "in his opening speech to the Jury," Davis wrote, "bore down savagely on the Defdt. who is now married, & who has been using extraordinary exertions to procure testimony, to prove that the woman had permitted the embrace of other men." Although the trial might last until midnight, Davis was determined "to sit it out tonight." By the end of the letter Davis could write, "It is now nearly 10 Oclk, & Lincoln to make his Closing Speech." After deliberation the jury declared, "We the Jury find that Albert G. Carle the Defendant is the real father of the Bastard child of the said Nancy Jane Dunn." The court ordered Carle to pay $50 per year for the support of the child from December 1849.[45]

Davis had planned to close the spring session of the court on Friday, May 2, but both Zephaniah Dunn and Carle "insisted on a trial in the seduction suit." Davis continued the term until Saturday so that there would be time to seat a jury and bring in witnesses. Witnesses, according to Davis, questioned Nancy Jane Dunn's virtue and "blacken[ed] her character desperately." After the trial began, Davis "felt sorry for her father." "I suppose," he wrote, "he thought her virtuous." Davis sarcastically observed, "The evidence disclosed a beautiful State of morals among the young men and young girls of this Grove." The jury found Carle guilty and awarded Zephaniah Dunn $180.41 in damages. However, Zephaniah Dunn remitted, or gave back, the damages in exchange for a promise from Carle that he would not seek custody of the child.[46]

Although some women entered the courts as litigants either because they had violated the ideal of sexual purity or because someone had wrongly accused them of doing so, more women came before the courts to resolve economic disputes surrounding debt, dower, and inheritance. In some cases women used the court system to recover debts that others owed them. When J. G. Cotton failed to pay Margaret Murphy her wages, for example, she went to Justice of the Peace J. P. Gauch to complain. After Cotton failed to appear, the justice of the peace awarded Murphy $6.86. Cotton appealed to the Champaign County Circuit Court, which dismissed the appeal and awarded Murphy the lower court's judgment and an additional 10 percent in damages.[47]

In December 1836 Charles Arnold and William Butler gave Eliza A. Kindoll a promissory note for $250, due one year later. In 1837 Eliza A. Kindoll married James E. Reed. In January 1838 James and Eliza Reed retained John Todd Stuart and his law partner, Abraham Lincoln, and filed a declaration in the Sangamon County Circuit Court. The Reeds declared that Arnold and Butler "(although often requested so to do) have not as yet paid the said sum of money in the said promissory note specified, or any part thereof, to the said Eliza A. whilst she was sole and unmarried, or to the said James E. Reed and Eliza A. his wife, or either of them since their intermarriage." When Arnold and Butler failed to appear at the March 1838 term, the court ruled for the Reeds and awarded $250. The court later sold five town lots that Arnold owned to satisfy the judgment in the case.[48]

When women married in antebellum America, their real and personal property became the property of their husbands, according to the common law.[49] According to Illinois law, before a man could convey his wife's lands to another person, a court official had to obtain her separate voluntary assent to the transaction.[50] Statutory law thus mitigated the harshest aspects of coverture by requiring a married woman to approve the sale of land she brought to the marriage and similarly to relinquish her dower rights to any land that her husband sold. This safeguard also had corresponding responsibilities. Creditors frequently sued both husband and wife to foreclose a mortgage when they proved unable to pay their debts. In April 1857 Joshua Davis gave A. R. Griffith a promissory note for $1,000, and Davis and his wife, Ellen, secured the note with a mortgage on 145 acres of land. Griffith assigned the note to a person named Bevan. After Joshua Davis failed to pay the note, Bevan sued Joshua and Ellen Davis in the Vermilion County Circuit Court to foreclose the mortgage. The court granted the foreclosure and ordered the Davises to pay the debt within twenty days, or the court would sell the land to satisfy the judgment. The Davises failed to pay the judgment, and the master in chancery sold their land at public auction.[51]

Gradually, states enacted statutes that gave women ownership of property that they brought into the marriage. Illinois did not pass its Married Women's Property Act until 1861. Herndon, Lincoln's third law partner, described the law as "allowing women (married women) all their property,— real, personal, mixed,—free from all debt contract, obligation and control of their husbands. This law puts man and woman in the same position, as far as property-rights and their remedies are concerned. This is right,—just as it should be." Caroline Healey Dall, a feminist orator and author, quoted Herndon's observation approvingly in her 1861 book, *Woman's Rights under the Law: In Three Lectures*. Dall found that "this expression of Mr. Herndon's opinion gains additional interest from the fact that he has been for seventeen years the legal partner of Abraham Lincoln, now President of the United States." Dall also commended "certain statutes of the State of Illinois" for their "unusual liberality." For example, Dall noted that in Illinois, the wife "in preference to all others" could administer her husband's estate. Furthermore, although an Illinois wife did not have "*legally* the first title to the guardianship of her child on the demise of her husband," she did have it "by a kind of *comity*, the consent of public opinion and the courts."[52]

The death of the head of a household frequently brought women into courts in a variety of roles related to the settlement of the estate. When a man died, his widow, daughters, and daughters-in-law often became parties to a variety of inheritance suits. The death of a husband also brought many widows before antebellum Illinois courts to assert their dower rights. Under the common law a widow in Illinois, as in most other states, was entitled to a life estate equal to one-third of all the lands that her husband owned at the time of his death. Illinois law went even further. If a widow had not relinquished her dower rights to *any* land that her husband sold before his death, she could also claim a one-third interest in those lands as well.[53] The heirs of a deceased man were to assign his widow her dower as soon after his death as possible. If the heirs failed to do so within one month or the widow was dissatisfied with the assignment of dower, she could sue for her dower rights. To help ensure that widows would be left with adequate support, a widow's dower in antebellum Illinois was not subject to creditors' claims against her husband's estate. A few other states restricted dower. In Pennsylvania, for example, insolvent estates provided no dower in land to widows; creditors' claims were paramount.[54] Lincoln and his partners' practice included sixty-eight dower cases.

Two cases in the Logan County Circuit Court arising from John Lucas's death in 1855 illustrate the general outlines of such litigation. John Lucas had stated in his will that his wife, Sarah Lucas, could have one-third of his land during her life or she could live with his son John A. Lucas, who would support her. Not wanting to live with and be supported by John A. Lucas, Sarah Lucas took her dower in land. Later she petitioned the court for her dower in an additional tract of land that her husband had bequeathed to his son Thomas Lucas. Sarah Lucas married Michael Mann while the case was still pending; now a *feme covert,* Sarah Lucas Mann had to add her husband as a plaintiff in the case. The court awarded her dower in the additional tract and appointed commissioners to execute the court's decree.[55]

In the same term that the court settled the dower issue, four of John Lucas's children contested his will. In the will that he prepared in 1854 John Lucas left most of his 760-acre estate and personal property to his wife, his three sons, and his youngest daughter. His three elder daughters received only $50 each, and another daughter received twenty acres of land. Because these four daughters were married, the husbands had to be parties to any legal action that their wives wished to undertake.[56]

The four elder daughters and their husbands sued their mother, Sarah Lucas Mann, her new husband, their three brothers, and their younger sister to set aside the will. They argued that their brothers had exerted "undue influence" over their father, who was "not of sound mind or judgment and . . . was suffering from imbecility" when he made his will. According to the four elder daughters, John Lucas had earlier expressed his intention of dividing his estate equally among his eight children. The four daughters and their husbands asked the court to set aside the will and to divide the estate equally. The defendants responded that John Lucas was "of sound mind and memory" when he made his will. The court obtained depositions from witnesses in Texas and continued the case for several terms. Finally, as with many such cases, the court dismissed the case when the parties reached a settlement.

Under the terms of the agreement Caleb Lucas, one of the sons, gave to his four sisters sixty-three acres, $700, and three horses worth $100 each.[57]

A widow often served either as the executrix of her husband's will, or if he left no will, the administratrix of his estate.[58] Sarah Carrico's experience is typical. When James Carrico died without a will in August 1834, the court appointed his widow, Sarah Carrico, as the administratrix of his estate. Even though she could not write her own name, Sarah Carrico administered her husband's estate. After tabulating the estate's debts, she found that her husband's personal assets could not pay them. She petitioned the court to sell some of the estate's land to satisfy the debts. As a formality, she made her three minor children defendants in the case. The court granted the petition, and Sarah Carrico sold ninety acres of land for $50.10 to apply to the estate's debts.[59]

Paternalistic legislators, judges, and juries attempted to protect women's economic interests by requiring that they accede to the sale of their real estate and to the relinquishment of their dower rights. To prevent women from becoming more economically vulnerable, antebellum Illinois courts released them from marriage to husbands who had deserted them, forced fathers to support their bastard children, and upheld women's dower and inheritance rights. However, the courts also held husbands and wives responsible for debts and mortgages.

Women also appeared in antebellum Illinois courts to fulfill other functions. Two hundred women appeared as witnesses in the cases in Lincoln's law practice.[60] Although many women appeared as witnesses in slander, divorce, and debt cases, they also appeared in criminal trials involving charges of murder, larceny, and assault; in chancery disputes about inheritance matters; and in a variety of other cases. Their testimony was crucial to legal proceedings and often critical to the verdict in individual cases. In the slander case between Tabitha Ann Edwards and Maria Patterson, for example, the court subpoenaed at least four women to testify as witnesses. At least two appeared before the Mason County Circuit Court in Havana, Illinois, and testified on behalf of the Edwardses. They also submitted to cross-examination by the attorneys for the Pattersons. One woman testified that Maria Patterson admitted that she had said that "Mrs. Edwards had had children by a negro." An unmarried Edwards daughter testified that on one occasion, Maria Patterson came to her house when only her father and some of the younger children were present. The daughter testified that Patterson told her that "her mother had had children by a negro and that all her children were negroes." The testimony of these two witnesses was likely critical to the jury's decision in favor of the Edwardses and the award of $220. The Pattersons' lawyers mentioned this testimony prominently in their bill of exceptions, which formed the basis of their appeal to the Illinois Supreme Court.[61]

When Cynthia Klein sued John Klein for divorce on the grounds of cruelty and repeated drunkenness, Anna Stacy Freeman proved to be a witness critical to the outcome of the case. Cynthia Klein insisted that John Klein had frequently beaten her and on one occasion threatened to kill her. Furthermore, he had frequently visited prostitutes. John Klein filed a cross-bill for divorce; he denied that he had beaten or threatened his wife, but he did admit he had visited "every house of ill fame in Springfield." The court ordered the master in chancery to take testimony and report his findings. Master in Chancery Antrim Campbell interviewed four witnesses before the attorneys for both parties. The last witness was Anna Stacy Freeman, who testified that she had known the Kleins for six or seven years and had lived in their home for three years. She knew that Cynthia Klein had struck John Klein "in anger more than once." She had also seen Cynthia Klein drunk and associating with "women of bad character." One prostitute, Nancy Doolittle, had come to the Kleins' home with Cynthia Klein's permission and when the Kleins' thirteen-year-old daughter was present. Freeman thought it would be "ruinous to the morals of the children . . . to associate with their mother, in consequence of her abandoned character and her corrupt associates." The court apparently found Freeman's testimony decisive. After Campbell filed his report, the court denied Cynthia Klein's petition for divorce. The court granted John Klein's petition for divorce, ordered him to pay $400 in alimony, and granted him custody of the couple's children.[62]

Other women gave testimony to the court through depositions, which also sometimes proved critical to the disposition of a case. In Piatt County, Illinois, in 1852 James Hollingsworth asked Deborah Ater to care for his wife, who was sick. Jacob Ater accompanied Deborah Ater to Hollingsworth's house, where Jacob Ater insisted that Deborah Ater leave town with him. She refused, and Jacob Ater knocked her down, kicked her, and threatened to kill her. Hollingsworth intervened, and he and Jacob Ater fought. Later, while Hollingsworth was accompanying Deborah Ater to his house, Jacob Ater confronted him in front of Hollingsworth's store and threw a bottle at him. Hollingsworth pointed his pistol at Ater, but the gun did not fire. Other parties intervened, but the grand jury indicted James Hollingsworth on a charge of assault with a deadly weapon. Deborah Ater's eyewitness testimony, given through a deposition nearly a year and a half later, was that Hollingsworth had acted in self-defense. This testimony convinced the state's attorney to drop the case.[63]

In antebellum Illinois, trials were also a form of entertainment and education, one of the few such opportunities to which rural Illinoisans may have had access. Women were among those who entered courthouses to observe the proceedings. In Danville, the county seat of Vermilion County in eastern Illinois, both William Fithian and George W. Casseday built "fine looking Brick seminaries" in 1850 or 1851 for the instruction of the young women of the area. As the two men promoted their rival schools, Casseday wrote an article in which he criticized Fithian and claimed that when Fithian's wife died, Fithian had left her body in Paris, Illinois, to be buried by others. Fithian sued Casseday in an action of slander, and the case promised to "excite a great deal of interest" if it went to trial. Fithian retained local attorney Usher Linder and a Springfield attorney with a growing reputation for public speaking, Abraham Lincoln. John Murphy and Edward A. Hannegan represented Casseday. Hannegan was a former U.S. senator from Indiana and former ambassador to Austria. The judge in the case found him to be "a beautiful speaker" with an education "as fine as any man that I ever heard." This cosmopolitan speaker "entertained greatly with descriptions of foreign courts." During the trial "the ladies of town in great number were present all the time." There were also six women among the forty-four witnesses in the trial. The jury in the case found for Fithian and awarded nearly $550 in damages.[64]

Attending court could even have political implications. When the nine women stood trial in De Witt County, accused of rioting in the prohibition case, between one hundred and two hundred "ladies" watched the proceedings. The defendants had physically and forcefully demonstrated their views on one of the great moral *and* political issues of the 1850s. Most, perhaps all, of the women who attended the trial did so in support of the defendants. A reminiscence of the event declared that when Lincoln finished his speech in defense of the women, "many were bathed in tears," demonstrating "his power in presenting truth and carrying his audiance [*sic*] with him." Newspapers that supported temperance or prohibition cheered the defendants, their female supporters in the courtroom, and the lawyers who defended the "fair daughters of Adam."[65]

Antebellum Illinois courts, then, were far from exclusively male domains; women often asserted and defended their interests there. Furthermore, the number and variety of antebellum cases involving women demonstrate that women were active participants in the antebellum Illinois legal system. Stepping into the "public realm," they brought suits, defended themselves against accusations, provided testimony, and participated in the community ritual of court days as spectators.

In response to women's participation, paternalistic judges and juries released them from bad marriages, upheld ideals of female sexual purity, and protected the interests of the economically vulnerable "weaker sex." In doing so, these men attempted to reinforce the cultural image and legal perception of women as dependents. Clearly, antebellum jurists and lawyers had a "gendered vision of law."[66] To assert that Illinois judges, lawyers, and jurors were acting in a paternalistic rather than patriarchal fashion is not to deny their subordination of women. Such an interpretation does, however, suggest that legislators and jurists recognized the "mutual obligations and reciprocal rights" that mitigated the harshest aspects of patriarchy.

Notes

1. "An Act declaring what Laws are in force in this State," 4 February 1819, *Laws of the State of Illinois* (1819), 3; St. George Tucker, *Blackstone's Commentaries, with Notes of Reference to the Constitution and Laws of the Federal Government of the United States and of the Commonwealth of Virginia,* 5 vols. (1803; rpt., New York: Augustus M. Kelley, 1969), 2:442, or William Blackstone, *Commentaries on the Laws of England,* 4 vols. (1765–69; rpt., Chicago: University of Chicago Press, 1979), 1:430.

Abraham Lincoln used Blackstone's *Commentaries* as his introduction to the study of law, but it is difficult to determine what edition, of multiple English and fourteen American ones, he might have used. St. George Tucker's 1803 edition had influence far beyond the borders of Virginia. Joseph Chitty's edition of Blackstone, first published in 1831, became known as the "frontier Blackstone." See Craig Evan Klafter, *Reason over Precedents: Origins of American Legal Thought* (Westport, Conn.: Greenwood, 1993); Dennis R. Nolan, "Sir William Blackstone and the New American Republic: A Study of Intellectual Impact," *New York University Law Review* 51 (November 1976): 731; Joe Luttrell, "Two Centuries of Blackstone's Commentaries," *AB Bookman's Weekly* (25 April 1994): 1808–13.

See also Cornelia Hughes Dayton, *Women before the Bar: Gender, Law, and Society in Connecticut, 1639–1789* (Chapel Hill: University of North Carolina Press, 1995), 19–22; Norma Basch, "Invisible Women: The Legal Fiction of Marital Unity in Nineteenth-Century America," *Feminist Studies* 5 (Summer 1979): 346–66.

2. Joan R. Gunderson and Gwen Victor Gampel find that even in eighteenth-century New York and Virginia, *femes covert* were "very much involved in the legal system. Consequently, the traditional Blackstonian concept of marital unity does not apply" ("Married Women's Legal Status in Eighteenth-Century New York and Virginia," *William and Mary Quarterly* 39 [January 1982]: 116). In contrast, Deborah A. Rosen, in her study of colonial New York, insists that "exceptions to the common law appear to be rare" in the treatment of married women and that the chancery court in New York "in practice . . . only rarely alleviated the weight of common law restrictions on women" (*Courts and Commerce: Gender, Law, and the Market Economy in Colonial New York* [Columbus: Ohio State University Press, 1997], 116).

3. "The Court House of Sangamon County," unidentified newspaper clipping, 19 February 1867, vertical files, Illinois State Historical Library, Springfield.

4. Paul M. Angle, *"Here I Have Lived": A History of Lincoln's Springfield, 1821–1865* (Chicago: Abraham Lincoln Book Shop, 1971), 43 (quotations); G. S. Rowe, "The Role of Courthouses in the Lives of Eighteenth-Century Pennsylvania Women," *Western Pennsylvania Historical Magazine* 68 (January 1985): 5–8.

5. Robert M. Spector, "Woman against the Law: Myra Bradwell's Struggle for Admission to the Illinois Bar," *Journal of the Illinois State Historical Society* 68 (June 1975): 239–40; Cynthia A. Bunting, "Elsah's Woman J.P.," *Elsah History* 15 (April 1976): 7, cited in Adade Mitchell Wheeler and Marlene Stein Wortman, *The Roads They Made: Women in Illinois History* (Chicago: Charles H. Kerr, 1977), 193–94 n. 5; Charlotte Adelman, *WBAI 75: The First 75 Years* (Paducah, Ky.: Turner Publishing, 1992), 14.

Midnineteenth-century Illinois law limited jury service to "all free white male taxable inhabitants in any of the counties in this State, being natural born citizens of the United States, or naturalized according to the constitution and laws of the United States, and of this State, between the ages of twenty-one and sixty years" ("An Act Prescribing the Mode of Summoning Grand and Petit Jurors, and Defining their Qualifications and Duties," 7 February 1827, *Revised Code of Laws of Illinois* [1827], 251).

6. Nancy F. Cott, *The Bonds of Womanhood: "Woman's Sphere" in New England, 1780–1835* (New Haven, Conn.: Yale University Press, 1977), 197–99.

7. Linda K. Kerber, *Women of the Republic: Intellect and Ideology in Revolutionary America* (Chapel Hill: University of North Carolina Press, 1980), 153; Rowe, "Role of Courthouses," 12–13. For an examination of women's participation in the public arena outside the courtroom, see Mary P. Ryan, *Women in Public: Between Banners and Ballots, 1825–1880* (Baltimore: Johns Hopkins University Press, 1990), and Elizabeth R. Varon, *"We Mean to Be Counted": White Women and Politics in Antebellum Virginia* (Chapel Hill: University of North Carolina Press, 1998).

Rosen finds that "women constituted only a small percentage of litigants in New York courts, and their percentage decreased over the course of the eighteenth century. . . . The number of women who came into court on their own, and on their own behalf, was small and declining" (*Courts and Commerce*, 96).

For women's encounters with the law in the South in the nineteenth century, see Laura F. Edwards, *Gendered Strife and Confusion: The Political Culture of Reconstruction* (Urbana: University of Illinois Press, 1997), 25–31, 215–17; Victoria E. Bynum, *Unruly Women: The Politics of Social and Sexual Control in the Old South* (Chapel Hill: University of North Carolina Press, 1992); and Peter W. Bardaglio, *Reconstructing the Household: Families, Sex, and the Law in the Nineteenth-Century South* (Chapel Hill: University of North Carolina Press, 1995).

8. William Henry Herndon, "Analysis of the Character of Abraham Lincoln," *Abraham Lincoln Quarterly* 1 (December 1941): 417; Michael Burlingame, *The Inner World of Abraham Lincoln* (Urbana: University of Illinois Press, 1994), 57–59, 74, 315.

9. Abraham Lincoln to Mary Owens, 16 August 1837, in *The Collected Works of Abraham Lincoln,* ed. Roy P. Basler, 8 vols. (New Brunswick, N.J.: Rutgers University Press, 1953), 1:94.

10. A guardian had legal custody of a child, protected the child's interests, and provided for his or her needs. A guardian *ad litem* was appointed by the court to represent a child or children's interests in a single case; this person was almost always a lawyer.

Table 1.1 includes twenty-four partition and dower cases in the dower category, but these are not included in the inheritance category. The eight bastardy cases were criminal prosecutions but were counted separately because the defendants were men in those cases, whereas women were defendants in those counted as criminal prosecutions. The identification of women as litigants was a difficult task for the staff of the Lincoln Legal Papers. When a person with a feminine first name was involved in some types of cases, especially those surrounding inheritance, it was difficult to determine whether she was older than eighteen and thus considered to be a woman in the eyes of the law. However, widows and married daughters could be clearly identified (Martha L. Benner and Cullom Davis et al., eds., *The Law Practice of Abraham Lincoln: Complete Documentary Edition* [DVD; Urbana: University of Illinois Press, 2000], hereafter cited as *LPAL*).

11. No women were litigants in admiralty or bankruptcy cases. Of the fifty-one probate cases in Lincoln's practice, twenty-four involved female litigants.

12. Gunderson and Gampel, "Married Women's Legal Status," 134; Mary R. Beard, *Woman as Force in History: A Study in Traditions and Realities* (New York: Macmillan, 1946), 136–44, 198–204.

13. Joseph Story, *Commentaries on Equity Jurisprudence, as Administered in England and America*, 2 vols. (1836; rpt., New York: Arno, 1972), 2:655.

14. Lawrence Stone, *Road to Divorce: England, 1530–1987* (New York: Oxford University Press, 1990); "An Act Respecting Divorce," 22 February 1819, *Laws of the State of Illinois* (1819), 35–37; "An Act Concerning Divorces," 31 January 1827, *Revised Code of Laws of Illinois* (1827), 181–83; "Divorces," 3 March 1845, *Revised Statutes of the State of Illinois* (1845), 196–97.

15. For the liberalization of divorce laws in nineteenth-century Massachusetts and Virginia and the continuing prohibition of divorce in South Carolina, see Michael S. Hindus and Lynne E. Withey, "The Law of Husband and Wife in Nineteenth-Century America: Changing Views of Divorce," in *Women and the Law: A Social Historical Perspective*, vol. 2: *Property, Family, and the Legal Profession*, ed. D. Kelly Weisberg (Cambridge, Mass.: Schenkman, 1982), 133–53.

16. See also the more extended treatment of divorce by Stacy Pratt McDermott in chapter 3; Nancy F. Cott, "Divorce and the Changing Status of Women in Eighteenth-Century Massachusetts," *William and Mary Quarterly* 33 (October 1976): 586–614; and Lawrence B. Goodheart, Neil Hanks, and Elizabeth Johnson, "'An Act for the Relief of Females . . .': Divorce and the Changing Legal Status of Women in Tennessee, 1796–1860," *Tennessee Historical Quarterly* 44 (Fall 1985): 318–39 and (Winter 1985): 402–16.

17. Bill for Divorce, 4 March 1853, *Beerup v. Beerup, LPAL*; Decree, 18 June 1853, *Beerup v. Beerup, LPAL*.

18. Bill for Divorce, Affidavit, 4 September 1854, *Brewer v. Brewer, LPAL*; Decree, 1 December 1854, *Brewer v. Brewer, LPAL*.

19. Lincoln and his partners handled 145 divorce cases between 1836 and 1861, 88 of which were in the Sangamon County Circuit Court. For an examination of the implications of divorce for women, see Norma Basch, "Relief in the Premises: Divorce as a Woman's Remedy in New York and Indiana, 1815–1870," *Law and History Review* 8 (Spring 1990): 1–24. For a discussion of child custody and the presumption of paternal right, see Michael Grossberg, *Governing the Hearth: Law and the Family in Nineteenth-Century America* (Chapel Hill: University of North Carolina Press, 1985), 234–85. For the implications of the "unwritten law" that a man could kill his wife's lover if he caught them in the act, see Hendrik Hartog, "Lawyering, Husbands' Rights, and 'the Unwritten Law' in Nineteenth-Century America," *Journal of American History* 84 (June 1997): 67–96.

20. Sangamon County Circuit Court, Judge's Docket database, 1836–1860, Lincoln Legal Papers, Springfield, Ill. This database records each appearance of a single case; therefore, a single case might have multiple appearances if it persisted through several terms of court. Of 3,077 appearances of criminal cases, 88 (3 percent) involved female defendants. There

is no indication that criminal cases with female defendants had fewer or more appearances per case than those involving male defendants.

Other charges on which the grand jury indicted women in Sangamon County included assault with a deadly weapon, bigamy, concealing the death of a bastard child, malicious mischief, perjury, poisoning, selling liquor without a license, riot, and threatening life. Statistics on Lincoln's practice are drawn from *LPAL*. Of the sixteen criminal cases with women defendants, only six cases involved women only. The others involved men and women charged with the same offense (e.g., adultery, assault, poisoning). Only four of the sixteen (25 percent) involved sexual crimes, but the Sangamon County sample is more reliable because of the larger sample size.

21. "Criminal Code," 6 January 1827, *Revised Code of Laws of Illinois* (1827), 125; Order, 12 June 1854, *People v. Hill, LPAL*. Robert Hill and Isabella Hill were African Americans who lived in Sangamon County. See G. S. Rowe, "*Femes Covert* and Criminal Prosecution in Eighteenth-Century Pennsylvania," *American Journal of Legal History* 32 (April 1988): 138–56.

22. Arrest Warrant, 7 December 1841, *People v. Babbitt, LPAL*; JP Transcript, 21 December 1841, *People v. Babbitt, LPAL*; Affidavit and Order, 30 December 1841, *People v. Babbitt, LPAL*; Order, 1 June 1842, *People v. Babbitt, LPAL*.

23. Order, 23 March 1850, *People v. McHenry and Graves, LPAL*; Judge's Docket, November term 1850, *People v. McHenry and Graves, LPAL*; Order, 19 March 1851, *People v. McHenry and Graves, LPAL*; Order, 25 March 1851, *People v. McHenry and Graves, LPAL*; Judge's Docket, March term 1851, *People v. McHenry and Graves, LPAL*.

24. A higher incidence of nolle prosequi (failure to prosecute) in criminal cases with women defendants than in those with male defendants was also evident in eighteenth-century Pennsylvania. See G. S. Rowe, "Women's Crime and Criminal Administration in Pennsylvania, 1763–1790," *Pennsylvania Magazine of History and Biography* 109 (1985): 335–68.

25. *(Springfield) Illinois State Journal*, 16 June 1856; Order, 18 November 1856, *People v. House, LPAL*; Order, 1 December 1856, *People v. House, LPAL*.

26. Order, 29 April 1857, *People v. House, LPAL*; *Daily Illinois State Journal*, 30 April 1857; *Daily Illinois State Journal*, 1 May 1857.

27. *Daily Illinois State Journal*, 2 May 1857.

28. Ian R. Tyrrell, *Sobering Up: From Temperance to Prohibition in Antebellum America, 1800–1860* (Westport, Conn.: Greenwood, 1979); Herbert Wiltsee, "The Temperance Movement, 1848–1871," *Papers in Illinois History and Transactions for the Year 1937* (Springfield: Illinois State Historical Society, 1938), 82–92; Daniel W. Stowell, "Staggering toward Reform: Temperance and Prohibition in Antebellum Illinois," paper delivered at the Illinois History Symposium, Springfield, 4 December 1998.

29. The criminal defendants included Elizabeth Shurtliff, thirty-eight, wife of a miner; Catherine Shurtliff, possibly seventeen, daughter of a miner; Rowena R. Herndon, twenty-six, wife of a farmer; Caroline Sawyer; Emily Lewis, forty, wife of a physician; Catharine Shinkle, twenty-five, wife of a carpenter; Martha Taylor; Helen Sawyer; and Caroline Taylor.

30. *(Springfield) Illinois State Register*, 27 May 1854; Judgment Docket, 16 May 1854, *People v. Shurtliff et al., LPAL*; A. H. Goodpasture to William H. Herndon, 31 March 1869, *People v. Shurtliff et al., LPAL*; Fee Book, May 1854, *People v. Shurtliff et al., LPAL*; "Criminal Jurisprudence," Division X, sec. 117, 3 March 1845, *Revised Statutes of the State of Illinois* (1845), 171.

Abraham H. Goodpasture (1812–85), who told Herndon the story of this trial in 1869, was born in Tennessee and moved to Illinois before 1850. He became the pastor of a Cumberland Presbyterian church near Petersburg, Illinois. He declared that he had heard the story directly from the Reverend R. D. Taylor, who was present at the trial. See Douglas L. Wilson and Rodney O. Davis, eds., *Herndon's Informants: Letters, Interviews, and Statements about Abraham Lincoln* (Urbana: University of Illinois Press, 1998), 572–73, 750.

31. The cases with women as plaintiffs and the slanderous accusations were *Allsop v. Sturgeon* (adultery, prostitution); *Beatty et ux. v. Miller et ux.* (adultery); *Blue v. Allen et ux.* (perjury); *Cantrall et ux. v. Primm* (adultery); *Cockrell et ux. v. Tainter* (unknown); *Fancher v. Gollogher* (fraud, fornication); *Hatch v. Potter et ux.* (fornication); *Jacobus v. Kitchell et ux.* (prostitution); *Keltner & Keltner v. Keltner* (unknown); *Kipper et ux. v. Davis et ux.* (unknown); *McDonough et ux. v. Donnelly* (unknown); *Martin v. Underwood* (fornication); *Mitchell et ux. v. Mitchell* (adultery); *Patterson et ux. v. Edwards et ux.* (adultery, fornication); *Preston et ux. v. Townsend et ux.* (unknown); *Regnier v. Cabot & Torrey* (fornication); *Sanders et ux. v. Dunham* (adultery); *Scott et ux. v. Ellis* (unknown); *Toney v. Sconce* (fornication); and *Warner v. Nisewander* (unknown).

In *Skinner v. Overstreet et ux.* Jane Overstreet was accused of making slanderous accusations of adultery. In *Chase v. Blakely & Blakely,* Phebe Blakely was accused of slanderous accusations of theft and of poisoning an animal.

32. Andrew J. King, "Constructing Gender: Sexual Slander in Nineteenth-Century America," *Law and History Review* 13 (Spring 1995): 65–66.

33. Mark E. Steiner, "The Lawyer as Peacemaker: Law and Community in Abraham Lincoln's Slander Cases," *Journal of the Abraham Lincoln Association* 16 (Summer 1995): 9.

34. Andrew J. King, "The Law of Slander in Antebellum America," *American Journal of Legal History* 35 (January 1991): 20–21; King, "Constructing Gender," 86; Steiner, "Lawyer as Peacemaker," 6.

35. Declaration, Plea, 20 October 1843, *Patterson et ux. v. Edwards et ux., LPAL.*

Reputation was as important to married women as to single women: "Whereas single women needed good reputations to join the community of women through marriage, married women needed to maintain such reputations to remain within the community" (King, "Constructing Gender," 105).

36. Tucker, *Blackstone's Commentaries,* 2:443; Declaration, Plea, 20 October 1843, *Patterson et ux. v. Edwards et ux., LPAL.*

37. Order, 7 June 1844, *Patterson et ux. v. Edwards et ux., LPAL.*

38. *Patterson et ux. v. Edwards et ux.,* 7 Ill. 720–24 (1845); Petition for Rehearing, 28 January 1846, *Patterson et ux. v. Edwards et ux., LPAL.*

Like many northern states, Illinois prohibited interracial marriages. "No person of colour, negro or mulatto, of either sex, shall be joined in marriage with any white person, male or female, in this State; and all marriages or marriage contracts, entered into between such coloured person and white person, shall be null and void in law" ("An Act Respecting Free Negroes and Mulattoes, Servants, and Slaves," 17 January 1829, *Revised Code of Laws of Illinois* [1829], 111). Punishments for violating this statute included fines, whippings, and imprisonment. See also David W. Fowler, *Northern Attitudes toward Interracial Marriage: Legislation and Public Opinion in the Middle Atlantic and the States of the Old Northwest, 1780–1930* (New York: Garland, 1987).

39. King, "Constructing Gender," 77–78.

40. "An Act to Provide for the Maintenance of Illegitimate Children," *Revised Laws of*

Illinois (1833), 334–36; "Bastardy," 3 March 1845, *Revised Statutes of the State of Illinois* (1845), 85–86.

In 1861 the Illinois legislature increased the required term of support to ten years and gave the mother custody of the child until the child was ten years old. See "An Act to Amend Chapter Sixteen of the Revised Statutes of 1845, Entitled 'Bastardy,'" 22 February 1861, *Public Laws of the State of Illinois* (1861), 171–73.

41. U.S. Census Office, Seventh Census of the United States (1850), Champaign County, Illinois, ms., 234, 422.

42. U.S. Census Office, Eighth Census of the United States (1860), Champaign County, Illinois, ms.

43. *Grable v. Margrave, LPAL; Anderson v. Ryan, LPAL.* Another example of paired cases involving claims of assumpsit (breach of marriage contract) and seduction was *Neighbor v. Hall* and *People ex rel. Neighbor v. Hall.* See *Neighbor v. Hall, LPAL; People ex rel. Neighbor v. Hall, LPAL.* The Sangamon County Circuit Court heard these cases in 1859. The 1851 Edgar County Circuit Court case of *Benson v. Mayo* likewise involved the breach of a marriage contract (*LPAL*). *Keenan v. Price,* an 1855 Vermilion County Circuit Court case, involved a mother's bringing a seduction action for the loss of her daughter's services (*LPAL*).

44. Order, 3 May 1850, *Dunn v. Carle, LPAL;* Order, 2 May 1850, *People ex rel. Dunn v. Carle, LPAL;* Order, 17 October 1850, *People ex rel. Dunn v. Carle, LPAL;* Order, 17 October 1850, *Dunn v. Carle, LPAL.*

45. David Davis to Sarah Davis, 1 May 1851, *People ex rel. Dunn v. Carle, LPAL;* Order, 2 May 1851, *People ex rel. Dunn v. Carle, LPAL.*

46. David Davis to Sarah Davis, 3 May 1851, *Dunn v. Carle, LPAL;* Order, 2 May 1851, *Dunn v. Carle, LPAL;* Order, 2 May 1851, *People ex rel. Dunn v. Carle, LPAL.*

47. JP Transcript, 14 January 1858, *Murphy v. Cotton, LPAL;* Judgment Docket, 11 November 1858, *Murphy v. Cotton, LPAL.* For a parallel case see *Dillon v. Cotton, LPAL.*

48. Declaration, 12 January 1838, *Reed et ux. v. Arnold & Butler, LPAL.*

49. Tapping Reeve, *The Law of Baron and Femme, of Parent and Child, Guardian and Ward, Master and Servant, and of the Powers of the Courts of Chancery,* 3d ed. (Albany, N.Y.: William Gould, 1862), 49.

50. "An Act establishing the Recorder's office, and for other purposes," 19 February 1819, *Laws of the State of Illinois* (1819), 21; "Conveyances," 3 March 1845, *Revised Statutes of the State of Illinois* (1845), 106.

51. Promissory Note, 21 April 1857, *Bevan v. Davis et ux., LPAL;* Mortgage, 21 April 1857, *Bevan v. Davis et ux., LPAL;* Bill of Complaint, May 1859, *Bevan v. Davis et ux., LPAL;* Decree, May 1859, *Bevan v. Davis et ux., LPAL;* Master in Chancery's Report, 17 August 1859, *Bevan v. Davis et ux., LPAL.* Lincoln's law practice encompassed more than one hundred cases of foreclosures of mortgages with women litigants (*LPAL*).

52. Caroline H. Dall, *Woman's Rights under the Law: In Three Lectures* (Boston: Walker, Wise, 1861), 127–29; "An Act to Protect Married Women in their Separate Property," 21 February 1861, *Public Laws of the State of Illinois* (1861), 143. See also Elizabeth Bowles Warbasse, *The Changing Legal Rights of Married Women, 1800–1861* (New York: Garland, 1987); Norma Basch, *In the Eyes of the Law: Women, Marriage, and Property in Nineteenth-Century New York* (Ithaca, N.Y.: Cornell University Press, 1982); Marylynn Salmon, *Women and the Law of Property in Early America* (Chapel Hill: University of North Carolina Press, 1986).

Reva B. Siegel argues that married women were also entitled to joint rights in family assets because of the household labor they performed, a claim asserted by some nineteenth-century women's rights activists ("Home as Work: The First Woman's Rights Claims Concerning Wives' Household Labor, 1850–1880," *Yale Law Journal* 103 [March 1994]: 1073–1217). Under this view married women's property acts fell far short of achieving equality.

53. "Dower," 3 March 1845, *Revised Statutes of the State of Illinois* (1845), 198–203; Reeve, *Law of Baron and Femme*, 98–103; Salmon, *Women and the Law of Property*, 141–47.

54. In eighteenth-century Pennsylvania, for example, the law "did not permit widows any inheritance when their husbands' estates were insolvent" (Rowe, "Role of Courthouses," 18). See also Salmon, *Women and the Law of Property*, 163–68.

55. Bill of Complaint, 17 February 1858, *Mann et ux. v. Lucas*, LPAL; Decree, 21 September 1858, *Mann et ux. v. Lucas*, LPAL; Decree, March 1859, *Mann et ux. v. Lucas*, LPAL; Decree, 30 March 1859, *Mann et ux. v. Lucas*, LPAL.

56. Bill of Complaint, 23 March 1859, *Reed et al. v. Mann et al.*, LPAL; Will, 11 December 1854, *Reed et al. v. Mann et al.*, LPAL.

57. Bill of Complaint, 23 March 1859, *Reed et al. v. Mann et al.*, LPAL; Answer, 2 August 1859, *Reed et al. v. Mann et al.*, LPAL; Decree, 23 April 1861, *Reed et al. v. Mann et al.*, LPAL; Agreement, 9 April 1862, *Reed et al. v. Mann et al.*, LPAL. One of Lucas's sons, Thomas K. Lucas, died after his father made the will but before his father died. Thomas K. Lucas's wife, their minor son, and his wife's new husband became defendants in this case in his stead.

58. From at least 1845 on, Illinois law stipulated that "Administration shall be granted . . . to the widow or next of kin to the intestate . . . but in all cases, the widow shall have the preference" ("Wills," 3 March 1845, *Revised Statutes of State of Illinois* [1845], 547). See also Dall, *Woman's Rights under the Law*, 127–28.

59. Affidavit, 28 August 1834, *Carrico v. Carrico et al.*, LPAL; Notice, Settlement, 15 March 1837, *Carrico v. Carrico et al.*, LPAL; Petition for Partition, 17 March 1837, *Carrico v. Carrico et al.*, LPAL; Guardian ad litem's Answer, 17 March 1837, *Carrico v. Carrico et al.*, LPAL; Decree, 17 March 1837, *Carrico v. Carrico et al.*, LPAL; Affidavit, 19 November 1837, *Carrico v. Carrico et al.*, LPAL. For other examples of women in the role of executrix or administratrix, see *Batterton v. Batterton et al.* (Sangamon County Circuit Court, 1842), *Brown v. Heredith* (Sangamon County Probate Justice of the Peace Court, 1840), *Case v. Virden* (Sangamon County Circuit Court, 1859), *Clark & Clark v. Hinthorn et al.* (McLean County Circuit Court, 1841), *Davenport v. Davenport et al.* (Sangamon County Circuit Court, 1839), *Dingman v. Derrin* (Sangamon County Circuit Court, 1837), *Dingman v. Derrin* (Sangamon County Circuit Court, 1838), *Ely v. Kirk* (Tazewell County Circuit Court, 1850), *Ex parte Finley & Black* (Macon County Circuit Court, 1840), *Goode v. Lucas* (Christian County Circuit Court, 1846), *Mathes v. Sampson & Sampson* (De Witt County Circuit Court, 1858), *Miller v. Miller et al.* (Menard County Circuit Court, 1848), *Ritter & Ritter v. Wagoner* (Menard County Circuit Court, 1849), *Scott v. Davenport* (Tazewell County Circuit Court, 1843), and *Steele v. Aiken* (Illinois Supreme Court, 1856), all in LPAL.

60. An analysis of the first names of witnesses yielded 202 women who served as witnesses. The use of initials for first names prevented gender identification for 1,657 of the 8,802 witnesses. Of the remaining 7,145 witnesses, 202 (2.8 percent) had identifiable female first names.

61. Various Subpoenas, October 1843, *Patterson et ux. v. Edwards et ux.*, *LPAL;* Bill of Exceptions, 7 June 1844, *Patterson et ux. v. Edwards et ux.*, *LPAL*. Subpoenaed female witnesses included Susan Barnes, Nancy Cavin, Maria Seimers (or Seymour), and Miss Edwards (daughter of the plaintiffs). At least Seimers and Edwards testified during the trial.

62. Master in Chancery's Report, October term 1859, *Klein v. Klein, LPAL*.

63. Deposition, 20 September 1853, *People v. Hollingsworth, LPAL*. James Hollingsworth and Jacob Ater had something of a history in the courts. In 1852 the grand jury indicted Hollingsworth in three separate cases alleging the sale of liquor to Ater in quantities of less than one quart. See *People v. Hollingsworth, LPAL*.

64. David Davis to Sarah Davis, 20 October 1851, *Fithian v. Casseday, LPAL;* David Davis to Sarah Davis, 27 October 1851, *Fithian v. Casseday, LPAL*.

65. W. H. Goodpasture to William H. Herndon, 31 March 1869, *People v. Shurtliff et al.*, *LPAL; Illinois State Register,* 27 May 1854.

66. King, "Constructing Gender," 67.

2

"For the Well-Being of the Child":
The Law and Childhood

DENNIS E. SUTTLES

The records of Illinois courts for the three decades before the Civil War provide excellent examples of how law and perceptions of the family interacted to protect the interests of the child in controversies involving family members. The conflict between the common law's interpretation of the father as patriarch of the family and society's more democratic view of that unit was different throughout the country. Although the common law heritage of patriarchy maintained pressure on Illinois courts to conform to that tradition, the records show that the courts were persuaded to follow society's lead in seeking the best interests of the child whenever possible.

For centuries the father and husband of the family held the position of patriarch—a place fashioned through history, made sacred by Scripture, and embodied within English common law. Economic and social changes accelerated by the American and French Revolutions fostered a change in the way Americans viewed the family and the roles of its members. The internal dynamics of families gradually changed from patriarchal to more democratic relationships. Each family member gained importance according to his or her socially prescribed role as an individual within the family unit.[1]

The writings of John Locke (1632–1704) and Jean-Jacques Rousseau (1712–78) ushered in a new awareness of childhood development, and the pressures of increasing urbanization and industrialization in the former British colonies altered society's views on marriage, children, and family life.[2] Society gradually began to view the family as a more private, introspective unit characterized by a companionate relationship between husband and wife. Attitudes toward children within the family became gentler, and child-rearing practices reflected the privatization of the family unit.[3] The father's absolute rule as patriarch, although supported by common law, diminished as society attributed some of his responsibilities to the mother. Children gradually lost their importance as a source of supplemental income and retirement security for their parents. They became economically worthless but intrinsically valuable as a future asset to a republican society. Concern for the child's nurture and education became the determinate factor in the worth of the child.[4] Parents instilled their children with values of good citizenship: order, responsibility, and self-discipline.[5]

The modern family of the post-Revolutionary era in the United States reflected the political and social changes in Europe and America.[6] The family emerged from this era democratic in nature. Individual family members developed clearly defined roles within the family. At the same time, it also took on the character of the "republican family" as it absorbed the essence of the political and social changes brought about in the birth of the new republic. This era was a formative one for both the family and the state.[7]

Not only did the family place more importance upon the child but the state began to exert its power over children as well. The courts exercised more control over children by expanding the English common law doctrine of *parens patriae*.[8] Originally, this doctrine gave the judiciary the power to intercede in specific situations in order to protect the child's property from misuse by his or her parents or guardians. The state increasingly expanded the scope of this doctrine to include custody matters on the ground that children existed as a public trust for the future of the nation. Nineteenth-century courts gradually interpreted the authority that families held over children as a power "held in trust" for the larger society and, as such, falling within the parameters of state regulation.[9]

During the nineteenth century categories of domestic relations law gradually evolved to reflect society's growing recognition of individualism within the family. At the beginning of the century statutes dealing with women and children were scattered within the categories of contract, tort, and property law. As the law developed, a distinctive legal concept emerged that viewed the family as a nucleus of separate legal individuals rather than an integral part of political society. With the rise of the republican family came the development of a body of law known as "domestic relations" law. By the late nineteenth century laws involving courtship, marriage, adoption, child custody, property rights of wives, and divorce became a united body of domestic relations law. Changes in those laws for children came about more slowly than they did for their mothers. Not until 1900 did the law begin to distinguish "children's rights."[10]

The statutes of Illinois during the period from statehood (1818) until the outbreak of the American Civil War reflected this tendency. Comparing the *Revised Statutes of Illinois* for 1827, 1845, and 1856, the number of laws dealing with "infants"—boys younger than twenty-one and girls younger than eighteen—increased dramatically over time.[11] No unified body of laws regarding minors existed; instead, such laws were scattered among sections pertaining to property, guardianship, tort, and custody, among others. The laws regarding guardianship far outnumbered those found in other divisions protecting the rights of the minor. Because of the large incidence of intestate estates, the importance of an equitable distribution of property, and the economic interests involved, the rights of minor heirs required particular protection.[12]

The number and variety of cases heard before the Illinois Supreme Court from 1819 until 1861 involving minors revealed a strong emphasis on the issues of guardianship, property, tort, custody, and morality. Of 267 cases involving children, 135 cases (51 percent) dealt with guardianship issues, sixty (23 percent) with property disputes, twenty-nine (11 percent) with questions of tort, twenty-seven (10 percent) with the consequences of parental divorce, and thirteen (5 percent) with infractions of laws legislating morality.[13] It was not unusual for a case to touch children in more than one way; for example, a dispute involving a child might include both guardianship and property issues. A closer look at these cases in relation to the court's interpretation of existing law reveals that the court emphasized the protection of the child's best interests.

The legal career of Abraham Lincoln (1836–61) provides a sampling of antebellum Illinois cases from all court venues involving the interests of children. Table 2.1 provides the distribution of such Lincoln partnership cases among a variety of topics.[14]

The laws governing the relationship between the guardian and her or his ward grew in number and specificity throughout the period. In 1827 the Illinois statutes stipulated in very broad terms the rules governing the appointment, powers, and removal of guardians, how and when guardians could sell the real estate of minors, and the appointment of a guardian *ad litem* for minors in chancery cases.[15] By 1845 the laws governing the relationship between guardian and ward in chancery cases became more elaborate. The number of laws specifying the duties and legal requirements of the guardian increased to protect further the interests of wards.[16] The Illinois statutes of 1856 incorporated even more detailed rules for guardians as well as rules in other areas in which the interests of children came before Illinois courts.[17]

Of the Lincoln partnership cases involving guardians and wards between 1836 and 1861, 97 percent dealt with issues in equity involving land. More than half dealt with the partition of estates due to the death of a father or the request of his widow for her dower rights. As a result of these actions, minors

Table 2.1. Types of Litigation Involving Minors, 1836–61

Type of Litigation	Number of Cases	Percentage
Inheritance (minor heirs)	492	78.2
Custody of children	47	7.5
Illegitimate children	26	4.1
Property disputes involving minors	15	2.4
Minors as laborers	11	1.8
Minors as victims of crime	11	1.8
Liability for the actions of minors	9	1.4
Orphans	4	0.6
Minors as perpetrators of crime	4	0.6
Debt collection involving a minor	4	0.6
Sale of real estate belonging to a minor	3	0.5
Other	3	0.5
	629	100.0%

Source: Martha L. Benner and Cullom Davis et al., eds., *The Law Practice of Abraham Lincoln: Complete Documentary Edition* (DVD; Urbana: University of Illinois Press, 2000).

received their inheritance in one of two ways. In some cases the court divided the real estate according to the wishes of the deceased as expressed in a will or, if the person died intestate, by order of the court. Each heir received a parcel of land after payment of the estate's debts. In other cases the survivors received a cash settlement from the sale of the land if the court-appointed commissioners determined that the land could not be divided equitably without financial loss. A close examination of these cases and the laws of Illinois illuminates the courts' commitment to protect the child's financial interests.

In the 1857 Menard County Circuit Court case of *Sheneman v. Goodpasture et ux.*, the court partitioned the estate of the late Joseph Smith by selling the land and dividing the proceeds among Smith's heirs. Joseph Smith's father, Enoch B. Smith, had died between 1830 and 1835 and left land to his son. When Joseph Smith died in 1850, he left behind a widow, two daughters, and a son, Enoch B. Smith II. Within seven years of Joseph Smith's death, his widow, Adelphia Smith, married William B. Goodpasture, who purchased the titles to the inherited land from the Smiths' two daughters, Mrs. James Rayburn and Frances M. Smith.[18]

On March 23, 1857, young Enoch B. Smith II's guardian, Adam Sheneman, filed a suit for the partition of his ward's share from the 157 acres of land in five parcels (5 acres, 40 acres, 61 acres, 11 acres, and 40 acres) left in Joseph Smith's estate.[19] During the May 1857 term of the Menard County Circuit Court, Sheneman's attorney, William H. Herndon, presented the evidence of affidavits, deeds, and titles to document the history of the estate. Although summoned to appear before the court, the Goodpastures appeared with their attorney only once. After hearing the evidence at a subsequent hearing and receiving no reply to the plaintiff's petition, the court decreed that it would take the bill "as confessed." The judge ordered the partition of the 157 acres "in one part for complainant as guardian for Enoch B. Smith and two parts to William B. Goodpasture." He further decreed that Adelphia Goodpasture would have "her fair and reasonable dower" from the lands to be divided.[20]

Following the law, the judge appointed three commissioners from Menard County to determine the best method to divide the land equitably. If the land were "susceptible of division," the law required the commissioners to report exactly how the land was to be divided. However, if they determined that a division of the 157 acres "would be injurious to the land or estate," they also had to report their findings to the court as soon as possible in order that it might decree further action.[21]

After examining each parcel and reaching a decision on their division, the three commissioners reported to the court on May 20, 1857, that the lands could not be divided equitably because they were "so small and so scattered that it would be to the detriment of the estate and an injury to all persons concerned or interest[ed] in the lands or estate." The commissioners also determined that one-third of the lands should be set aside as Adelphia Goodpasture's "reasonable" dower.[22]

The court approved the report of the commissioners and ordered the master in chancery, Albert I. Brooks, to sell the remaining land at public auction. After public notification of the sale Brooks conducted the auction on the steps of the Menard County courthouse in Petersburg on August 20, 1857. Enoch Smith's stepfather, William B. Goodpasture, was the highest bidder and purchased the land for $19.10 per acre.[23]

In this particular case the commissioners determined that the land could not be divided fairly without harm to both parties to the partition suit.[24] By approving the report of the commissioners, the court decided that a monetary settlement would be most equitable. By recommendation of the commissioners the court ordered the land sold and the proceeds divided among the remaining heirs. The guardian of Enoch B. Smith received $1,021.78 for his ward, and William Goodpasture received $1,976.92 for his wife's dower and her daughters' portions of the estate. However, not all partition suits ended in this manner.

In some cases the minor heirs received land as a result of the partition of their father's estate. The 1853 Woodford County case of *Fields v. Fields et al.* resulted in the partition of an estate in which both minor heirs and their mother received land as their inheritance and dower, respectively. Sometime before 1850 Gilbert Fields, a farmer in Woodford County, died intestate, leaving behind his wife, Rhoda Fields, and their six children: John H. (an adult, no age given in the census); Philander, 24; Sophia Fields Ames, 23; Hyram, 19; Sarah, 17, and Melissa, 13. In 1850 forty-seven-year-old Rhoda Fields owned approximately $2,000 in real estate. Their eldest son, John H. Fields, lived outside Woodford County, whereas Philander remained at home to maintain the 240-acre family farm. Sophia, the eldest daughter, had married David Ames, a blacksmith, who lived in Woodford County; they had three sons.[25] When Hyram came of age in 1852, he demanded his share of the inheritance, which made it necessary for the family to partition the estate.

At the Woodford County courthouse in Metamora, John H. Fields petitioned the circuit court to partition the estate of his late father on behalf of his family. Circuit clerk Peter Doty summoned John's mother, brothers, and sisters to appear in court to begin the proceedings.[26] By the spring of 1853 only two of the Fields children were still minors. John's attorney requested that the court appoint a guardian *ad litem* to represent both Sarah, then twenty, and Melissa, sixteen; the age of majority then was twenty-one. On April 25, 1853, Judge David Davis appointed Abraham Lincoln as their guardian *ad litem*, and he immediately composed an answer on behalf of Sarah and Melissa Fields to John Fields's petition for partition.[27] As one of several attorneys riding the circuit, Lincoln may or may not have known the Fieldses or their particular situation, but as a court-appointed guardian *ad litem*, Lincoln declared that he was "entirely ignorant of the matters and things in said petition alleged & that he knows of no reason why the prayer thereof should not be granted, but requires that full proof be made."[28] In 1853 the case law of Illinois stated that no court could pass judgment in a case involving minor children without sufficient proof of the matters involved duly recorded in the court record.[29]

That same day the court called the adult defendants three times to appear before the judge, but none came forward to answer the petition. Their failure to appear simply signified their compliance with the petition and their desire to avoid costly legal fees. Judge Davis read the plaintiff's petition, heard the oral evidence presented by John Fields's attorney, considered the failure of the adult defendants to appear, and weighed the answer of the guardian *ad litem*. After considering these materials, Judge Davis awarded dower to Rhoda Fields equal to one-third of the estate. The court awarded each child in the suit one-fifth of the remaining land.[30]

In order to distribute the land equitably among the heirs in a way that would not damage the value of the estate, Judge Davis appointed three men from the community to serve as commissioners to view the land and determine the best way to partition it. He ordered them to report their findings at the next term of court.[31]

On September 26, 1853, the three commissioners returned to court to report that they had complied with Judge Davis's instructions as prescribed by law. A few days earlier they had visited the land in question, estimated its value, and found that they could partition the land in proportion to its value without damaging the total value of the estate. In their report the commissioners specified the exact location of each heir's inheritance and the land set aside as the widow's dower.[32] Each of the five children and their mother shared equally in the expenses of the suit.[33]

These examples demonstrate how guardians or guardians *ad litem* protected the financial interests of minor heirs in a court of law. The law protected children's inheritance and simultaneously averted a financial burden for the community. It ensured that children received a proper portion of their parent's estate. The courts' active preservation of each minor's inheritance may be viewed as an extension of the English common law principle of *parens patriae*. The courts prevented the misuse of a child's inheritance by guardians or parents in order to hold children as a public trust for the young Republic.

While the child in the republican family gained a more favored status within the family, the common law still placed the ownership and control of the child and the child's personal property firmly in the hands of the father or, in his absence, the mother. The Illinois Supreme Court case of *Parmelee et al. v. Smith* provides a good example of this practice.

In August 1856 fifteen-year-old Kate C. Smith left her home in Monroe, Michigan, where she lived with her mother, Alvira F. Smith, to spend some time with her brother, Winfield Smith, in Milwaukee, Wisconsin. She packed her clothing, family daguerreotypes, school books, and other personal belongings in a common leather russet trunk and traveled on the Michigan Southern Railroad to Chicago. She checked her trunk with the railroad when she left Monroe and saw it the next day during a stopover at Adrian, Michigan, where baggage handlers transferred her trunk from the Monroe train to the Adrian-to-Chicago train. Upon arrival at the Michigan Southern and Northern Indiana Railroad Depot in Chicago, Kate gave her baggage claim ticket for her trunk and her omnibus ticket to the omnibus line agent. Upon her arrival at the Milwaukee steamboat, she found that her baggage had not made it to the steamer, and she in fact never saw it again. Kate's mother accused the carrier of losing her daughter's trunk between the train and the steamer.

Kate's mother brought an assumpsit suit against Frank Parmelee and other common carriers in Chicago to recover the cost of her daughter's personal property along with damages. Cook County Circuit Judge George Manniere presided at the jury trial in Chicago during the special June 1858 term of the court. Kate Smith stated in her deposition that she had packed in her trunk "one silk dress, two colored muslin dresses, two Swiss muslin dresses, one barege dress, two basques, one white merino cape, one bonnet, one embroidered handkerchief, one fan, twelve pairs of stockings, one lot of underclothes, twelve collars," several school books, and other personal belongings.[34]

Kate's sister, Evaline Smith, testified that she had helped her sister pack her trunk. She verified that the value of the contents did approach $500 and that none of the articles belonged to others. Evaline swore that "all the articles had been used by Kate, my sister, more or less, and they were exclusively in her charge, and were generally articles of apparel and ornament, for her, necessary in traveling."[35]

Once Evaline concluded her testimony, neither side of the controversy provided additional evidence. The jury found Frank Parmelee and the other carriers guilty and assessed Alvira Smith's damages at $146.92. Even though the court awarded Mrs. Smith only a third of the amount of her loss, the defendants motioned the court to set aside the verdict and order a new trial. However, the court refused the motion. The carriers thereupon registered an exception to the verdict and appealed the case to the Illinois Supreme Court.[36]

During the trial in Chicago the attorneys for Frank Parmelee and the other carriers had argued that the clothing and other personal belongings were the sole property of fifteen-year-old Kate. Her mother had no right to sue for damages to property she did not use nor own. At its April 1859 term in Ottawa the Illinois Supreme Court reviewed the case and affirmed the judgment of the lower court. In his written opinion for the court Justice Pinckney Walker supported the ownership of a child's property not as an absolute right granted the parent but as an entitlement of that parent whose duty it was to support the child.

According to Walker, parents furnished their minor children with clothing for the child's use at the will of the parent. Children were not given unlimited freedom to do what they wished with it. The parents held the "right of property and possession," and they might take the clothing away at any time. The duty of parents to support their child gave them the right to control the benefits the child received from personal property. The parents controlled the means of that support. Clothing, services, and the earnings of a minor child belonged to the parents. Their duty and obligation to support their children, as recognized by tradition, entitled the parents to these benefits. "The duty of supporting the idle and prodigal child, without the power of controlling the means," the court concluded, "has never been recognized either as a moral or legal duty."[37]

According to the courts, the personal property of minor children belonged to the parents, whose duty it was to provide their children with the necessities of life. Although the child exclusively used the property, clothing in this case, the parents retained ownership as an entitlement for their support of that child. This concept was in keeping with the inability of children directly to bring suit in court. An adult always represented them, either as a guardian, a guardian *ad litem,* or a next friend (similar to a guardian) in court.[38] In fact, to a limited degree the law still considered children as a kind of property of the parent. This case reaffirmed the idea that children had no legal existence apart from their parents.

Custody cases disturbed this harmonious view of families, just as divorce destroyed it for marriages. Traditionally, fathers, as the ruling patriarchs of the family unit, retained custody of their offspring. As the republican family gained strength and the courts exercised their power to protect the child as a public trust through the English common law doctrine of *parens patriae,* the patriarchal family declined. In child custody cases the judges considered the needs of the child, as against the interests of the parents, the maternal rights of the mother, and the suitability of both parents in determining who would best care for the child in question. In some cases the court gave custody of children to strangers who proved to be better guardians than the children's natural parents.[39] The court records reflect a strong reliance on this "best-interests-of-the-child" doctrine and in several cases even refer to the doctrine specifically.[40]

The Illinois Supreme Court case of *Cowls v. Cowls* (1846) emphasized the best-interests-of-the-child doctrine and served as a precedent in future Illinois cases involving the welfare of children.[41] In an earlier decision the Edwards County Circuit Court had granted Ann Cowls a divorce from her husband, Thomas Cowls, but made no provision for the custody of their two children, Mary Jane, six, and Thomas, four. The children continued to live with their father, who allegedly lived with a woman "in a state of fornication" until he married her a few weeks before Ann Cowls filed a suit against him. In April 1845 Ann Cowls filed a bill in chancery against Thomas Cowls for an increase in alimony and for custody and maintenance of their two young children. Ann Cowls characterized Thomas Cowls's new wife as a "woman of notoriously bad character, and unqualified in any manner for the proper care and education" of the children. She described her former husband as "negligent of the education and moral welfare of the children, and addicted to excessive and frequent intoxications, and . . . in the habit of quarreling with the [stepmother] in the presence of the children, and driving her from home, that Thomas habitually uses profane, indecent, immoral, and vulgar language as well in the presence of the children as elsewhere, and is in other respects wholly disqualified from educating the children in a respectable and moral manner."[42] On April 15, 1846, Ann Cowls gained custody of the children with a maintenance allowance of $30 per month for five years.[43]

Thomas Cowls hired Abraham Lincoln to represent him and appealed the court's decision to the Illinois Supreme Court. In his argument before the supreme court Lincoln relied upon a citation of a custody case in which the court awarded the children to their mother, who had continued to live with a man in an unmarried state. The court viewed the position of Thomas Cowls in a different light. The woman in the case Lincoln cited gained custody of her children on the weight of the "tender years" doctrine, despite her moral irresponsibility.[44]

Chief Justice John Caton saw in Thomas Cowls "grouped together into one disgusting and revolting picture, those features of a father's character who has become unworthy of the charge of his own offspring."[45] He defended the court's right to become involved in the custody of Thomas Cowls's children by the English common law doctrine of *parens patriae*. Caton stated that power aptly in this case. It was not a new idea for the chancery court to exert its power to control and interfere with the custody of minors. It was an ancient tradition that the supreme court could not question. A regulated society governed by republican principles considered it important that a child be "reared and educated under such influences that he may be qualified to exercise the rights of freemen and take part in the government of the country." The country owed it to the child, as well as to itself, to protect the child from abuse, fraud, and neglect. The child had a right to this protection. If the father conducted himself in a manner that upheld the child's right to this protection, the court would not interfere with the parent's control. However, a father who neglected and abused that charge for his natural offspring would find the courts ready to intercede for the child. The court would take measures to remove such children from their natural father, appoint a guardian to care for the children, and might even consider placing the children in the care of a person outside the natural family sphere.[46]

To bolster his opinion Caton referred to the treatise on equity jurisprudence by the late Joseph Story, associate justice of the U.S. Supreme Court. According to Story, the chancery court extended its control over the person of the child for the child's protection and education, and over the child's property to manage and preserve it in order to take care of the future needs of the child. The court assumed that parents would take seriously the responsibility entrusted to them. Parents were expected to care for their children properly; to educate them in literature, morals, and religion; and to treat their offspring with kindness and affection. If parents did not live up to this assumption, Story warned that "the court of chancery will interfere, and deprive [parents] of the custody of [their] children, and support a suitable person to act as guardian, and to take care of them, and superintend their education."[47] The Illinois Supreme Court thus upheld the decision of the lower court to award the children to Ann Cowls and agreed that the $30-per-year maintenance for each child was reasonable.[48]

In the case of *Cowls v. Cowls,* then, the court exercised the doctrine of *parens patriae* to justify intervention where the custody of children was at stake. Three years later the court reaffirmed the father's common law right to the custody of his children unless he gave up that right or lost it because of his misbehavior, misfortune, or some other extraordinary circumstances.[49] The case of *Miner v. Miner* (1849) delineated the hierarchy of rights within a child custody case. In it the Illinois Supreme Court established its right to determine the best interests of the child over the rights of both father and mother.

Laura L. Miner filed her bill for divorce at the May 1848 term of the Jersey County Circuit Court. She complained that her husband, Martin B. Miner, treated her with extreme and repeated cruelty. After a change of venue to Greene County, Martin withdrew his defense to a divorce "reserving to himself the right of contesting before the court all her legal claims, to the custody, care and maintenance of his daughter, Charlotte H. Miner, and any claim which might be set up by [his wife] for alimony." The court granted Laura Miner a divorce and, after hearing both sides regarding the custody of their child, awarded the mother custody of their daughter and decreed that she keep as payment of alimony certain articles of personal property in her possession, some of which may have been Martin Miner's. The court made no mention of monetary alimony payments but ordered Martin Miner to pay Laura Miner $15 at the end of each month to offset any further expense in litigating the case until the court rendered its final decision. Martin Miner appealed to the Illinois Supreme Court on all these decrees except the divorce.[50]

Martin Miner's attorney, David J. Baker, argued that his client had a common law right to the custody of his daughter out of his duty to maintain and to educate her. He also had a right to her labor. Even though Charlotte Miner was only seven years old, Martin Miner had primary custody rights to his daughter over those of her mother. He could enforce these rights through the power of a writ of *habeas corpus.*[51]

Laura Miner's attorney, William Thomas, based his client's claim to custody of Charlotte on six points. First, Laura Miner's father was a very wealthy man who welcomed his daughter and granddaughter to his home with his support. Second, Laura Miner appeared well qualified to educate and care for her child. Third, the child needed the special care only a mother could give. Fourth, the child's father owned no property, which limited his capacity to prepare his daughter for her duties in life. Fifth, even though the father kept a housekeeper at home, she was ignorant and not capable of caring for or educating the child. Sixth, based upon the nature of her case and the law governing the custody of children, the lower court could not have erred in granting Laura Miner custody of her daughter. William Thomas relied upon the court's decision in *Cowls v. Cowls* and a host of other decisions as authorities to support his contentions.[52]

Illinois Supreme Court Justice John Caton, in his opinion for the court, stated that the only question submitted in this case was the custody of the child. The court had to be exclusive in its examination of the records from the divorce proceedings to take into consideration only that evidence touching upon the child's custody. In that respect the *Miner* case was significantly different from *Cowls v. Cowls*. Regardless of the differences in the examination of evidence, *Cowls v. Cowls* established the court's chancery powers in child custody decisions that applied directly to this case. Caton expressed his compassion for the litigants, as they both clearly and honestly exhibited a strong attachment to their daughter.[53]

As to the father's legal right to the custody and the control of his child, Caton stated that contradictory decisions abounded. Nevertheless, the court believed that the father retained primary custody of his child unless he forfeited or lost his right through circumstances making him an unfit father. In a divorce one parent had to be given custody of the child or the resulting conflict between the parents could result in violence.

Caton stated that the mother's rights to the custody of her daughter were secondary to those of the father. However, in the eyes of the court the custody rights of both father and mother were "subject to the control of the courts of chancery, and when its aid is invoked, while it may not disregard the natural rights of parents, and the ties of blood, the best interest of the child must be primarily consulted."[54] He went on to reason that on this consideration a child of "tender years" was usually awarded to the care of the mother, if she was of good character. Even if the father had no fault, the court usually chose the mother, primarily because she was endowed with those natural qualities that were important in the nurture of young children. This circumstance was especially true in relation to the custody of daughters at an impressionable age. Caton explained that "while the affection of parents for daughters may be equal, yet the mother, from her natural endowments, her position in society, and her constant association with them, can give them that care, attention and advice so indispensable to their welfare; which a father, if the same children were left to his supervision, would be compelled in a great degree to confide to strangers."[55] As Caton's opinion makes clear, the court assumed that the mother had the opportunity to be at home to care for her child, while the father, as family provider, would not be able to care for the child while working. He would be compelled to hire someone to exercise his parental duties in his absence. As Laura Miner's attorney argued, Martin Miner's housekeeper was not an acceptable substitute for Charlotte's natural mother.

Caton knew of no instance where a father, granted a divorce due to his misconduct, gained custody of his children. If the possibility ever existed, the statute removed it from occurring in chancery court.[56] According to the statutes, once a divorce was granted, the chancery court was compelled to issue a decree affecting the "care, custody and support of the children, or any of them, as from the circumstances of the parties and the nature of the case shall be fit, reasonable and just."[57]

A review of the facts of the case revealed that the court had granted the divorce on the ground that the father ill-treated his wife. Martin Miner was a man who lost control of his violent temper often. His conduct toward his wife was "unreasonable, oppressive, and we may add cruel, as to render her life miserable, and to cause her health to be seriously impaired."[58] Because she came from a wealthy household and lived in conditions well below that to which she was accustomed, she frequently criticized or complained about her husband. Caton, however, did not use Laura Minor's complaints to justify Martin Miner's abuse of his wife. Although Martin Miner consistently showed the affection toward his child normally exhibited between father and daughter, it was not enough in the eyes of the court.

Caton summed up the sentiments of the court that justified its favoring the mother over the father in this case. The court did not expect Martin Miner to be able to give the personal care and attention a young girl of seven or eight years required. Her mother was more qualified in that regard, and there did not seem to be any objections against her. If Martin Miner gained custody of Charlotte, he would have to leave her with another while he was working. The court surmised that Martin Miner's daughter would want to associate with other young girls in whose company she would grow and mature in the ways of a woman. Her father could not supply the necessary "womanly guidance." His work would prevent him from keeping a watchful eye on his daughter while he was away from home. The court believed that Charlotte's upbringing would be better served by a "vigilant and tender mother."[59]

In the opinion of the Illinois Supreme Court young Charlotte belonged with her mother. The court affirmed the lower court's decision and modified the other conditions of the circuit court's decree regarding court costs. The court warned Laura Miner that it would not tolerate any intentions she held of taking the child out of the state if it awarded custody of Charlotte to her. The court guaranteed the father's right to visit his daughter whenever reasonably possible. Even though the court awarded custody of Charlotte to her mother, Charlotte's interests and development remained a concern of the court. The court warned both parents that it would view any attempt to alienate the child from the other parent as contempt of court and would impose the prescribed judgment.[60]

In those cases involving very young minors the judges considered the tender years of the child by awarding custody to the child's mother rather than to the father.[61] The court clearly supported the notion of the republican family in which the child held a unique, yet vulnerable, position that deserved special protection within the family. In many cases the court disregarded the patriarchal assertions of the father and gave preference to the subordinate members of the family. However, the patriarchal authority of the father did not always give way to the desires of the mother or the child.[62]

A good example of these limitations is the Menard County case of Maria Bennett, who brought suit against her husband, Richard E. Bennett, for divorce on the ground of adultery. In her April 1855 bill for divorce Maria Bennett claimed that her husband carried on an adulterous affair with another woman for several years. She had resigned herself to his infidelity until he became "bold enough to declare & avow his love for his mistress" to her. She stated that "he even went farther [to] declare that the woman with whom he lived in adultery was as good as any member of his family alluding to the daughters of [his wife] and he even insisted on bringing his strumpet to live in the same house with [her] because he said he would support her anyhow & he could thus do it better." Maria Bennett further accused her husband of cursing her in fits of rage and attempting to destroy her good name in the community by insinuating that she was a prostitute and an unfit wife. In addition to adultery, she accused Richard Bennett of collecting his debts and assigning his property to a trust in an attempt to defraud her of every possible means of support. Maria and Richard Bennett had produced five living offspring from their marriage: a married daughter and four younger children, two boys and two girls, who lived at home. Maria Bennett sought an absolute divorce from Richard Bennett, custody of their four minor children, an injunction to restrain the trustees from disposing of the proceeds of a sale of land until the court decided the case, and alimony from the estate to provide for her and the children.[63]

Richard Bennett denied his wife's charges of adultery and abuse. He admitted that he "could never again live with" his wife and would welcome a divorce from her. He objected to her request for custody of their children. Richard Bennett sought to vindicate himself of what he claimed were false charges.[64]

Maria Bennett hired William H. Herndon to argue her cause before the Menard County Circuit Court during the spring 1855 term. Even though Richard Bennett submitted his answer to the court on May 3, 1855, he failed to appear in court at the October 1855 term. Judge David M. Woodson called a jury to hear the evidence in the trial. The jury found Richard Bennett guilty of adultery, as charged in Maria Bennett's bill of complaint. Woodson awarded her a divorce and, based upon the testimony of witnesses in the case, decreed that the Bennett's three-month-old daughter and her older sister still at home be awarded to "the exclusive control" of their mother. While Maria Bennett gained possession of all the personal property, she lost custody of her two sons to their father. She may have lost "exclusive control" over the boys, but the court "expressly ordered and decreed . . . that the boys have free access at all times and places" to their mother. For the support of Maria Bennett and her two daughters the court ordered Richard Bennett to pay his ex-wife $100 a year in four installments of $25 a quarter, as well as the court costs involved in the divorce.[65]

In the case of *Bennett v. Bennett* the court considered the tender years and sex of the daughters in awarding custody of them to their mother. In the earlier decision in *Cowls v. Cowls* Caton had written that after a divorce was decreed, the court found that it also had to decide where to place the children. When the court had to remove all or some of the children from the custody of the father, it would place them with the mother if she was not objectionable. The court thought that she would be a better caregiver than a stranger. In fact, the court concluded, it might be the case that "when no serious objection can be urged against the father, that it would be advisable to give to the mother the care of a portion at least of the children, especially if they be daughters of very tender years."[66]

The court believed that the mother's nurture of daughters and babies outweighed the paternal rights of the father. Richard Bennett, although denying the charges of adultery, failed to prosecute his case. By not contesting the evidence in open court, he allowed the court to grant the divorce and infer his guilt. The court likely granted him custody of his two sons on the strength of a father's paternal and economic right to his sons.

The court considered the tender years of the illegitimate child as well as the legitimate child, but loopholes allowed unscrupulous fathers to escape their responsibility for the care and education of their offspring. In such cases the court expressed its frustration with the law. The court's irritation became quite evident in the 1844 case of *Wright for the use of Davidson v. Bennett and Bennett,* which also involved Richard Bennett's infidelity.

On June 4, 1844, a Menard County jury convicted Richard E. Bennett of being the father of Jane Davidson's illegitimate child. The justice of the peace ordered Bennett to pay "forty dollars annually from the 6th day of November, A.D. 1843, for the period of seven years, for the support, maintenance and education" of his illegitimate child. Richard Bennett posted the required bond, with his brother John Bennett serving as surety according to the statutory provisions.[67] Richard Bennett failed to pay child support and on June 8, 1844, he demanded that Jane Davidson surrender the custody of the child to him, which she refused to do. The statute governing the support of illegitimate children stated that if the mother of the illegitimate child refused to surrender it to the father, his obligation under the bond would cease. Jane Davidson's attorney, Thomas L. Harris, argued that the law required the father to post a second bond for the support of the child. However, Judge Samuel H. Treat of the Menard County Circuit Court decreed that the law supported the Bennetts' position. Probate Justice of the Peace Asa Wright, to whom Bennett was to pay the child support payments for distribution to Jane Davidson, appealed to the Illinois Supreme Court on her behalf.

The Illinois Supreme Court heard the case during its December 1845 term. Jane Davidson's attorney continued his argument for a second bond. Abraham Lincoln, on behalf of the Bennetts, argued that the law required the father to post only one bond. He admitted that although the common law did not permit the father of an illegitimate child to obtain custody, the statute in the case did.[68]

Writing for the Illinois Supreme Court, Justice Norman H. Purple, after "a careful and attentive consideration of the law," came to the conclusion that the statute plainly required only one bond. If the father "unnaturally and unfeelingly" demanded the child from its mother and she refused, he was freed of all obligation to support his child. This provision of the Illinois statute intended to give the father custody of his child, making him responsible for its education, support, and maintenance until the child reached majority, just as it would if the child were legitimate. By acknowledging his child in this manner, the father could not deny his parental obligation to that child. The legislature did not intend for the father to take custody of the child from its mother, only to "thrust it forth upon the world's charity, friendless and unprotected" after supporting the child for seven years as stipulated by his bond.[69] Although the intent of the law and the court favored the child and its mother, delinquent fathers like Bennett, who sought to avoid their financial responsibility, could circumvent it.

Shortly after the resolution of the *Bennett* case, the Illinois General Assembly closed this loophole in the law by passing a new bastardy law. The father of an illegitimate child had to wait until the child reached the age of three before demanding custody. As a result, he had to support the child financially for the first few years of its life. In 1861 the Illinois legislature raised the age at which the father could demand custody from three to ten.[70]

Although in extraordinary cases loopholes frustrated the courts' application of the best-interests-of-the-child doctrine, antebellum Illinois courts generally upheld the principle. The courts also expanded its use into the realm of the guardianship of orphans. In 1852 the Illinois Supreme Court applied this doctrine to prevent the removal of two orphans to an unsuitable guardian in the case of *Smith v. Shoup and Handsby*.

In December 1851 widower Augustus Alexander died, leaving thirteen-year-old Mary and eight-year-old John as orphans. During the course of his last illness Augustus Alexander asked Thomas Shoup to care for and educate his daughter and asked John Handsby to do the same for his son. When the court appointed William W. Smith as guardian for the children in January 1852, he claimed that his position gave him the right to control the children. Both Shoup and Handsby resisted his efforts to do so. Smith brought suit in the Logan County Circuit Court on a writ of habeas corpus to gain custody of Mary and John. The evidence revealed that the two children preferred their father's choice of guardians because of the "proper care and attention" given them. Additional evidence revealed that although the court had appointed him, Smith was not fit to serve as guardian for the minor children.

The judge of the circuit court felt compelled to "consult the best interests of the children; and that would not be done by putting them under the control of the petitioner. Under the circumstances of the case the children are not improperly detained, and the application of the guardian must be refused."[71] The court upheld Augustus Alexander's wishes for his orphaned children by considering their best interests.

The record declares that Alexander's two children preferred their father's choice of guardians but gave no hint as to how the children conveyed their feelings in the matter to the court. The record did not list them as witnesses, nor did the case file include depositions from the children, although their preferences and the court's perception of their interests had a profound influence on the case. The question of just how much the courts allowed children to participate personally in the legal proceedings remains unclear. Little evidence suggests their active involvement in the courtroom.

When their testimony became important to a case, the court subpoenaed both men and women to testify in person or by deposition as a witness in court. Rarely did children ever receive the same privilege, although courts summoned children to appear as litigants.[72] Their names accompanied those of adult men and women on summonses and other writs requiring their presence in court. Although minor litigants may have attended court proceedings, their interests were generally represented and expressed by their guardian or guardian *ad litem*.

In many cases children who had a vital interest in the progress of a case found themselves as the central focus of the legal proceedings with no opportunity to speak for themselves. The case of *Pea v. Williams* illustrates the amount of control guardians held in legal proceedings. In August 1855 twenty-five-year-old Greenberry Williams promised to marry sixteen-year-old Nancy Pea on the first day of September, 1855. Nancy Pea looked forward to her wedding day with anticipation, only to find to her chagrin that her fiancé had married Harriet Baker in Iowa. On behalf of the angry, brokenhearted young woman, her adult representative, Abner M. Watson, sued Greenberry Williams in the Sangamon County Circuit Court in an action of assumpsit and requested $2,000 in damages for breaking the marriage contract. Watson called upon Abraham Lincoln and William H. Herndon to prosecute the suit on behalf of Nancy Pea.[73]

The court called several witnesses to the stand but never heard the oral testimony of Pea and Williams. After hearing the evidence, the jury delivered a verdict in favor of Nancy Pea and awarded her $211 in damages. Significantly, Pea and Williams also did not participate in the final distribution of the judgment. Elias Williams, the father of Greenberry Williams, paid the judgment to Ezekiel Pea, the father of Nancy Pea.[74]

For the most part the court records also remain silent about the involvement of children in criminal proceedings. A minor younger than seven was deemed incompetent to commit criminal acts. However, between the ages of seven and fourteen children could be punished for a crime they committed. After fourteen, the court judged children as adults accountable for their criminal behavior.[75] Abraham Lincoln and his law partners did not take part in many criminal cases pertaining to children. In most of these cases the children were the victims. Most involved the sexual assault of minor females, the use of children to mask landownership to defraud those who sought payment of debts, or the recruitment of minors into committing criminal acts.[76]

One exception is the case of *People v. Dunning,* in which a minor participated. In 1860 Moses Dunning bribed a young servant girl, Joanne Riley, to steal jewelry for him. Riley complied with his request by stealing $160 worth of valuables from a Mrs. Anderson and took the goods to Moses Dunning. Gripped with the fear that he would be caught, Moses Dunning urged Joanne

Riley to return the stolen jewelry to Mrs. Anderson to avert suspicion. The young servant girl returned the jewelry but perhaps out of fear that she would bear sole responsibility for the theft, Riley relayed the complete story to a police officer, Moses Warner. Soon thereafter the police arrested both Joanne Riley and Moses Dunning. The grand jury later indicted Moses Dunning on a charge of larceny.

During the trial Joanne Riley maintained her story under a "severe cross-examination" by the defense attorney. Dunning produced a witness that accused Officer Moses Warner of being the young girl's co-conspirator. According to that witness, Moses Warner disliked Moses Dunning so much that he urged his young accomplice to testify against the defendant in court. From the testimony presented, the jury could not find enough evidence to convict Moses Dunning of larceny. They acquitted him of the charges, and the court released him.[77] Riley's testimony was so crucial to the case that the court allowed her to testify against Dunning, yet her testimony ultimately failed to sway the jury. For the most part minors did not participate in legal proceedings apart from their guardians or guardians *ad litem*, but in rare instances children were called upon to present testimony in court.

Minors were not completely silent when it came to governing their legal affairs. Louis Kirsch died in 1853, leaving to his widow and seven children real estate worth $1,675. His widow, Barbara Kirsch, did not have a lot of money, so she had to contract out to feed and clothe her seven children. Upon the application of George Huntington, mayor of Springfield, to the Sangamon County Circuit Court, the court appointed William H. Herndon as the guardian of Barbara Kirsch's seven children. When the widow presented her account for the care of her children to Herndon, he could not pay her. In order to satisfy the unpaid debt Herndon brought suit as guardian against the children and their mother during the April 1863 term of the Sangamon County Circuit Court to sell real estate from Louis Kirsch's estate to pay the debts for the care of the children. At the next term of court the judge ruled in favor of Herndon and ordered the sale of the real estate to pay the debt.

On April 18, 1863, George Kirsch, Elizabeth Kirsch, Frederick Kirsch, and Charles Louis Kirsch, all minors older than fourteen, signed a document petitioning the Sangamon County Court to appoint their mother, Barbara A. Kirsch, as their legal guardian. During the August 1867 term of this court, which had jurisdiction over the appointment of guardians, fourteen-year-old Julia A. Kirsch followed the lead of her older siblings and filed a personally signed petition acknowledging that although she was a ward of the court-appointed guardian William H. Herndon, she wished to have him removed as her legal guardian and replaced by her mother, Barbara Kirsch. On September 6, 1867, Sangamon County Court Judge Prescott approved her formal request for a change in guardian.[78] According to an 1845 Illinois statute, minors older than fourteen could choose their own guardian if their father was dead.[79]

An examination of Illinois statutes, the documentary evidence of Abraham Lincoln's legal practice, and reported Illinois Supreme Court cases during the period before the American Civil War reveals a legal system committed to upholding *parens patriae,* the best-interests-of-the-child, and the tender years doctrines to protect Illinois's children as a public trust. Judges were cognizant of the tradition of patriarchy in the common law, but they were also influenced by society's changing perspective of the family. Antebellum courts called upon traditions of common and chancery law to uphold the rights of fathers and mothers to nurture and educate their offspring. Nevertheless, the courts did not hesitate to intervene for the public good to counter threats to the nation's future, its children.

Notes

1. Steven Mintz and Susan Kellogg, *Domestic Revolutions: A Social History of American Family Life* (New York: Free Press, 1988), 43–45.

2. According to Edward Shorter, this change in the perception of the family took root in a shift from a traditional "moral" economy to market capitalism in Europe and America (*The Making of the Modern Family* [New York: Basic Books, 1975], 255–68). At about the same time Locke and Rousseau awakened adults to a new appreciation of childhood that included a better understanding of a child's intellectual and emotional development. See Bernard Wishy, *The Child and the Republic: The Dawn of Modern American Child Nurture* (Philadelphia: University of Pennsylvania Press, 1968), vii.

3. Mintz and Kellogg, *Domestic Revolutions,* 46; Lawrence Stone, *Family, Sex, and Marriage* (New York: Harper and Row, 1977); Randolph Trumbach, *The Rise of the Egalitarian Family: Aristocratic Kinship and Domestic Relations in Eighteenth-Century England* (New York: Academic Press, 1978), 1–5; Philippe Aries, *Centuries of Childhood: A Social History of Family Life* (New York: Alfred A. Knopf, 1952); and Lloyd deMause, *The History of Childhood* (New York: Psychohistory Press, 1962).

4. Viviana A. Zelizer, *Pricing the Priceless Child* (New York: Basic Books, 1985), 5.

5. Mintz and Kellogg, *Domestic Revolutions,* 45.

6. Aries, *Centuries of Childhood.* Around 1700 the theory that love rather than authority should characterize family cohesiveness heralded the emergence of the modern family.

7. Michael Grossberg, *Governing the Hearth: Law and the Family in Nineteenth-Century America* (Chapel Hill: University of North Carolina Press, 1985), 6–7.

8. The term *parens patriae* literally means "the political father of his people." The doctrine received its name from a parenthetical "as a father" that referred to the crown as a parent. See Lawrence B. Custer, "The Origins of the Doctrine of *Parens Patriae,*" *Emory Law Journal* 27 (Spring 1978): 201.

9. Kermit L. Hall, *The Magic Mirror: Law in American History* (New York: Oxford University Press, 1989), 164; Jamil S. Zainaldin, "Emergence of a Modern American Family Law: Child Custody, Adoption, and the Courts, 1796–1851," *Northwestern University Law Review* 73 (February 1979): 1084–85.

10. Hall, *Magic Mirror*, 151; Grossberg, *Governing the Hearth*, 304; Jamil S. Zainaldin, *Law in Antebellum Society: Legal Change and Economic Expansion* (New York: Alfred A. Knopf, 1983), 210.

11. Ages at which boys or girls were legally liable for certain actions or agreements varied by state of residence and sex of the minor.

12. *Revised Code of Laws of Illinois* (1827); *Revised Statutes of the State of Illinois* (1845); Norman H. Purple, *A Compilation of the Statutes of the State of Illinois* (Chicago: Keen and Lee, 1856).

13. These figures come from a compilation of reported Illinois Supreme Court cases located by searching the indexes of the *Illinois Reports*, vols. 1–26 (1819–62), for subject headings concerning children.

14. The staff of the Lincoln Legal Papers indexed most cases involving children under the broad heading of "Children" with subheadings of "Adoption," "Custody of Children," "Illegitimate," "Laborer," "Minor Heirs," and "Orphans." An additional subject heading valuable to the collection of cases involving children is that of "Guardian and Ward." To avoid duplication the handful of cases found under more than one subheading are placed within the subject area most relevant to the case. See Martha L. Benner and Cullom Davis et al., eds., *The Law Practice of Abraham Lincoln: Complete Documentary Edition* (DVD; Urbana: University of Illinois Press, 2000), hereafter cited as *LPAL*.

15. A guardian was a person to whom the court gave the legal authority to supervise the care of a minor. The court-appointed guardian *ad litem* defended a minor's interests in a particular case before a court of law. The two guardians were not always the same person. The court-appointed guardian *ad litem* was usually an attorney familiar to the court. See John Bouvier, *A Law Dictionary, Adapted to the Constitution and Laws of the United States of America*, 3d ed., 2 vols. (Philadelphia: T. & J. W. Johnson, 1848), 1:622–23; *Revised Code of Laws of Illinois* (1827).

16. *Revised Statutes of the State of Illinois* (1845).

17. Purple, *Compilation of the Statutes . . . of Illinois*.

18. Order of Reference, 18 May 1857, *Sheneman v. Goodpasture et ux.*, *LPAL*.

19. Petition, 23 March 1857, *Sheneman v. Goodpasture et ux.*, *LPAL*.

20. Decree, 18 May 1857, *Sheneman v. Goodpasture et ux.*, *LPAL*.

21. Ibid. See also *Revised Statutes of the State of Illinois*, Partitions, ch. 79, sec. 11 (1845), 401.

22. Commissioners' Report, Plat Map, *Sheneman v. Goodpasture et ux.*, *LPAL*.

23. Master in Chancery's Report, 13 April 1859, *Sheneman v. Goodpasture et ux.*, *LPAL*.

24. Ibid.

25. U.S. Census Office, Seventh Census of the United States (1850), Woodford County, Illinois, ms., 479.

26. Summons, 12 March 1853, *Fields v. Fields et al.*, *LPAL*.

27. Decree, 25 April 1853, *Fields v. Fields et al.*, *LPAL*.

28. Guardian *ad litem*'s answer, 25 April 1853, *Fields v. Fields et al.*, *LPAL*.

29. *Enos et al. v. Capps*, 12 Ill. 255 (1850): "Neither a default, nor a decree *pro confesso*, can be taken against an infant. A guardian *ad litem* should be appointed, who should file

an answer, after which the complainant must make full proof, whether the answer filed, admits or denies the allegations of the bill."

30. Decree, 25 April 1853, *Fields v. Fields et al., LPAL.*

31. Ibid. See also *Revised Statutes of the State of Illinois,* Partitions, ch. 79, sec. 9 (1845), 400–1.

32. Commissioners' Report, 26 September 1853, *Fields v. Fields et al., LPAL.* Rhoda Fields received one-third of the value of the estate, which equaled 160 acres in land.

33. Writ of Execution, 9 November 1853, *Fields v. Fields et al., LPAL.*

34. *Parmelee et al. v. Smith,* 21 Ill. 620–21 (1851).

35. Ibid., 622.

36. Ibid.

37. Ibid., 623–24.

38. *Revised Statutes of the State of Illinois* (1845), 93, 99 (by guardian and next friend), 201 (by guardian *ad litem* in dower), 260 (in law and equity proceedings), and 559 (in sale of real estate as part of estate settlement).

39. Hall, *Magic Mirror,* 166.

40. The "best-interests-of-the-child" doctrine originated from an opinion offered by the commercial-law reformer Lord Mansfield in the English case of *Rex v. Delaval* (1763). American judges used the broad discretionary power presented in this opinion to settle custody suits as they determined the welfare of the child. See Grossberg, *Governing the Hearth,* 209–10.

41. *Cowls v. Cowls,* 8 Ill. (3 Gilman) 435 (1846).

42. Bill of Complaint, 14 April 1847, *Cowls v. Cowls, LPAL.*

43. Decree, 15 April 1846, *Cowls v. Cowls, LPAL.*

44. *Cowls v. Cowls,* 8 Ill. (3 Gilman) 439 (1846).

45. Ibid.

46. Opinion, 9 February 1847, *Cowls v. Cowls, LPAL.*

47. Joseph Story, *Commentaries on Equity Jurisprudence as Administered in England and America,* ed. Isaac F. Redfield, 2 vols. (Boston: Little, Brown, 1861), 2:1341.

48. *Cowls v. Cowls,* 8 Ill. (3 Gilman) 442 (1846).

49. *Miner v. Miner,* 11 Ill. 43 (1849).

50. Ibid., 43–44.

51. In making his argument, Baker cited the New York case of *The People v. Mercien,* 3 Hill 399 (1842), to which the state supreme court referred in its decision: "In the People v. Mercien, it was held as a general rule of law, that, as between husband and wife, the claim of the former to the custody of their infant children is paramount, and will be enforced on *habeas corpus,* though the child be a daughter under five years of age" (*Miner v. Miner,* 11 Ill. 45 [1849]).

52. *Miner v. Miner,* 11 Ill. 47–48 (1849). The six points outlined in William Thomas's argument in support of Laura Miner's custody of her daughter reflected those presented earlier in the Pennsylvania Court of General Sessions during the legal battle of Ellen Sears D'Hauteville and Gonzalve D'Hauteville about the custody of their infant son, Frederick. According to Michael Grossberg's account of the case, the judge's decision to grant custody of the child to his mother gave "support to maternal preference, the tender years rule, and the best interests of the child doctrine as governing rules of American custody law" (Grossberg, *A Judgment for Solomon: The D'Hauteville Case and Legal Experience in Antebellum America* [Cambridge: Cambridge University Press, 1996], 231–32).

53. *Miner v. Miner*, 11 Ill. 49 (1849).

54. Ibid.

55. Ibid., 50.

56. Ibid.

57. *Revised Statutes of the State of Illinois* (1845), Divorce, ch. 33, sec. 6, 197.

58. *Miner v. Miner*, 11 Ill. 50 (1849).

59. Ibid., 51.

60. Ibid.

61. This tender years doctrine assumed that mothers were the best caretakers of children younger than seven, the "tender years" of a child's development. See Danaya C. Wright, "Forum—Constructing Patriarchy: The Development of Interspousal Custody Law in England: *De Manneville v. De Manneville:* Rethinking the Birth of Custody Law under Patriarchy," *Law and History Review* 17 (Summer 1999): 248.

62. While many historians believe that the struggle for women's rights progressed on a straight line toward equality, Wright opposes that view by concluding that women tended to lose custody cases after the *De Manneville* case of 1804. For an excellent study of women's custody rights, see Wright, "Forum—Constructing Patriarchy," 247–308.

63. Bill of Complaint, 19 April 1855, *Bennett v. Bennett, LPAL*.

64. Answer, 30 May 1855, *Bennett v. Bennett, LPAL*.

65. Decree, 3 October 1855, *Bennett v. Bennett,* Menard County Circuit Court, Chancery Record 1, 335–36, *LPAL*.

66. *Cowls v. Cowls*, 8 Ill. (3 Gilman) 440 (1846).

67. *Wright v. Bennett & Bennett*, 7 Ill. 588 (1845).

68. Ibid.

69. Opinion, 5 February 1846, *Wright v. Bennett & Bennett, LPAL*.

70. *Revised Statutes of the State of Illinois,* Bastardy, ch. 16, sec. 5 (1845); An Act to Amend Chapter Sixteen of the Revised Statutes of 1845, entitled "Bastardy," 22 February 1861, *Laws of Illinois* (1861), 171–72.

71. Judgment and Opinion Record, 19 January 1852, *Smith v. Shoup & Handsby, LPAL*.

72. For an example of a child subpoenaed as a witness in a case, see Susan Krause's essay, chapter 7 in this volume.

73. Declaration, 8 November 1855, *Pea v. Williams, LPAL*.

74. *Pea v. Williams, LPAL*.

75. Frank Crosby, *Everybody's Lawyer and Counsellor in Business* (Philadelphia: J. E. Potter, 1860), 258.

76. For examples of sexual assaults on minors, see *People v. Delny* and *People v. Percival, LPAL*. For examples of the use of children to mask the ownership of lands from creditors, see *Harris Lime Rock Co. v. Harris et al., Harris v. Feagans & Feagans,* and *Hill v. Feagans & Feagans, LPAL*. For an example of a minor's being recruited to commit a crime, see *People v. Dunning, LPAL*.

77. Ibid.

78. *Herndon v. Kirsch et al., LPAL*.

79. *Revised Statutes of the State of Illinois,* Guardian and Ward, ch. 47, sec. 1 (1845), 265.

PART 2

Marriages, Families, and Property in Conflict

3

Dissolving the Bonds of Matrimony: Women and Divorce in Sangamon County, Illinois, 1837–60

STACY PRATT MCDERMOTT

In 1838 Maria and George Chapman married in Sangamon County, Illinois. During their thirteen-year marriage they had five children. In 1851, when Maria Chapman discovered George Chapman's infidelity, she sued him for divorce on the ground of adultery. George Chapman hired a lawyer and denied his wife's charges. The court, however, found George Chapman guilty, granted Maria Chapman a divorce, and gave her custody of the children. The court also ordered George Chapman to pay $19.90 in court costs.[1]

Maria Chapman was only one of 167 women who were divorced in Sangamon County between 1837 and 1860. Divorce cases were not rare occurrences on the Sangamon County Circuit Court docket. During that twenty-three-year period female and male plaintiffs presented 220 divorce petitions to the circuit court judge in Springfield, and the court granted divorces in 76 percent of the cases.[2] The court dismissed only forty-four of the divorce cases that appeared in those years.[3] Women filed for divorce 139 times (63 percent) in Sangamon County, and the court granted them divorce decrees in 110 of their petitions (79 percent). By comparison, men filed only eighty-one suits for divorce (37 percent), and the circuit court granted them divorce decrees in fifty-seven (70 percent) of those cases.

Divorce was a viable legal option for antebellum Illinois women. The Illinois legislature provided liberal access to divorce, and many Illinois women chose divorce as a remedy for marital difficulties. By 1850 the number of divorced Americans was rapidly increasing; however, the legal structure of divorce and the occurrence of divorce in Illinois were not typical.[4] Illinois circuit courts applied divorce laws liberally, and by 1860 the state was leading the nation in granting divorce decrees.[5]

Divorce legislation in the United States differed widely from state to state, and legislation in no state exactly matched that of another.[6] Drastic state and regional variations in antebellum America demand more local studies to gain a broader understanding of the history of American divorce. While a number of studies examine the legal status and experiences of women in New England during the colonial and early national periods, studies of divorce in the nineteenth century are few, and not many consider divorce outside New England and the South. No studies of the law in the Midwest exist, and, as Norma Basch has stated, scholars have done little work on divorce in the county courts during what she terms the formative stage of the development of divorce law.[7] An examination of the Sangamon County Circuit Court is an important step in filling those gaps, especially in addressing the absence of midwestern legal studies. The rich history and impressive county documentary materials available offer an excellent opportunity to analyze divorce in an interesting locale within both a statewide and a national context.[8]

The changes apparent in the legislative and judicial process of divorce law in Illinois reveal much about the changing economic, social, and legal environment of antebellum America.[9] Divorce in antebellum Illinois fit neatly in the transition from Puritan to Victorian standards that Nancy Cott describes in her two studies of divorce in the eighteenth century.[10] As ideas surrounding women's legal status as property holders gradually changed, legal and social attitudes about divorce also changed. The interesting and unique circumstances of divorce law in Illinois illustrate those changes.

This case study of Sangamon County seeks to accomplish four related goals. First, it explores individual circuit court divorce cases in order to understand how individual women fared under the law. Second, it analyzes the occurrence and overall experience of divorce for a group of women in a particular locale over time, putting the individual women into a local, statewide, and regional perspective. Third, it examines the divorce caseload of a partnership of attorneys during the tenure of their practice in order to get a sense of how members of the bar litigated divorce cases. Fourth, and most significantly, it examines the experience of divorce in antebellum Illinois within the context of legal history and women's history and questions the reigning paradigm that confines scholarly inquiry of the history of women and the law within a patriarchal framework.

In Sangamon County women enjoyed easier access to divorce than did most women outside the state. A relatively urban county on the Illinois prairie, Sangamon County represented an intersection of northern and southern influences and population and depicted the mobility of a frontier community. Sangamon County also had a relatively mature legal profession in which lawyers and judges prospered. Antebellum Illinois litigants could choose among several experienced attorneys-at-law who accepted both great and small challenges. As home to Springfield, Sangamon County combined the political and social energy of a bustling state capital with the economic exuberance of a prosperous agricultural community that offered antebellum Illinois residents a unique blend of urban and rural characteristics. Springfield, which had a growing population of more than twenty-five hundred by 1840, attracted many well-educated, industrious individuals from across the state and the region, and local residents reaped the benefits of their influence in business, politics, and the social issues of the day.[11] In addition, the county served as a diverse commercial crossroad between the growing cities of St. Louis and Chicago, offering residents increased economic opportunities and greater mobility. The county seat and state capital of Springfield boasted two politically competitive newspapers, a vast assortment of businesses and manufacturers, and a growing network of railroads and highways. The city was a vibrant social, economic, and political center. A place where statewide interests converged at the capital, Sangamon County was a local legal community illustrative of both state and regional trends in American law.[12]

The question of jurisdiction is a case in point. In comparison to other states, the Illinois legislature made divorce more readily available earlier. Illinois gave the circuit courts jurisdiction over divorce in 1819 and completely abandoned the use of divorce by legislative act after 1839. Maryland and Ohio did not relinquish jurisdiction to the lower courts until 1842 and 1843, respectively.[13] Missouri abandoned legislative divorce earlier than Illinois, giving full jurisdiction to the circuit courts in 1818, but the Missouri courts granted a substantially smaller percentage of divorce decrees from 1840 to 1860.[14]

Throughout the antebellum period legislative divorces were increasingly expensive, time consuming, and difficult to obtain, and more and more states moved to alter the divorce process. The Virginia General Assembly, for example, was so overwhelmed by the number of divorce petitions during each legislative session that it abandoned the practice in 1850.[15] The legislatures of northern states tended to place jurisdiction for divorce within the circuit court structure long before those in southern states, and divorce laws were more fluid in newly settled western states. Norma Basch notes that during the nineteenth century, "east-west distinctions became even more pronounced, states tending to render divorce more readily accessible to their restless new inhabitants."[16]

The shift of divorce jurisdiction from the legislature to the circuit courts symbolized, as one scholar has put it, "the lessening role of families as a central organizing force of religion, politics, and the economy."[17] Another scholar writes that as American couples began to view marriage within a companionate ideal, their "new desire for intimacy and companionship displaced a domestic patriarchy in which men wielded authority over other members of the immediate and extended family."[18] Because patriarchy within the American family was breaking down, the extension of that patriarchy within the U.S. court system was breaking down as well. In essence, a gradual rejection of patriarchy as a ruling force in U.S. law was becoming apparent in the legal structure and adjudication of divorce.

This study of nineteenth-century Sangamon County challenges the assertion that nineteenth-century law was uniformly patriarchal. Patriarchy does not adequately explain the legal circumstances of women in antebellum Illinois. Stressing a paternalistic framework rather than a patriarchal one for divorce in Illinois does not imply that the courts treated women equally or that women shared equally in the legal status of men. In fact, a paternalistic interpretation suggests that Illinois legislators carefully crafted divorce law in order to protect women legally, economically, and physically, because they perceived women as incapable of protecting themselves. Illinois legislators recognized divorce as a necessary remedy for women and instituted a divorce law that was strategically designed to protect them. Judges added another layer of paternalism with their own liberal interpretation of the divorce law as they applied it in courtrooms across the state.

Although most antebellum Americans continued to view marriage as a lifetime commitment, many were beginning to recognize that divorce was necessary in some circumstances.[19] As a result, women's access to divorce in many states increased by varying degrees during the period between the American Revolution and the Civil War. As Cornelia Hughes Dayton demonstrates in her legal history of eighteenth-century women in Connecticut, women were beginning to encounter "a less intimidating and burdensome divorce process" and were seeing their requests "granted by the judges with a minimum of fuss."[20] Connecticut was leading the way during the 1700s, but by the nineteenth century Illinois, Indiana, and Ohio were in the forefront of the "easy" divorce movement, with Ohio granting one hundred divorces in 1850 alone.[21] During the period between 1776 and 1850 divorce rates were much higher in western states and territories than in the Northeast and the South.[22] Absolute divorce with the right to remarry, rare in the colonial period, continued to be uncommon or unavailable in some eastern and southern states throughout the antebellum period. Even in states that allowed divorce, like Massachusetts, the legal process was expensive.[23] By comparison, Illinois divorce statutes provided for women in dire economic circumstances by exempting them from paying the court costs associated with divorce cases.[24]

Just before Illinois emerged as a leader in granting divorce, Indiana was in the national spotlight. In 1824 Indiana became the first state to pass an omnibus, or incompatibility, clause that allowed petitioners to obtain divorces for any misconduct that resulted in unhappiness and destroyed the marriage relationship. Iowa had allowed a short-lived incompatibility clause in 1845, but Illinois did not institute one until 1862.[25] Indiana gained a national reputation as a divorce mill, attracting the attention of prominent social commentators of the day.[26] In a *New York Daily Tribune* editorial in 1860 Horace Greeley chastised the state as a "paradise of free-lovers" where the "lax principles of Robert Dale Owen" supported the establishment of a "state of law which enables men and women to get unmarried nearly at pleasure."[27] While the influence of radical utopian leaders like Owen at New Harmony, Indiana, may have contributed on some level to the state's high rate of divorce, notoriously lax procedure in the courts played a more prominent role in creating a legal environment that attracted migrants seeking divorce.[28] Indiana's divorce rate was high but not the highest in the country. Although Illinois's divorce law and practice did not receive the national attention that Indiana's did, by 1857 Illinois—which in 1859 took the bold legal step of allowing divorced women to take back their maiden name—was leading the nation in divorce, granting more divorce decrees per capita than Connecticut, Maine, Massachusetts, Missouri, or Ohio, states that were historically less restrictive in statute and in practice than other states.[29]

During the antebellum period women assumed new economic and social roles that altered and began to transform their familial relationships. As Norma Basch argues in her study of the emerging legal history of women in the United States, access to divorce certainly helped to redefine "women's legal relationship to the family and provided women with some form of limited legal relief."[30] Legal issues, like divorce and child custody, were becoming more frequent occurrences in local courts across the country. More and more women became participants in the legal system as society addressed new challenges that the expanding roles of women created. Family law was moving to the forefront of legal discourse and legal practice; in states like Illinois, it was becoming a larger part of the chancery docket.

For example, county circuit courts throughout Illinois heard increasing numbers of divorce petitions. Both rural and urban counties reflected this trend. Although the economic, social, and political nature of Illinois counties and the diverse religious, ethnic, and geographical origins of their inhabitants differed significantly, divorce was a common occurrence in courts throughout the state. Circuit courts struggled with complex legal family issues associated with the dissolution of marriages. Between 1837 and 1869, 281 couples divorced in Kane County in northern Illinois. The county's proximity to Chicago attracted a migratory population that experienced the familial disruption associated with westward migration.[31] In the Knox County Circuit Court in Galesburg, Illinois, plaintiffs filed twenty-three divorce suits during the 1840s. This is particularly interesting considering that this rural frontier community had an 1840 population of only 1,210.[32]

By comparison, Sangamon County's population in 1840 was 14,716, and by 1850 the county had grown to 19,228 people. Sangamon County was home to the busy state capitol, whereas Knox County remained remote and bucolic, and Kane County's population was transitory and therefore unstable. Despite their differences, however, the three counties had virtually identical rates of successful divorce petitions. The Kane County Circuit Court granted divorce decrees in 76 percent of divorce petitions filed between 1837 and 1869. The Knox County Circuit Court granted divorces in 70 percent of the cases filed there during the 1840s.[33] Sangamon County divorce petitioners obtained decrees 76 percent of the time. The similar circumstances of divorce cases in these three diverse localities reflect the willingness of antebellum Illinois circuit courts to grant divorces. Although atypical in some ways, Sangamon County was representative of the state in the practice of divorce, and for that reason it is an excellent locality through which to study divorce in the antebellum era.

Nancy Cott's study of divorce in eighteenth-century Massachusetts forms the foundation for any analysis of divorce in the United States before 1900. Her work demonstrates the importance of community studies of law and focuses attention on the richness of legal proceedings and their importance in any historical investigation of women.[34] Analysis of the independent details of individual divorce cases offers a rich perspective for a local history of women and illuminates the circumstances of divorce at the local level, where most women experienced it. Mining nuggets from individual divorce cases, reviewing some of the social and political discourse of the period, and examining the census and marital records for an individual county help bring the women who experienced divorce in Lincoln's Illinois to life. Careful examination of those resources provides a wealth of detail that the statutes and the state supreme court precedents cannot. For example, of the 220 female litigants in divorce actions in Sangamon County between 1837 and 1860, five were black, six remarried their husbands after going to the legal trouble of divorcing them, one worked as a cook in the Illinois governor's mansion, at least four reclaimed their maiden name following their divorce, at least a dozen chose not to remarry after the court granted their divorce decree, and one remarried despite her failure on two separate occasions to obtain a legal divorce from her first husband.[35]

In an effort to understand the experience of divorce broadly, historians must engage in the painstaking work of collecting the minutiae of individual divorce cases from an entire corpus of divorce cases. With the use of data extracted from an entire group of cases, patterns emerge that form an outline for understanding the typical experience of divorce in a given locale. A detailed database forms the foundation of this study's statistical portrait. However, the statistics must be understood within the legal framework. The very structure of divorce in Illinois reveals much about women's experiences.

All divorces in Illinois were *a vinculo matrimonii*, total severance of the marriage tie, rather than *a mensa et thoro*, separation from bed and board, which essentially served as a legal separation that did not leave the parties free to remarry.[36] Full divorce with the right to remarry was rare in some southern states, and some eastern states granted more legal separations than full divorce decrees. Because the circuit courts granted only *a vinculo matrimonii* divorces, all Illinois women who obtained divorce decrees were free to remarry, though not all chose to do so.

Full divorce was available in Illinois, but the grounds for divorce were at first narrowly defined; they increased in number from 1818 to 1845. Illinois law at statehood in 1818 provided for divorce on the grounds of adultery, bigamy, or impotence. In 1824 Illinois legislators added willful desertion and, in 1827, included fraud and extreme and repeated cruelty for two years and habitual drunkenness for two years. Conviction on a felony charge became an additional ground in 1845.[37] By 1845 the Illinois legislature provided for a relatively liberal number of grounds for divorce, the most significant of which was extreme and repeated cruelty. In Illinois, circuit courts granted divorce decrees solely on the ground of cruelty, whereas historically cruelty could not stand alone, and petitioners could cite it only in combination with another ground.[38] Even given the two-year stipulation, Illinois's provision for cruelty as a viable stand-alone ground for divorce as early as 1827 placed it ahead of most other states.

The *Illinois Revised Statutes* of 1833 contained seven brief sections on divorce. These provisions stipulated the grounds, court jurisdiction, and residence of petitioners. They warned against collusion of the parties, insisted on the proof of grounds, and provided for the payment of court costs for poor women, a feature that the Illinois General Assembly added in 1827. In 1845 the legislature added an eighth section that provided the circuit courts with the power to grant divorces on grounds other than those that the law specified.

Illinois divorce law declared explicitly that divorce did not affect the legitimacy of children. Illinois law gave the circuit courts the power to settle questions of alimony and child custody as "shall be fit, reasonable, and just."[39] The Illinois statutes were, however, more specific with regard to grounds. To sue on grounds of willful desertion, extreme and repeated cruelty, or drunkenness, the complainant had to prove to the court through witness testimony or depositions that the accused spouse had, for example, been a habitual drunkard for at least two years. The law in Illinois, as in many other states, required women whose husbands abandoned them to wait two full years before filing for divorce. Furthermore, a woman living with a physically abusive husband could not expect to obtain a divorce until she had suffered the abuse for two years, or she could leave her husband and wait for him to sue her for divorce on the ground of desertion.[40]

Illinois's statutory waiting period suggests that the legislative structure of divorce, at least as it applied to the two-year waiting period for desertion, cruelty, and drunkenness, was patriarchal. The legislators who crafted divorce law in Illinois may have attached the waiting period as a way to maintain male control over families or perhaps the waiting period was a compromise among legislators who disagreed about how to legislate divorce. Whatever the reason, that the legislature allowed for divorce on those grounds at all, when other states allowed divorce only on the ground of adultery, suggests a step away from a strictly patriarchal structuring of the law.

Throughout the 1840s and 1850s the Illinois Supreme Court strictly interpreted the statutes pertaining to divorce. In the case of *Schillinger v. Schillinger* in 1852 the court reversed a decree of divorce in the Morgan County Circuit Court because the master in chancery charged with proving the allegation of desertion recommended the divorce decree without sufficient evidence.[41] The supreme court decided that the complainant, George Jacob Schillinger, had failed to prove that the defendant, Elizabeth Schillinger, had willfully deserted him for the period of two years or more, as the statute required. The court plainly stated that even in cases in which the defendant confessed to having behaved as accused, the proof of grounds was still mandatory. In the opinion Justice Lyman Trumbull wrote: "It is clear that a court has no authority to decree a divorce on a bill being taken for confessed, without proof to sustain its allegations."[42]

In 1853 in *Birkby v. Solomons et al.* the Illinois Supreme Court reversed a decree of divorce in Macoupin County because the grounds on which the circuit court had granted the decree were insufficient. The decision spoke directly to the eighth section of the statute on divorce, which allowed the circuit courts "full power and authority to hear and determine all causes for a divorce not provided for by any law of this state."[43] In the opinion Justice

John Caton wrote: "We have no hesitation in saying that the law does not confer upon the courts an unlimited discretion to grant divorces in all cases. . . . Where the legislature has prescribed one measure of guilt as necessary, the courts cannot say that less shall be sufficient."[44]

In the Macoupin County Circuit Court case Ann Birkby had filed for divorce against John Birkby, who then filed a cross-bill against his wife, also asking for a divorce. The court found for the defendant in the original bill and for the complainant in the cross-bill, thus granting the divorce on the grounds that John Birkby had cited. John Birkby accused his wife of threatening to kill him and to destroy his property and of refusing to attend to household duties and absenting herself from the house for days and weeks at a time. The Illinois Supreme Court took issue with the circuit court's decree, deciding that "the causes of the complaint are of the same character as some of those specified in the statute, but less in degree than the legislature has seen fit to prescribe."[45] The eighth section of the divorce law provided for grounds not covered in the statutes, but the supreme court clearly did not allow for a liberal interpretation of this section or of the grounds specifically mentioned in the statutes.

The Illinois Supreme Court adhered closely to the statutes in deciding issues in divorce cases and showed no tolerance for a wide interpretation of the statute pertaining to grounds. Regardless of the individual circumstances in the case, the state's high court was unwilling to stretch what the legislature had put forth in the statutes covering divorce. The decisions in *Schillinger v. Schillinger* and *Birkby v. Solomons et al.* illustrate the court's strict interpretation of Illinois's divorce laws. From 1837 to 1860 six other significant appeals in divorce cases came before the state's highest court. In all the cases the court allowed the circuit courts little room for interpretation of the statutes.[46] Most Illinois divorce cases, however, never reached the Illinois Supreme Court, and studies of divorce based on those appellate cases alone would be inaccurate. For the majority of women the experience of divorce came within the framework of the circuit courts, which tended to be much more flexible in applying the statutes. In fact, circuit court judges, masters in chancery, and juries demonstrated a much more paternalistic perspective toward divorce, often, for example, granting decrees without sufficient evidence of the two-year rule. In every Sangamon County Circuit Court case in which litigants cited desertion, cruelty, or drunkenness but failed to prove that the offense had been ongoing for two years, the court granted a divorce decree anyway. It was within that local context that most women litigants experienced divorce.

The circuit court experiences of Maria Dutch are more illustrative of women's experience of divorce than the Illinois appellate cases. Her divorce case was typical of most of those on the Sangamon County Circuit Court docket. Examining her case in detail provides a glimpse of how the courts handled divorce cases. In 1848, when she was nineteen, Maria L. Moore married Ebenezer Dutch Jr. Together, they had four children and by 1860 had amassed real estate holdings totaling $5,800 and personal property totaling $1,850. Ebenezer prospered, probably as a farmer, and the family was financially secure. The family's economic prosperity, however, did not mirror the internal dynamics of the marriage. In 1860 Maria Dutch retained a lawyer and sued her husband for divorce in the Sangamon County Circuit Court on the grounds of extreme and repeated cruelty and adultery.[47]

In the bill for divorce Maria Dutch's attorney, James C. Conkling, wrote: "Humbly complaining showeth unto your honor your oratrix Maria L. Dutch that . . . she was married to Ebenezer Dutch Jr. in the state of Illinois where she has continued to reside ever since her marriage."[48] The Illinois statutes required that the complainant in an action of divorce prove that the marriage did occur and that the complainant was a resident of the state.

Conkling went on to write: "Ever since her marriage to said Dutch she [conducted] herself as a dutiful and affectionate wife and discharged all her duties faithfully toward him. But your oratrix charges that the said Ebenezer Dutch Jr. has wholly disregarded his obligations toward her and that he has been guilty of extreme and repeated cruelty toward her since their marriage and that subsequently to their marriage and during the years 1858, 1859, 1860 he has committed adultery on several occasions."[49]

Adhering to the statutes, Conkling laid out the grounds in the case as both adultery and extreme and repeated cruelty. He stated that the cruelty began in 1858 and continued up until the filing of Maria Dutch's divorce suit in 1860, thus satisfying the two-year span that the law required. Conkling also clearly stated that Ebenezer Dutch was guilty of adultery as well.

Conkling went on to list the names and ages of the children, three boys and one girl, ranging in age from two to nine years, and noted that Ebenezer Dutch had custody and control of the children and had forcibly taken the youngest from Maria Dutch's care. Conkling also stated that Maria Dutch owned a piece of land of which Ebenezer Dutch had possession. His client wanted the land returned to her and requested custody of the children and alimony payments. Conkling concluded the bill: "In tender consideration . . . may it please your honor that said Ebenezer Dutch Jr. be made defendant to this bill of complaint . . . and that upon the final hearing of this cause a decree be rendered dissolving the bonds of matrimony."[50]

Conkling filed the bill with the circuit court clerk on August 16, 1860, and the clerk docketed the case in the August 1860 term of the court. On the same day the clerk issued a subpoena in chancery ordering Ebenezer Dutch to appear in court and subpoenas for nine witnesses to appear to testify in the case. The county sheriff served the subpoenas. On September 3 the court ordered that the allegations of Maria Dutch's bill be taken as confessed against the defendant, who had failed to appear, and ordered that "the cause be referred to the master in chancery to take and report the testimony herein."[51] The master took the testimony, verified the complainant's accusations, and recommended to the court that it grant the divorce decree.

On September 5, twenty days after Maria Dutch filed the case, the court decreed the divorce on both grounds charged in the bill, granted her custody of her nine-year-old daughter and two-year-old son, and ordered Ebenezer Dutch to give her a seventy-six-acre tract of land in lieu of alimony payments. Ebenezer Dutch received custody of the other two children, and the court ordered him to provide for the education of the two children in Maria Dutch's custody and pay the court costs of $21.95. At thirty-one Maria Dutch was legally divorced from an abusive husband, responsible for two children, in possession of a good portion of land, and legally free to remarry. Maria Dutch probably left Sangamon County sometime after the divorce, perhaps after selling the alimony property. She disappeared from the county's census records and does not appear to have remarried in Sangamon County. One can only speculate as to the social difficulty she faced as a divorced woman, but she had chosen to face that difficulty in order to free herself from Ebenezer Dutch's brutality and infidelity.

The Sangamon County Circuit Court heard Maria Dutch's case within one term of the court, as was typical in most divorce cases, and divided the children in characteristic fashion. The tender years doctrine, which provided that younger children were best kept with their mother, probably motivated the court's decision to allow Maria Dutch custody of the two-year-old boy. Ebenezer Dutch's status as a farmer may have played a role in the court's decision to grant him custody of the two older boys. Sons were particularly important to the economic success of family farms, and custody decisions in divorce cases bowed to those economic concerns. The courts also tended to divide the children along gender lines: sons went to live with their fathers, daughters with their mothers. This practice probably explains why Maria Dutch gained custody of her daughter.[52]

Regarding grounds, judgment, procedure, and issues of alimony and child custody, Maria Dutch's case was typical of the divorce cases that appeared on the Sangamon County Circuit Court docket. Hers was one of 107 divorce cases appearing between 1856 and 1860, and it provides an excellent example of the pleading and practice of a typical divorce case in Illinois during the antebellum period. Socially and economically, divorce in Illinois was no less difficult for a woman than in any other state. Most women litigants in divorce cases in Sangamon County were farmers' wives, and most were not wealthy by antebellum standards. Only twelve of the couples involved in divorces cases from 1837 to 1860 had combined personal and real property valued at more than $1,000.[53] Divorced women in Illinois were still subjected to the potential economic hardships of life without husbands, and certainly the social stigma of divorce loomed large.[54] However, the legal process in Illinois was relatively simple and proceeded quite expeditiously.

The most common ground for divorce cited in divorce petitions in Sangamon County was desertion (see table 3.1). Of the 195 cases (which cited 295 grounds) appearing on the Sangamon County Circuit Court docket between 1837 and 1860 in which the surviving documentation lists the grounds, 108 (55 percent) of the complainants cited desertion as the ground or one of the grounds for divorce. The court granted divorce decrees to women who cited desertion in 88 percent of their cases. Men were less successful, obtaining divorce for desertion in only 74 percent of their cases (see table 3.2). The large discrepancy between female and male divorce decrees based on the ground of desertion suggests the paternalistic nature of divorce outcomes. In antebellum Illinois society many women needed the economic support of a husband, whereas men were more readily employed and able to earn income without the aid of a spouse. Therefore, the courts more readily offered divorce decrees to abandoned wives so that they might legally remarry.

Table 3.1. Grounds in Divorce Cases by Gender of Plaintiff, 1837–60

Grounds	All Plaintiffs		Female Plaintiffs		Male Plaintiffs	
	Number	Percentage	Number	Percentage	Number	Percentage
Desertion	108	55	61	44	47	59
Cruelty	57	29	54	39	3	4
Adultery	55	28	25	18	30	38
Drunkenness	43	22	42	30	1	1
Cruelty and drunkenness	23	12	23	17	0	0
Bigamy	5	3	5	4	0	0
Fraud	2	1	1	1	1	1
Impotence	1	0.5	1	1	0	0
Felonious conviction	1	0.5	1	1	0	0

Total cases[a] = 195

a. Many cases cited more than one ground for divorce; hence number columns add up to more than the total number of cases and percentage columns add up to more than 100 percent.

Source: Martha L. Benner and Cullom Davis et al., eds., *The Law Practice of Abraham Lincoln: Complete Documentary Edition* (DVD; Urbana: University of Illinois Press, 2000).

Table 3.2. Success Rate of Divorce Petitions by Grounds and by Gender of Plaintiff, 1837–60

Grounds	All Plaintiffs	Female Plaintiffs	Male Plaintiffs
All grounds	76%	79%	70%
Desertion	82	88	74
Cruelty	72	70	100
Adultery	78	80	77
Drunkenness	74	74	100
Cruelty and drunkenness	65	65	n.a.
Bigamy	40	40	n.a.
Fraud	0	0	0
Impotence	0	0	n.a.
Felonious conviction	100	100	n.a.

Source: Martha L. Benner and Cullom Davis et al., eds., *The Law Practice of Abraham Lincoln: Complete Documentary Edition* (DVD; Urbana: University of Illinois Press, 2000).

Note: Virtually all divorces were granted on the grounds alleged; if the divorce was granted on different grounds, it was counted as an unsuccessful petition because the plaintiff's ground(s) did not prevail.

In 1848 Elizabeth Baker married Thomas Pike, a successful farmer with real estate holdings totaling $1,300. The Pikes lived together until 1852, when Thomas Pike deserted his twenty-two-year-old wife and the couple's two small children. Elizabeth Pike apparently enjoyed the comfort of supportive parents and did not pursue a divorce from her husband in 1854, when she could have filed for divorce on the ground of desertion. In early 1857 Elizabeth retained Abraham Lincoln and William H. Herndon and filed for divorce. The court granted the decree on the ground of desertion and gave her custody of the children. A proposal of marriage obviously provided the incentive that Elizabeth needed to sue Thomas for divorce, for in December of that year she married Squire Cross.[55]

In almost all the cases of desertion the defendant failed to appear or could not be located. However, the complainant still had to prove, as the statute required, that the desertion had occurred two or more years earlier and that the deserting spouse had not returned. In most instances one witness to the desertion was sufficient in the eyes of the circuit court judge. Typically, family members, neighbors, and friends appeared as witnesses in divorce cases. In the Pike divorce case Harrison Baker, Elizabeth's father, attested to his son-in-law's desertion. The master in chancery in the case summarized Baker's testimony by stating that "the defendant left the state of Illinois in April 1852. He abandoned the complainant without any cause at all and has ever since failed and refused to provide for her. Defendant went to California."[56]

Charging and proving desertion was certainly the most successful and perhaps the easiest way to obtain a divorce in Sangamon County. The number of divorces granted on the ground of desertion reflects the mobility of the county's population and particularly that of Springfield, an urban city on the Illinois prairie. Westward expansion appears to have played a significant role in desertion cases. As husbands traveled west to scout out land and other economic opportunities, such as those surrounding the California gold rush, they left wives behind. Death, disease, or personal reasons kept many men from returning home, leaving women alone with children and often destitute.

Many abandoned women chose divorce. Others simply began new relationships without the benefit of a legal dissolution of the marriage. Some women who faced loneliness and dire economic circumstances sought divorce so that they might remarry. Others pursued divorce only after receiving a marriage proposal. Perhaps surprisingly, some women who wanted to gain legal control of any real property they held chose divorce to regain *feme sole* status. The law allowed single women full legal control of their own real property. Illinois courts granted divorced women control of property they had brought to their marriages, regardless of the degree of their own culpability in the divorce. The Sangamon County Circuit Court case of *Plunkett v. Plunkett* illustrates this proclivity; the court allowed Ann Plunkett to keep her real property even though she had deserted her husband and the marriage. Such a ruling was not the norm; states like New York, which had stricter divorce laws, did not give women control of their own property until they proved that their husbands were at fault in the divorce.[57]

Adultery was another common ground for a divorce, and both men and women cited it in their petitions. Of fifty-five petitions in which adultery appeared as one ground for divorce, men brought 30 (55 percent) of the cases. Of all the grounds that men cited in their petitions for divorce, they were most successful in obtaining divorce decrees when they cited adultery.[58] The court granted the divorce in 77 percent of those cases. On the surface such a result suggests a sexual double standard, but women were even more successful in obtaining divorce decrees when they cited adultery in their petitions, receiving a divorce 80 percent of the time. Illinois's extremely high rate of divorce decrees based on adultery illustrates one commonality that Illinois divorce law shared with other states during the antebellum period and represents one point at which the state did not depart from the past. Antebellum Americans did not condone sexual misconduct. Many jurists perceived adultery as "the worst offense against the sanctity of the family" and recognized plaintiffs' right to free themselves from an unfaithful spouse.[59]

The *Hampton* and *Waddell* cases illustrate the various uses of adultery as a ground in divorce pleading and practice. Both cases shed light on how individuals viewed their options when marital discord arose. The *Hampton* case is particularly illustrative. After twenty-one years of marriage Catherine and Samuel Hampton divorced in 1845. Catherine Hampton had accused her husband of drunkenness, desertion, and adultery. She charged that in his drunkenness he had often "failed to provide for her competent subsistence but wasted his means in drinking" and that he had abandoned her in 1840.[60] At the time she filed for divorce Catherine Hampton, who was then living in a household with two of her grown sons, also believed that Samuel Hampton was living in a state of adultery with a woman to whom he professed to be married but legally was not.

After hearing the evidence, the court granted Catherine Hampton her divorce.[61] Regardless of the specific ground or grounds that the court recognized to grant a divorce in the *Hampton* case, Catherine Hampton's legal representation, the law firm of Stephen T. Logan and Abraham Lincoln, wisely included all the grounds that applied to her case. The bill for divorce filed in this case carefully focused on Samuel Hampton's guilt, while declaring that Catherine Hampton "discharged all the duties of a wife whilst the said Samuel Hampton lived with her."[62] This strategy of emphasizing the innocence of the complainant was common in actions of divorce as the plaintiff's attorneys worked to ensure a divorce decree based on the guilt of the defendant. In an era long before "no-fault" divorces, assigning blame was necessary to meet the statutory requirements for a divorce and contributed to determining the amount of alimony and to the resolution of custody issues.

The *Hampton* case depicts two distinct options in dealing with marital difficulties. The remedy for marital difficulties did not necessarily mean legal divorce.[63] Samuel Hampton extricated himself from an unhappy marriage to Catherine Hampton by physically leaving the household. Following that desertion, he entered into another relationship with a woman and was apparently content to go on with his life, regardless of the adulterous and perhaps bigamous situation. For him legal separation was unnecessary. Unhappy in his marriage to Catherine Hampton, he left and effectively "married" a new "wife." In contrast, Catherine Hampton used a suit for divorce to dissolve her relationship with her husband. For her legal divorce was necessary in severing the ties to her errant husband.

Rebecca Waddell also dealt with an unhappy marriage through extralegal means. In 1847, when she was seventeen, Rebecca Johnson married twenty-two-year-old Squire Waddell, a struggling young farmer. They had two children during the next few years. In 1851 Squire Waddell left on a trip to California to make his fortune. When he returned in September 1853, after an absence of at least a year, he learned that Rebecca Waddell was involved in an adulterous affair with William Welles.[64] Men who went west during the

California gold rush in the early 1850s anticipated hardships for themselves in their travels but perhaps overlooked the reality that their lengthy absences left their wives at home to face hardships as well.[65] Squire Waddell later claimed that he had left financial support for his family during his absence, but the support may have been insufficient or perhaps loneliness motivated Rebecca Waddell. Many "49er widows" like Rebecca Waddell experienced financial and emotional voids during prolonged absences of husbands.[66]

In 1853 Squire Waddell retained the law firm of Lincoln and Herndon and filed for divorce on the ground of adultery. Rebecca Waddell failed to answer the charges. Numerous witnesses then testified to her adulterous activities, and the court granted Squire Waddell a divorce and custody of the children.[67] After the divorce Rebecca Waddell disappeared from Sangamon County, perhaps having left with her lover. Squire Waddell remained in Sangamon County, prospered as a farmer, and raised his and Rebecca Waddell's two children with his new wife.[68]

The *Waddell* case is a gender reversal of the *Hampton* divorce. In this case the husband was the one who attached importance to the legal dissolution of the marriage. Squire Waddell did not leave the marriage as Samuel Hampton had. Perhaps his interest in his children kept him from desertion, but certainly Rebecca Waddell's adultery gave him incentive to pursue a legal separation. Although it is possible that Squire Waddell forced his wife into a situation that led to her eventual abandonment of her own children, it appears from the evidence that she chose another man over Squire Waddell and willingly allowed the divorce and relinquished her children to him. Perspectives of marriage and divorce in antebellum America were not necessarily gender specific.

Cruelty as a ground cited in divorce petitions was, however, very gender specific. Of the fifty-seven cases in which cruelty appeared as one ground for divorce, women filed fifty-four of them. Seventy percent of the women who cited cruelty as at least one ground in seeking a divorce were successful. Fourteen cases (25 percent) were either dismissed at the complainant's request or by decree of the court. In contrast, only three men filed for divorce based on cruelty, but all three obtained divorces. Women were more likely to cite cruelty as a ground for divorce.

Following the American Revolution, judges interpreted matrimonial cruelty using English theories and precedents. Divorce laws typically required petitioners to prove actual physical violence in order to obtain a divorce decree. By the 1840s judges were beginning to move away from that traditional interpretation and to examine seriously charges of threatened violence. However, even within that changing framework, many states refused to grant absolute divorce with the right to remarry, even when a woman's physical health was in jeopardy.[69] Whereas physically abused women in the eighteenth century had little legal recourse against their husbands, women in antebellum Illinois did.[70] Illinois legislators, in paternalistic fashion, designed divorce statutes with the personal welfare of women and children in mind, and the court adjudicated accordingly to protect them.

One Sangamon County case provides evidence that Illinois circuit courts' liberal practice of granting divorce decrees to women who charged their husbands with extreme and repeated cruelty saved some women from serious injury or death. Not long after Margaret and Robert Matthews married in 1851, he began behaving erratically and treating her cruelly. Margaret Matthews hired an attorney later that same year and filed for divorce. Although she had not been married for at least two years and therefore could not prove repeated cruelty for two years, as the Illinois statute required, the court considered the charge in light of Robert Matthews's sanity, which was not a recognized legal ground for divorce. The evidence bore out Margaret Matthews's claims, and the court, probably invoking the discretionary eighth section of the 1845 *Revised Statutes,* granted her a divorce.[71]

Another, more extreme example of cruelty is the case of Josephine Stierlin. She married Henry Stierlin in March 1853 and shortly after the marriage learned that her husband had not only falsely represented himself to her as a wealthy, respected man but also that he had an "intolerable ill temper." He drank constantly, failed to provide necessities, and treated his wife with "the most barbarous, extreme and repeated cruelty."[72] In the June 1855 term of the Sangamon County Circuit Court, Josephine Stierlin sued her husband for divorce. Her husband hired a lawyer, denied the charges of cruelty and drunkenness, and asked the court to dismiss the case. However, the court found him guilty of extreme and repeated cruelty and granted Josephine Stierlin a divorce.[73]

Women's petitions for divorce were more likely than men's divorce petitions to cite habitual drunkenness as a ground. In forty-one cases drunkenness appeared as at least one ground. Women filed all but one of these bills. Women were nearly as successful in obtaining divorces for drunkenness as they were for cruelty. In 74 percent of the cases the court granted the decree. The court dismissed four cases at the request of the complainant.[74] Faced with the economic uncertainties of life without a husband, women sometimes chose to remain married to drunkards.

The Williamson divorce is an interesting case involving a husband who had a serious problem with alcohol. On March 1, 1850, Dorothy and George Williamson married in Sangamon County. By the fall of 1851 George Williamson had become a habitual drunkard and was unable to provide for his new wife. His drinking continued, and Dorothy Williamson soon found out that at the time of their marriage, her husband was still legally married to his first wife, who was living in Iowa and with whom he had children. Dorothy Williamson retained a lawyer and sued her husband for divorce in the Sangamon County Circuit Court in Springfield. The evidence proved that George Williamson was guilty of both bigamy and drunkenness. The court granted the divorce in the fall of 1853. Freed from her unhappy marriage, Dorothy paid the court costs of $13.35.[75]

Women often cited both cruelty and drunkenness as grounds in their petitions for divorce. Of twenty-three such cases, the court granted the divorce in fourteen. A success rate of 65 percent suggests that women were slightly less successful in obtaining a divorce when they cited both as grounds. However, a woman was more likely to obtain custody of her children if she cited both drunkenness and cruelty than if she cited only drunkenness.

Martha Ann Jones's experience illustrates this curious pattern. She and Abel Jones married in 1831. Abel Jones was a farmer, and by 1850 he and his wife had nine children and owned $3,000 in real property.[76] Abel Jones was repeatedly jailed for public drunkenness. Martha Jones suffered with Abel Jones's drinking problem throughout the marriage and apparently endured repeated cruelty at the hands of her drunken husband. In 1852 Martha Jones hired a lawyer and sued her husband for divorce on the grounds of cruelty and drunkenness. In her bill for divorce she stated that she remained with her husband and endured "treatment most brutal and outrageous" for the sake of her large family and "continued to do so up until last June when [her husband] threatened to cut her throat."[77]

In his answer Abel Jones denied the charges. He also pointed out that "for a long time after said acts and transactions took place said complainant lived with him as his wife and condoned all said offenses."[78] In the ensuing trial the jury found for the plaintiff, and after twenty-one years of marriage the Joneses were divorced. The court granted Martha Jones custody of three of the children, probably the youngest three, and ordered Abel Jones to pay her $300 annually in support.[79] Although the court record is silent regarding the remaining children, at least two of the nine were probably grown by the time of the divorce. Abel may have maintained custody of the older boys, as their presence on the farm would have been imperative to its economic success. In the end, Martha Jones, after years of abuse, viewed legal separation from her husband as an appropriate remedy for her marital troubles.

Women were more likely than men to cite desertion, extreme and repeated cruelty, and habitual drunkenness. However, adultery, the most notoriously gender biased of grounds in the colonial and early national period, was applied nearly equally in antebellum Illinois. In regard to adultery the court was able in a complicated economic and legal transitional period to strike a balance. While the law compelled plaintiffs who cited adultery to prove the guilt of their errant spouse and deny any culpability on their own part, the Sangamon County Circuit Court granted divorces to plaintiffs who cited adultery essentially without regard to the gender of the plaintiff or the alleged adulterer. The situation in Illinois represented a definite shift away from the sexual double standard that many eastern and southern laws traditionally imposed and that supported the patriarchal ideal of a higher moral standard for women.[80]

Adultery, desertion, extreme and repeated cruelty, and habitual drunkenness represented the majority of grounds in divorce cases appearing in Sangamon County Circuit Court, but Illinois law also provided additional bases for ending marriage difficulties. Bigamy, felonious conviction, fraud, and impotence were uncommon grounds, although all appeared in the Sangamon County Circuit Court at least once. Illinois law also recognized the unique situation of individual cases with regard to issues of economics and family dynamics. The law left alimony and child custody questions in divorce cases to the discretion of the circuit courts. As a result, the law charged circuit court judges with the difficult task of reaching equitable settlements with no direct guidelines.

Although the Sangamon County Circuit Court records of child custody are quite spotty, the court generally awarded women custody of their children. Especially in cases in which the grounds were desertion or cruelty and/or drunkenness, women were successful in keeping their children. In the thirty-four cases in which custody settlements are known, women retained custody 76 percent of the time. The court awarded only five men custody of their children. In two cases the court split custody between the parties. In another the court awarded custody of the children to the maternal grandmother. In all but one of those cases in which the grounds included adultery, the court denied custody to the guilty party.

Alimony was a much more difficult issue, and the records are nearly silent. During the twenty-three-year period of this study the record fully details alimony settlements in only ten cases. Martha Ann Jones and Maria Brown are two of the women whose alimony settlements appear in the court record. When Martha Ann and Abel Jones divorced in 1852, the court awarded her $300 in annual support.[81] Maria Brown obtained a parcel of land worth $500 in lieu of alimony when her husband, James Brown, divorced her in 1841.[82] The court had found Maria Brown guilty of adultery, but despite her sexual transgression, the court provided her with economic support.

One can draw few conclusions from such a small sample, especially without detailed research on the economic standing of the men in the cases. One result, however, is striking. In three of the nine cases men found guilty of adultery were required to pay support. On the other hand, when the court found the wife guilty of adultery, she still received some form of alimony settlement, though not usually custody of her children. This result suggests a proclivity on the part of the court to punish economically men who committed adultery but to ignore the "sins" of the adulterous wife in favor of her economic support.

The wildly independent and sometimes creative differences in alimony and child custody settlements attest to the latitude that circuit court judges had in making these crucial family decisions. In that capacity judges held a great deal of power in determining settlements that certainly represented one of the most important events in the lives of litigants in divorce cases. In Sangamon County two circuit court judges decided the alimony and child custody arrangements in almost every divorce case during the period of this study. The judicial tenures of Samuel H. Treat and David Davis spanned the late 1830s through the 1850s on the judicial circuits that included Sangamon County. The personal and judicial opinions of those two individuals formed the basis for their individual decisions in such matters.

In terms of divorce decrees Treat and Davis granted a nearly equal percentage of decrees, 77 percent and 78 percent, respectively. However, in terms of the gender of the plaintiff, the record of the two judges is strikingly different. Treat's court granted divorces in only 53 percent of the thirty-six divorce cases with female plaintiffs, whereas Davis's court granted divorces in 71 percent of the 125 divorce cases with female plaintiffs. Although the alimony and child custody records are incomplete, it appears that the divorce decrees that Davis's court granted tended to mention alimony and child custody matters more frequently. That tendency may again signal a greater sensitivity on Davis's part. However, those differences may have simply reflected the different periods in which the men sat on the bench. Treat presided from 1840 to 1848, whereas Davis sat on the bench in the latter years of this study, when divorce petitions and decrees were increasing and the issues of child custody and alimony were becoming more prominent components of the business of Illinois circuit courts.[83]

The personal characteristics of judges is suggestive. Showing their paternalistic face, Sangamon County Circuit Court judges, and probably most Illinois circuit court judges, rarely ordered women to pay court costs. The court generally ordered men, whether they were plaintiffs or defendants, to assume responsibility even in cases in which their wives were the guilty party in the divorce. For example, when Squire Waddell accused his wife of adultery and sued her for divorce in 1853, the court accepted his charge against her and granted the divorce. Although the judge ruled that Rebecca Waddell was the party at fault, Squire Waddell paid the costs.[84] Sangamon County women could expect to obtain divorce decrees without having to incur the costs. If in a rare circumstance the court did order her to pay, she could be exempted from payment if she were poor.[85]

Illinois law recognized the difficult economic situation some women might face in the aftermath of divorce and legislated accordingly. Furthermore, circuit courts across the state recognized that they were probably most likely to obtain fees from men. Part of the reason that judges ordered men to pay was that women were financially less able to pay. At any rate, the law exempted women from incurring what amounted to an average of $16.11 in court costs per divorce case filed in the Sangamon County Circuit Court in Springfield.[86]

While attitudes toward women's financial independence remained relatively static throughout the period, marital expectations were changing, and men and women were beginning to perceive their roles differently. The era of romantic love fostered the notion that marital union should be emotionally as well as economically beneficial.[87] The proliferation of novels that dealt with issues previously considered outside the bounds of polite discourse influenced antebellum society, and many focused on divorce and warned readers to avoid loveless and hasty marriages based solely on the economic or social position of the potential spouse.[88] Women's periodicals and publications also proliferated and contributed to the notion that women deserved more than mere economic support from a husband. In 1838 Sarah Grimké, a nineteenth-century antislavery and feminist reformer, wrote in *Letters on the Equality of the Sexes* that God intended wives to be companions and helpers rather than housekeepers and that women were equal to men.[89]

In her 1846 book *Life in Prairie Land* Eliza Farnham captured the changing expectations that women brought to their marriages in antebellum Illinois. In relaying a conversation she had with a man during her travels to the Prairie State, she detailed his marital expectations and shared her own. She reported that the man had said that "every man ought to have a woman to do his cookin'" and that if he ever decided to marry, he would "give her enough to eat and wear" so long as she tended to all domestic duties. Farnham's retort illustrated her belief that marriage was a moral contract. She wrote that when a man took a woman away from home and family, he was morally required to treat her as a human being and not as an animal or machine: "The parties promise to study each other's happiness and endeavor to promote it."[90]

THE
SEVEN STAGES
or
MATRIMONY.

1. One look at beauty such as that
   Has placed a lover under his hat.
2. She reads – she smiles – her fluttering heart
   Is now transfix'd by Cupid's dart.
3. He raves – he swears – she plights her word :
   The fowler snares the silly bird !
4. The fatal knot has tied them fast.
   Oh, happiness too sweet to last!
5. The baby dear delights its Ma :
   Because it looks just like its Pa :
6. But now the leaves desert the rose
   And ragged thorns themselvs disclose.
7. She sues her lord – she's bound to win,
   She leaves his house, but keeps his tin!

QUIZZING.

A LOVE LETTER.

POPPING THE QUESTION.

THE MARRIAGE.

THE BABY.

THE QUARREL.

THE DIVORCE.

ATTORNEY AT LAW.

Bill of COST.

Annuity.

Those changing expectations of marriage resulted in changing perceptions about the acceptability of divorce. The legal philosopher Joel Prentiss Bishop wrote in 1852: "Marriage is in every view the most important institution of human society; it involves the most valued interests of every class; awakens the thoughts and engages the care of nearly every individual; and how it may be entered into, or how dissolved, or what is the effect of a pretended dissolution, is a matter of almost constant legal inquiry and litigation."[91] Legal, social, and political discussion on marriage and divorce in antebellum America represented a lifting of past prohibitions on public discourse of private matters and ushered in new attitudes and ideals. As couples began to view marriage within a romantic context, they felt more cheated by unhappy unions than the generation before them had. In turn, divorce became more attractive to people experiencing marital difficulties. One scholar has argued that during the nineteenth century, familial relationships were becoming increasingly companionate rather than patriarchal in nature, which fostered higher marital expectations.[92] The legal, religious, and social implications of marital perceptions and the commitment to the institution of marriage itself did not affect all women or men the same way. However, more and more women and men who experienced unhappy marriages chose legal and extralegal separations.

The historian Norma Basch speculates that a disproportionate number of women who chose to sue their husbands for divorce "enjoyed some financial independence outside of marriage."[93] This assertion does not apply in Illinois, where the majority of women litigants in divorce cases were farmers' daughters with little or no personal or real wealth. While it is true that several Sangamon County women who divorced their husbands had some familial economic assistance after their divorce, most chose divorce despite the tenuous nature of their future financial circumstances as divorced women. Furthermore, the majority of female petitioners were seeking divorces from husbands who had abandoned them and were failing to provide economic support in the first place.

Regardless of their economic circumstances, Illinois women had a variety of reasons for pursuing divorce. Economic, social, religious, and personal considerations no doubt contributed to the way they coped with difficult marriages. However, their gender did not necessarily dictate the course of action they eventually pursued. Neither did social pressures yield predictable choices. Women's motivation to pursue divorce decrees is not immediately obvious in most cases. What is certain, however, is that once they decided to pursue divorce, women in Illinois experienced few legal problems in obtaining a divorce. Access to divorce was more limited in most other states. The most extreme example was South Carolina, which had no provision for divorce until 1868.[94]

While examination of Sangamon County divorce cases across the period of this study offers clues about the experiences of antebellum Illinois women, analysis of the divorce practice of Abraham Lincoln and his three law partners provides a view through the eyes of members of the bar who handled many divorce cases. Investigation of those partnership cases as a whole provides another window into antebellum divorce. Lincoln's personal perspective of and professional involvement with divorce litigation, wedded with the statistical analysis of the entire corpus of divorce cases in Sangamon County, provides a unique marriage of historical resources.

The divorce cases that Abraham Lincoln and his law partners handled reflect the occurrence of divorce throughout the state and provide a basis for comparison to the divorce cases in Sangamon County as a whole. The pleading of Lincoln's divorce cases and the statistical breakdown of his divorce practice offer another perspective from which to interpret the legal representation that women received in actions of divorce. The attitude of Lincoln and his peers at the bar toward women in divorce cases provides further evidence that Illinois law and lawyers viewed women litigants within a paternalistic context.

Between 1837 and 1860 Lincoln and his three successive law partners—John Todd Stuart, Stephen T. Logan, and William H. Herndon—handled 145 divorce cases across central Illinois.[95] During his nearly twenty-five-year law practice Lincoln and his partners handled eighty-eight divorce cases in Sangamon County alone, 40 percent of the 220 divorce cases that appeared on the Sangamon County Circuit Court docket during that time.[96] Fifty-four percent of the divorce litigants they represented were women. Of the divorce cases that they handled, female plaintiffs brought 63 percent of the cases.

That Lincoln and his partners handled such a high percentage of the divorce cases appearing on the Sangamon County Circuit Court docket may suggest the eagerness with which Lincoln's law firms sought to gain business. It may also reflect Lincoln's reputation as a compassionate person when dealing with clients' personal and family problems. It could mean that fewer lawyers in Sangamon County were engaged in divorce practice or family-related litigation. Whatever the reason, Lincoln took many divorce cases, and his contemporaries may have considered him a divorce lawyer.[97]

Lincoln's divorce practice in Sangamon County parallels the pattern of all divorce cases in the county and throughout the state. In Lincoln's cases more women than men filed for divorce. Desertion was the most common ground, cited in 46 percent of all petitions. Petitioners rarely cited the grounds of bigamy, impotence, and felonious conviction. Women were more likely to cite desertion, cruelty, or drunkenness as grounds in their petitions. Male and female plaintiffs cited adultery as the ground in nearly equal proportions. The number of divorce petitions in Sangamon County increased over time, with the largest number appearing in the late 1850s. During Lincoln's law practice the per capita divorce rate nearly doubled, from an average of 2.10 divorce decrees per 10,000 people in the late 1830s and 1840s to an average of 4.13 divorce decrees per 10,000 people during the 1850s.[98] In 1860 the rate was three divorces per 10,000 people, putting Sangamon County well ahead of the national rate.[99] Family-related cases also became a larger percentage of chancery dockets. Women were taking advantage of their access to divorce in Illinois, which was indicative of their expanding legal options within the context of their rapidly changing social, legal, and economic roles.[100] Lincoln's practice reflected those changes.

Lincoln no doubt experienced conflicting feelings about divorce, as did his contemporaries at the bar. Many years after Lincoln's death Herndon wrote that Lincoln hated divorce practice most of all. On one hand, Lincoln appreciated that divorce was a necessary remedy for some couples. Yet he felt sadness about the dissolution of the marriages of his clients.[101] At any rate, it appears that Lincoln, as a respected man in the community and a capable lawyer, was a popular choice as counsel in legal issues regarding families, specifically in divorce cases. It is difficult to extrapolate Lincoln's personal feelings from the dry, formulaic pleading documents filed in legal cases. However, looking across the case documentation, a sense of Lincoln's perspective on women and his feelings about divorce emerges.[102]

The case of Samuel and Polly Rogers is an excellent example of Lincoln's personal, internal struggle regarding the issue. Samuel Rogers complained that his wife deserted him and that she was also guilty of adultery.[103] He retained the law partnership of John T. Stuart and Abraham Lincoln in August 1838. Lincoln convinced his client that the desertion of his wife was sufficient as a ground for divorce and recommended that the allegation of adultery against his wife be "muted . . . through tender consideration to the said defendant's character."[104] Lincoln was, in effect, sparing the defendant the embarrassment of the adultery allegation, but his decision was a legal blunder. When the court granted the divorce, it ordered Samuel to pay Polly $1,000 in alimony, quite a large lump-sum payment for the period.[105]

In an attempt to reduce the alimony Stuart and Lincoln filed an amended bill for divorce in which they added the adultery allegation. Lincoln also filed an affidavit attesting that his client had previously disclosed his wife's adultery. Upon reviewing the allegations against Polly, the jury found for the plaintiff, and the court reduced the alimony to an initial payment of $126 and subsequent $39 semiannual payments.[106] Lincoln's approach in this case was perhaps partially the result of inexperience. He had been licensed to practice law for little more than one year before taking Samuel Rogers's case. Yet examination of the case documentation of Lincoln's divorce practice over time reveals Lincoln's gentle nature regarding women. Lincoln's personal relationship with Mary Lincoln, particularly Lincoln's gentle acceptance of his wife's temper tantrums and other childlike behaviors, reflected his deep paternal streak.[107] Lincoln showed concern about the economic and social dangers that divorced women faced, and his respect for the women who entered into his personal and professional life reflected that tenderness.

Lincoln's personal feelings about women and divorce and the nature of his divorce practice offer another clue about the paternalist perspective with which men at the bar approached divorce litigation. Women made up the larger percentage of complainants in divorce cases, and defendants rarely hired opposing counsel to answer the charges. Antebellum Illinois attorneys were therefore more likely to be representing the legal interests of women in divorce cases. While not all Illinois attorneys considered themselves great protectors of women in divorce cases, Illinois women had both legal and personal advocates in the process. Because the law exempted most women who petitioned for divorce from paying court costs and attorney fees, lawyers certainly had little financial incentive for taking on divorce cases. Because many male defendants were deserters whose whereabouts were unknown, the lawyers were unlikely to collect their fees from the husbands. Perhaps a sense of obligation to protect women compelled some attorneys to represent women filing for divorce.

With the help of their lawyers antebellum Illinois women navigated the complexities of the Illinois court system and availed themselves of their legal right to seek divorce decrees, gain custody of their children, and obtain alimony settlements. The prevalence of divorce cases on the Sangamon County Circuit Court docket reflected the growing numbers of Illinois couples who were disillusioned with their marriages and were willing to seek legal remedies to their personal problems. Divorce in antebellum Illinois was accessible, and the legal framework on which it was based allowed judges considerable leeway in granting divorce decrees and determining crucial family questions of alimony and child custody.

As antebellum Illinois judges and juries rendered their verdicts in divorce cases across the state, the social and economic context of divorce was in a formative period. The trend of states' shifting divorce from legislative to judicial jurisdiction, the expansion of grounds for divorce, and growing social acceptance of divorce, as one scholar notes, "contributed to divorce rates which more accurately reflect the extent of marital conflict and disruption in the early frontier states."[108] Another scholar asserts that the decline of religion and the secularization of divorce was "the principal motor of modernization."[109] Changing economic opportunities for women and the increased public attention to women's issues, which public forums like the Seneca Falls Convention of 1848 helped to spotlight, contributed to the lessening of the negative stigma attached to divorce. The Seneca Falls delegation split on the issue of divorce because many delegates in attendance opposed divorce on moral or religious grounds. Others, like Elizabeth Cady Stanton, believed that secular and religious laws should not regulate marriage and divorce, which they viewed as private matters.[110] The debate about the issue increased public discussion of the legal and social aspects of divorce, a subject that Americans had previously considered taboo. The opening of a public forum for debating the issue challenged the very notion of the traditionally subordinate legal status of antebellum American women and set the stage for social and legal changes.

Antebellum women in Sangamon County benefited from those sweeping changes. Although the paternalistic structure of the law of divorce in Illinois prevented equal legal status for women, women did benefit from the willingness of Illinois courts to grant them divorces. Few places in the country allowed women or men as many different reasons for which they could end a marriage as did Illinois. Maria Chapman had benefited from liberal divorce provisions when she chose to leave her adulterous husband in 1851. Illinois women of all economic backgrounds had more access to divorce in the antebellum period than ever before. While many circumstances of divorce came with initial embarrassment and shame to the families facing it, the legal process of divorce in Illinois was relatively simple.

The paternalism of divorce law in Illinois, while viewing women as incapable of protecting themselves, provided women with a level of access to divorce in the name of a protective umbrella that, ironically, opened legal doors for Illinois women and set the stage for increased legal opportunity. In fact, the paternalist structure of divorce offered women a legal remedy to marital difficulties and placed in women's hands some power to act as agents in their own lives. Many women in Sangamon County chose that legal remedy and applied it to their unique economic, social, and familial situations. In exercising their legal option of dissolving the bonds of matrimony, women accepted responsibility for themselves and their children and asserted themselves despite the notion that they were incapable of handling those challenges.

Notes

1. Bill for Divorce, 24 July 1851, *Chapman v. Chapman;* Decree, 28 August 1851, *Chapman v. Chapman;* Fee Bill, August term 1851, *Chapman v. Chapman,* all in *The Law Practice of Abraham Lincoln: Complete Documentary Edition,* ed. Martha L. Benner and Cullom Davis et al. (DVD; Urbana: University of Illinois Press, 2000), hereafter cited as *LPAL.*

2. Of the 220 divorce cases that appeared in Sangamon County Circuit Court, surviving documentation records the judgment in only 212. One woman obtained an annulment of her marriage, but this study does not include her case.

3. This study derives all the statistics for Sangamon County Circuit Court divorce cases from a database incorporating information from the case files, judge's dockets, court records, and fee books from 1837 to 1860. Lincoln handled no divorce cases in the first (1836) and final (1861) years of his law practice. The information collected for the database included the names of the cases, litigants, and attorneys, the judgments and judgment dates, the grounds for divorce, the gender of each plaintiff, court costs, and alimony and child custody settlements.

4. Roderick Phillips, *Putting Asunder: A History of Divorce in Western Society* (Cambridge: Cambridge University Press, 1988), 439.

5. William Forrest Sprague, *Women and the West: A Short Social History* (Boston: Christopher Publishing, 1940), 97; *Appleton's Annual Encyclopedia and Register of Important Events for 1870* (New York: D. Appleton, 1871), 392–93.

6. Joel Prentiss Bishop, *The Law of Marriage and Divorce and Evidence in Matrimonial Suits* (Boston: Little, Brown, 1852), 279.

7. Norma Basch, *Framing American Divorce: From the Revolutionary Generation to the Victorians* (Berkeley: University of California Press, 1999), 100. In their edited collection, *A Shared Experience: Men, Women, and the History of Gender* (New York: New York University Press, 1998), Laura McCall and Donald Yacovone call for more gender-related studies in the West.

8. Complete court docket records and chancery case files, a wealth of census and marriage records, and abundant county histories, biographies, and genealogical indexes make Sangamon County an excellent county through which to examine the experience of divorce for Illinois women generally.

9. For the changing characteristics of womanhood, see Nancy F. Cott, *The Bonds of Womanhood: "Woman's Sphere" in New England, 1780–1835* (New Haven, Conn.: Yale University Press, 1977).

10. Nancy F. Cott, "Divorce and the Changing Status of Women in Eighteenth-Century Massachusetts," *William and Mary Quarterly* 33 (October 1976): 586–614; Nancy F. Cott, "Eighteenth-Century Family and Social Life Revealed in Massachusetts Divorce Records," *Journal of Social History* 10 (Fall 1976): 20–43.

11. John Mack Faragher, *Sugar Creek: Life on the Illinois Prairie* (New Haven, Conn.: Yale University Press, 1986), 102.

12. Paul M. Angle, in *"Here I Have Lived": A History of Lincoln's Springfield, 1821–1865* (Chicago: Abraham Lincoln Book Shop, 1971), offers glimpses of the economic, social, and political environment of Springfield and Sangamon County.

13. Marylynn Salmon, *Women and the Law of Property in Early America* (Chapel Hill: University of North Carolina Press, 1986), 64; Martin Schultz, "Divorce in Early America: Origins and Patterns in Three North Central States," *Sociological Review* 25 (Autumn 1984): 511–26.

14. Illinois courts granted divorces in 68.1 percent of the petitions filed in 1840, 70.4 percent of those in 1850, and 68.5 percent of those in 1860. By comparison, Missouri granted divorces in 48.2 percent of petitions filed in 1840, 55.7 percent of those in 1850, and 61.3 percent of those in 1860. See Schultz, "Divorce in Early America," 520.

15. Glenda Riley, "Legislative Divorce in Virginia, 1803–1850," *Journal of the Early Republic* 11 (Spring 1991): 51.

16. Basch, *Framing American Divorce*, 23.

17. Richard H. Chused, *Private Acts in Public Places: A Social History of Divorce in the Formative Era of American Family Law* (Philadelphia: University of Pennsylvania Press, 1994), 11.

18. Anya Jabour, *Marriage in the Early Republic: Elizabeth and William Wirt and the Companionate Idea* (Baltimore: Johns Hopkins University Press, 1998), 2.

19. Glenda Riley, *Divorce: An American Tradition* (Lincoln: University of Nebraska Press, 1991), 34.

20. Cornelia Hughes Dayton, *Women before the Bar: Gender, Law, and Society in Connecticut, 1639–1789* (Chapel Hill: University of North Carolina Press, 1995), 113.

21. Mary Somerville Jones, *An Historical Geography of the Changing Divorce Law in the United States* (New York: Garland, 1987), 23–24.

22. Jane Turner Censor, "Smiling through Her Tears: Antebellum Southern Women and Divorce," *American Journal of Legal History* 25 (January 1981): 24–47; Lawrence B. Goodheart, Neil Hanks, and Elizabeth Johnson, "'An Act for the Relief of Females . . .': Divorce and the Changing Legal Status of Women in Tennessee, 1796–1860," *Tennessee Historical Quarterly* 44 (Fall 1985): 318–39 and (Winter 1985): 402–16. For a contemporary account of divorce see Henry Folsom Page, *A View of the Law Relating to the Subject of Divorce in Ohio, Indiana, and Michigan* (Columbus, Ohio: n.p., 1850).

23. Jane H. Pease and William H. Pease, *Ladies, Women, and Wenches: Choice and Constraint in Antebellum Charleston and Boston* (Chapel Hill: University of North Carolina Press, 1990), 31.

24. Riley, *Divorce*, 49.

25. Jones, *An Historical Geography*, 23. Iowa's incompatibility clause allowed for divorce in cases "when it shall be made fully apparent to the satisfaction of the court that the parties cannot live in peace or happiness together, and that their welfare requires separation between them" (Riley, *Divorce*, 47). This provision remained in effect until 1851.

26. Neal R. Feigenson, "Extraterritorial Recognition of Divorce Decrees in the Nineteenth Century," *American Journal of Legal History* 34 (April 1990): 148–49.

27. Greeley's editorial ran on March 1, 1860. See Richard Wires, *The Divorce Issue and Reform in Nineteenth-Century Indiana* (Muncie, Ind.: Ball State University, 1967), 17.

28. Wires's *Divorce Issue and Reform* focuses on Indiana's reputation as a "divorce mill."

29. Martin Schultz, "Divorce Patterns in Nineteenth-Century New England," *Journal of Family History* 15 (1990): 101–15. See also Schultz, "Divorce in Early America," 511–26.

30. Norma Basch, "The Emerging Legal History of Women in the United States: Property, Divorce, and the Constitution," *Signs: Journal of Women in Culture and Society* 12 (Autumn 1986): 107.

31. Rebecca Looney, "Migration and Separation: Divorce in Kane County, 1837–1869," *Illinois Historical Journal* 89 (Summer 1986): 70–84.

32. Terry Wilson, "The Business of a Midwestern Trial Court: Knox County, Illinois, 1841–1850," *Illinois Historical Journal* 84 (Winter 1991): 252.

33. Looney, "Migration and Separation," 72 (for Kane County); Wilson, "Business of a Midwestern Trial Court," 252 (for Knox County).

34. Cott, "Divorce and the Changing Status of Women," 586–614; Cott, "Eighteenth-Century Family and Social Life," 20–43. Along with Cott's two studies of divorce, two of the best studies dealing specifically with divorce are Basch, *Framing American Divorce*, and Chused, *Private Acts in Public Places*.

35. The women mentioned were litigants in the following Sangamon County Circuit Court divorce cases: *Shelby v. Shelby, Chavers v. Chavers, Radford v. Radford, Wallace v. Wallace, Dennis v. Dennis, Noyes v. Noyes, Moro v. Moro, Lanterman v. Ross, Brockman v. Popper, Gentry v. Gentry*. The 1830, 1840, 1850, and 1860 census indexes and marriage indexes compiled by the Sangamon County Genealogical Society were most helpful.

36. Sabin D. Puterbaugh, *Puterbaugh's Chancery Pleading and Practice* (Chicago: Callaghan and Cutler, 1867), 710.

37. "An Act Respecting Divorce," 22 February 1819, *Laws of the State of Illinois*, 35–37; "An Act to Amend 'An Act Respecting Divorces,'" 17 January 1825, *Laws of the State of Illinois*, 169; "An Act Amending the Law Concerning Divorces," 12 January 1827, *Revised Code of Laws of Illinois* (1827), 180–81; "An Act Concerning Divorces," 31 January 1827, *Revised Code of Laws of Illinois* (1827), 181–83; "Divorces," 3 March 1845, *Revised Statutes of the State of Illinois* (1845), 196–97.

38. Elizabeth Pleck, *Domestic Tyranny: The Making of Social Policy against Family Violence from Colonial Times to the Present* (New York: Oxford University Press, 1987), 23. For an examination of marital cruelty see Merril D. Smith, *Breaking the Bonds: Marital Discord in Pennsylvania, 1730–1830* (New York: New York University Press, 1991), 27.

39. "Act Concerning Divorces," 182.

40. In 1816 Tapping Reeve wrote "that if a husband turns his wife out of doors, and so abuses her, that she cannot live with him safely, and she departs from him; that this is not a willful absence on her part, but that it is so on his" (*The Law of Baron and Femme, of Parent and Child, of Guardian and Ward, of Master and Servant, and of the Powers of Courts of Chancery* [New Haven, Conn.: Oliver Steele, 1816], 207–8). Such was not the case in Illinois, however. Illinois courts found women who chose this route to divorce at fault. However, fault did not dictate custody and alimony settlements, so women who deserted their husbands did not necessarily lose custody of their children or fail to obtain alimony.

41. *Schillinger v. Schillinger, LPAL*.

42. *Schillinger v. Schillinger*, 14 Ill. 149 (1852). George Schillinger finally got his divorce in 1853, when his wife sued him in Sangamon County Circuit Court on the ground of desertion.

43. "Divorces," 196–97. Lewis Solomons was the administrator of the estate of John Birkby, who died before his divorce case reached the Illinois Supreme Court.

44. *Birkby v. Solomons et al.*, 15 Ill. 122 (1853).

45. Ibid., 121–22.

46. *Reavis v. Reavis*, 2 Ill. 242 (1835); *Clark et al. v. Lott et al.*, 11 Ill. 105 (1849); *Vignos v. Vignos*, 15 Ill. 186 (1853); *Stewartson v. Stewartson*, 15 Ill. 146 (1853); *Howey et al. v. Goings*, 13 Ill. 101 (1851); and *Wren v. Moss et al.*, 6 Ill. 560 (1844).

47. Bill for Divorce, 16 August 1860, *Dutch v. Dutch, LPAL*; U.S. Census Office, Eighth Census of the United States (1860), Sangamon County, Illinois, ms.

48. Bill for Divorce, 16 August 1860, *Dutch v. Dutch, LPAL*.

49. Ibid.
50. Ibid.
51. Decree, 16 August 1860, *Dutch v. Dutch, LPAL.*
52. For child custody in the nineteenth century see Michael Grossberg, *Governing the Hearth: Law and the Family in Nineteenth-Century America* (Chapel Hill: University of North Carolina Press, 1985), 234–85; and Peter W. Bardaglio, *Reconstructing the Household: Families, Sex, and the Law in the Nineteenth-Century South* (Chapel Hill: University of North Carolina Press, 1995), 79–112.
53. Occupational and economic data are from the 1850 and 1860 U.S. censuses. For the 1850 census see U.S. Census Office, Seventh Census of the United States (1850), Sangamon County, Illinois, ms.
54. For a local social perspective of marriage and divorce, see Faragher, *Sugar Creek,* 79–87.
55. Sangamon County Genealogical Society, *Marriage Records of Sangamon County, Illinois, 1821–1840* (Springfield, Ill.: Sangamon County Genealogical Society, 1977); Sangamon County Genealogical Society, *Marriage Records of Sangamon County, Illinois, 1841–1850* (Springfield, Ill.: Sangamon County Genealogical Society, 1977); Sangamon County Genealogical Society, *Marriage Records of Sangamon County, Illinois, 1851–1860* (Springfield, Ill.: Sangamon County Genealogical Society, 1981).
56. Master in Chancery's Report, 27 October 1857, *Pike v. Pike, LPAL.*
57. Norma Basch, *In the Eyes of the Law: Women, Marriage, and Property in Nineteenth-Century New York* (Ithaca, N.Y.: Cornell University Press, 1982), 21.
58. Although male plaintiffs who cited cruelty (three) and drunkenness (one) obtained divorce decrees in every case, the low number makes conclusions difficult.
59. Salmon, *Women and the Law of Property,* 68.
60. Bill for Divorce, 10 May 1844, *Hampton v. Hampton, LPAL.*
61. Decree, 24 March 1845, *Hampton v. Hampton, LPAL.*
62. Bill for Divorce, 10 May 1844, *Hampton v. Hampton, LPAL.*
63. For an explanation of women's remedies to marital difficulties nationally, see Hendrik Hartog, "Marital Exits and Marital Expectations in Nineteenth-Century America," *Georgetown Law Journal* 80 (October 1991): 95–129, and Riley, *Divorce.*
64. Bill for Divorce, November term 1853, *Waddell v. Waddell, LPAL.*
65. Malcolm J. Rohrbough, *Days of Gold: The California Gold Rush and the American Nation* (Berkeley: University of California Press, 1997), 35.
66. Ibid., 244.
67. Decree, 25 November 1853, *Waddell v. Waddell, LPAL.*
68. Census Office, Eighth Census (1860), Sangamon County, Illinois.
69. Robert L. Griswold, "Law, Sex, Cruelty, and Divorce in Victorian America, 1840–1900," *American Quarterly* 38 (Winter 1986): 723. For a study of cruelty in England see A. James Hammerton, *Cruelty and Companionship: Conflict in Nineteenth-Century Married Life* (London: Routledge, 1992).
70. Dayton, *Women before the Bar,* 62.
71. Bill for Divorce, 3 August 1852, *Matthews v. Matthews, LPAL;* Judge's Docket, August term 1852, *Matthews v. Matthews, LPAL.*
72. Bill for Divorce, 15 April 1855, *Stierlin v. Stierlin, LPAL.*
73. Answer, 18 June 1855, *Stierlin v. Stierlin, LPAL;* Decree, 18 June 1855, *Stierlin v. Stierlin, LPAL.*

74. In one case the husband charged the wife with drunkenness. The court granted the divorce decree.

75. Bill for Divorce, 12 October 1853, *Williamson v. Williamson, LPAL;* Master in Chancery's Report, 29 November 1853, *Williamson v. Williamson, LPAL;* Fee Book, November term 1853; *Williamson v. Williamson, LPAL.*

76. Census Office, Seventh Census (1850), Sangamon County.

77. Bill for Divorce, 2 August 1852, *Jones v, Jones, LPAL.*

78. Answer, 6 September 1852, *Jones v. Jones, LPAL.*

79. Decree, 9 September 1852, *Jones v. Jones, LPAL.*

80. Cott, "Divorce and the Changing Status of Women," 599.

81. *Jones v. Jones, LPAL.* A typical Sangamon County family, consisting of three adults and four children in 1856, required approximately $405 a year to survive. Good pay for a workman was $10 per week, and rent (or housing) averaged about $120 annually. See Angle, *"Here I Have Lived,"* 173.

82. *Brown v. Brown, LPAL.*

83. The statistics included in this paragraph are drawn from the same database that informs the rest of this study (see note 3). The biographical information comes from *LPAL.*

84. *Waddell v. Waddell, LPAL.*

85. Illinois law also allowed poor plaintiffs, regardless of gender, to file lawsuits without cost. The statute directed the court to allow poor litigants all the necessary writs, process, and proceedings without fees or charge and assign legal counsel as well. See "An Act Concerning Costs," 16 January 1827, *Revised Code of Laws of Illinois* (1827), 103.

86. In the cases in which the court costs are known, the lowest court fee charged in a divorce action was $2.75 and the highest was $69.10. Circuit clerks based costs primarily on the number of terms of the court and the number of witnesses called. For example, a case that began and ended in one term of court and required only one witness cost considerably less than a case that lasted for several terms of court and required multiple witnesses.

87. For a detailed account of the implications of romantic love on the state of marriage in the United States, see Riley, *Divorce.*

88. Cathy N. Davidson, *Revolution and the Word: The Rise of the Novel in America* (New York: Oxford University Press, 1986); James Harwood Barnett, *Divorce and the American Divorce Novel, 1858–1937: A Study in Literary Reflections of Social Influences* (New York: Russell and Russell, 1939), 96.

89. Sarah Grimké, *Letters on the Equality of the Sexes* (Boston: I. Knapp, 1838).

90. Eliza W. Farnham, *Life in Prairie Land* (1846; rpt., New York: Arno, 1972), 37.

91. Bishop, *Law of Marriage and Divorce,* v.

92. Robert L. Griswold. *Family and Divorce in California, 1850–1890: Victorian Illusions and Everyday Realities* (Albany: State University of New York Press, 1982). Jabour's *Marriage in the Early Republic* examines one couple in the context of companionate marriage.

93. Norma Basch, "Relief in the Premises: Divorce as a Woman's Remedy in New York and Indiana, 1815–1870," *Law and History Review* 8 (Spring 1990): 9.

94. For an overview of divorce in the South see Censor, "Smiling through Her Tears."

95. Stuart and Lincoln were partners from 1836 to 1841; Logan and Lincoln were partners from 1841 to 1844; and Lincoln and Herndon were partners from 1844 to 1861.

96. *LPAL.*

97. James C. Conkling, a prominent member of the Sangamon County bar, also han-

dled a large number of divorce cases. The percentage of cases that he handled during the same period seems to be lower than Lincoln's (Sangamon County Circuit Court judge's docket database, Lincoln Legal Papers, Springfield, Ill.).

98. These per capita figures are based on the 1830, 1840, 1850, and 1860 U.S. censuses and the 1845 and 1855 state censuses and extrapolated across the period from these points.

99. Phillips, *Putting Asunder,* 459.

100. The best work on the emerging legal status of American women includes Basch, "Emerging Legal History of Women," 97–117; Dayton, *Women before the Bar;* and Salmon, *Women and the Law of Property.*

101. Jesse W. Weik, *The Real Lincoln: A Portrait* (Boston: Houghton Mifflin, 1922), 148–49.

102. David Herbert Donald's *Lincoln* (New York: Simon and Schuster, 1995) provides a thorough overview of Lincoln's life on a variety of levels.

103. Bill for Divorce, 14 August 1838, *Rogers v. Rogers, LPAL.*

104. Affidavit, 20 October 1838, *Rogers v. Rogers, LPAL.*

105. Judge's Docket, October term 1838, *Rogers v. Rogers, LPAL.*

106. Amended Bill for Divorce, 20 October 1838, *Rogers v. Rogers, LPAL;* Affidavit, 20 October 1838, *Rogers v. Rogers, LPAL;* Decree, 15 March 1839, *Rogers v. Rogers, LPAL.*

107. Michael Burlingame: *The Inner World of Abraham Lincoln* (Urbana: University of Illinois Press, 1994), 315. For a more detailed account of the Lincolns' marriage, see Jean H. Baker, *Mary Todd Lincoln: A Biography* (New York: W. W. Norton, 1987).

108. Schultz, "Divorce in Early America," 523.

109. Phillips, *Putting Asunder,* 192.

110. Elizabeth Cady Stanton, "Appeal for the Maine Law," in *Elizabeth Cady Stanton and Susan B. Anthony: Correspondence, Writings, Speeches,* ed. Ellen Carol DuBois (New York: Schocken, 1981), 40–43.

4

Inheriting the Earth: The Law of Succession

JOHN A. LUPTON

In 1853 William McDaniel wanted to disinherit Sally Correll and Martha McIntyre, two of his daughters. In order to accomplish this McDaniel authored a will in which he specifically left no property for them. Illinois inheritance laws dictated that if a person died without a will, the heirs would inherit the real and personal property of the estate equally. After the death of their father and upon hearing the conditions of the will, the daughters sued their siblings to set aside the will in order to inherit an equal share of the property. What ensued was an eight-year legal battle between brothers and sisters with three jury trials and an appeal to the Illinois Supreme Court. The *McDaniel* case illustrates one of several types of inheritance issues decided by the courts of antebellum Illinois.

Inheritance is the transmission of property from a deceased person to assigned heirs in the case of a will (testamentary disposition) or to legal heirs in a statutory mode of distribution in the absence of a will (intestate succession).[1] Because the transfer of property has always been a complicated issue, governing bodies have created many laws to oversee the process. These laws give courts the power to rule on real and personal property transfers in inheritance-related matters. Most inheritance laws in the early American Republic originated in England, and colonial American courts adopted and modified them to conform to their own situations.[2] This evolutionary process continued into the antebellum period.[3]

Walter B. Scates, a justice of the Illinois Supreme Court from 1841 to 1847 and 1853 to 1857, commented on the differences between English and Illinois inheritance laws in an 1845 court opinion.[4] English laws placed many encumbrances on the land to sustain an aristocracy. Scates noted that the only remaining encumbrance in Illinois was dower. Land in Illinois had "become a species of capital," and the inheritance "laws of England have been wholly changed with us."[5] Real property constituted wealth in antebellum Illinois. Susan Gray notes that the frontier economy in neighboring Michigan resulted in "land-rich and cash-poor" settlers.[6] Illinois followed the same pattern. Paper currency, bank notes, and promissory notes were unreliable, and specie was rare. However, the land itself and agricultural production yielded income and wealth for the landowner. Whether a person died wealthy or poor, the laws and the courts dictated how that person's assets would be distributed to beneficiaries and to creditors.

Married women possessed few rights in the legal system, but women in general were active participants in the inheritance process: administering estates, choosing the most beneficial inheritance for themselves, and acquiring their property. The courts protected children's rights to property and allowed them to voice their concerns through a guardian *ad litem,* a temporary guardian. Women and children used these lawful rights to obtain their rightful property. Statutes and courts provided for the well-being of women and children after the death of a husband or father because society did not. Welfare was virtually nonexistent. By maintaining an interest in part of a husband's estate, a widow did not have to rely on social provisioning for her support.[7] Real property also provided money for a child's education and clothing, so that society did not have to bear that responsibility. Courts recognized these rights and provided women and children with a strong voice in inheritance-related matters.

The process of inheritance in Illinois through the court system was strict and straightforward. The judges and juries who implemented the statutory provisions relating to inheritance consistently followed the letter of the law. Jurists deferred to precedent and followed the "doctrines or rules."[8] Within this rigid court system women and children took an active role in protecting their interests in the inheritance process. Despite the rigidity of the legal system on these matters, problems arose within the distribution of inheritance that required judicial resolution. While the majority of families had few problems in inheriting land and personal possessions, some families experienced bitter struggles to inherit the earth.

Several cases during Abraham Lincoln's twenty-five-year legal career illustrate some difficulties that occurred during the inheritance process. Of the nearly fifty-two hundred cases that Lincoln and his partners handled between 1836 and 1861, nearly nine hundred, or 17 percent, concerned inheritance. In these cases four times as many people died without a will than those who had written wills. John Mack Faragher found that most husbands on the Illinois prairie died without a will.[9] Ironically, Lincoln, an accomplished lawyer, also failed to write a will, and Illinois's mechanical intestacy laws dictated the distribution of his estate's assets.

Not surprisingly, men possessed most of the estates in cases in which

Lincoln was involved. However, unmarried (*feme sole*) women also owned property and wrote wills to distribute their possessions. For example, Anna Duncan of Morgan County, Illinois, wrote her will shortly before her death in 1851. She left everything that she owned, which included 548 acres of land and all her personal property, to her brother-in-law Charles Price to hold in trust for the benefit of her parents. After the death of her parents, she wanted the land and personal property to be divided equally between her two sisters, Caroline Price and Margaret Snow. Anna Duncan's father and mother died in 1854 and 1858. Charles Price had sold all the land after 1854 to support Duncan's mother, but Margaret Snow and her husband, Daniel, believed that Price had kept the money for himself; they sued Charles and Caroline Price to account for the money. The court later dismissed the case because of a technicality.[10] The Price and Snow families used the legal system to attempt to settle their inheritance dispute.

The experiences of five other families in Sangamon County, Illinois, illustrate the types of legal battles that arose over inheritance. The Bell family dealt with an indebted estate. The McDaniel family divided over the issue of a will. The Hillman family responded to an ineffective will. The Hinkle family wanted equal distribution of an estate's assets. The Glynn family faced an unexpected challenge. In all five examples the male head of the family died and left his widow and/or children to deal with different problems through the legal system. Anyone who had an interest in an inheritance-related matter—men, women, and children—had access to the courts.

The death of James Bell and the administration of his estate offer one example of estate settlement in antebellum Illinois. The inheritance process remained fairly static during the first decades of statehood; however, the structure of probate courts changed several times. The county commissioners' court in 1819, the probate court in 1821, the probate justice of the peace court in 1837, and the county court in 1849 each in turn began to exercise jurisdiction over estate settlements in antebellum Illinois.[11] Bell's estate settlement occurred within the framework of the probate justice of the peace court, and it was fairly typical of the period.

James Bell died intestate on December 21, 1842, in Springfield. An active businessman in Springfield in the 1830s and 1840s, Bell maintained different business partnerships with Seth Tinsley, Abner Y. Ellis, Joshua Speed, and Charles Hurst. At one point in the late 1830s Bell had run his own general store.[12] At his death he left a widow and three children younger than ten. A family member or close friend had to notify the probate court of a person's death, and Abraham Lincoln reported to Probate Justice of the Peace Thomas Moffett that Bell had died.[13] The first right to administer the estate belonged to the next of kin.[14] James Bell's widow did not apply for letters of administration, which was the formal authorization from the court to proceed to settle the estate. The next right belonged to a creditor, but since none appeared, the administration of James Bell's estate would normally have fallen to the public administrator. However, Lincoln appeared on behalf of Joshua Speed, one of Bell's former business partners, and requested that the court appoint William H. Herndon to administer the estate. A legal clerk in the Logan and Lincoln law office, Herndon would later become Lincoln's third law partner. No one objected to Herndon as administrator, and the court issued letters of administration to him. Herndon filed a $4,000 penal bond, which was twice the size of the estate's estimated value and a statutory requirement, to ensure that he would honestly perform the duties of administrator.[15]

Herndon's first responsibility was to make a full and complete inventory of all real and personal property and of all debts that were due the estate.[16] The court then appointed three people who did not have a claim on the estate to appraise the personal property. John Canfield, J. A. Hough, and Caleb Birchall valued James Bell's personal property, which included mostly furniture, books, a cooking stove, and a cow, at $288.50. Several months later Herndon sold the property for $257.67.[17] Herndon also calculated the debts owed to Bell's estate to be worth $102.29.

During his lifetime Bell had acquired many debts. As administrator, Herndon advertised that James Bell had died and that creditors should file their claims against the estate. Some claims were more important than others, and the Illinois statutes provided a hierarchical structure to rank them according to importance. Herndon divided the many claims into classes. First-class demands consisted of funeral and last sickness expenses. Second-class demands were administration expenses. Third-class demands only applied if the deceased possessed funds from an estate in which he or she were an administrator or executor. The fourth and last class was all other debts and demands against the estate.[18] After calculating the debts, Herndon discovered that Bell's estate owed $6,076.94.

The very first claim on the estate belonged to Bell's widow, Jane Bell.[19] Dower was a well-protected right that gave a widow a life interest in one-third of her deceased husband's real property.[20] Jane Bell was entitled to dower in the real property that her husband owned at any time during their marriage. In the March 1845 term of the Sangamon County Circuit Court, she filed her petition for dower. According to the statutes, the heir or heirs had to set off the dower for the widow. Because Bell's young children were the only heirs and because they obviously could not divide the land themselves, she had to sue her three children—Benjamin Bell, David Bell, and Elizabeth Bell—to claim her right to one-third of the land.[21]

James Bell owned 880 acres of land in Woodford, Logan, and Menard Counties in Illinois and three city lots in Springfield. Jane Bell wanted her dower to be the three lots in Springfield where she and her husband had lived, rather than portions of land in three separate and distant counties. The court appointed John T. Stuart as the guardian *ad litem* to look after the interests of the Bell children. A guardian *ad litem* served as a special guardian for the interests of minors in a specific lawsuit.[22] Stuart examined the records and stated that Jane Bell should have her dower. The court granted the petition and appointed three commissioners to assign her dower. The commissioners examined the property, decided that the three lots equaled one-third of the value of the total property, and awarded the three lots to her as her dower, which was not subject to creditors' claims.[23]

The law of dower was a protective right for women. Wives generally outlived husbands, and courts strictly enforced dower rights because without real property most widows did not have the means to provide for themselves. Dower allowed widows an opportunity to live without relying on the local community for support. While dower was not necessarily equitable in that a woman could bring more into a marriage than she might later receive in dower, most widows in Illinois were able to support themselves modestly. Family members helped if the widow needed additional financial assistance. A widow's dower also protected minor children, whom the widow had to support until they reached adulthood. For a woman the real power occurred during her husband's life. He could not sell any property on which she had not relinquished her dower rights. If a husband sold land without her consent, she could sue the buyer to gain her rightful third after her husband's death. In antebellum Illinois many women understood the importance of their dower rights and exerted those rights if treated unfairly. For example, Margaret Porter, a widow who lived in Sangamon County, sued dozens of people all over the state to acquire her dower in lands that her husband had sold without her consent.[24]

The personal property that Herndon sold and the debts that he collected were not enough to pay the debts of James Bell's estate. Herndon would have to sell as much of Bell's land as was necessary to pay the debts.[25] In September 1844 Herndon retained Lincoln and sued Jane Bell, Benjamin Bell, and David Bell in a chancery action to sell the land to pay the debts of the estate.[26] The court appointed James H. Matheny as guardian *ad litem* to protect the interests of the minor children. Matheny examined the records and agreed that Herndon should sell the lands. The court ordered the sale. Herndon sold different tracts between October 1846 and July 1847, adding $1,185.15 to the assets of the estate.[27] Herndon compiled the totals of the estate's assets and debts. The $1,545.11 in assets and the $6,076.94 in debts left a deficit of $4,531.83. Herndon reported that the assets were sufficient to pay the first- and second-class claims fully and to prorate the fourth-class claims. The court agreed, and Herndon paid the first- and second-class claims in full. Fourth-class claimants only received 3 percent of their claims. For example, Mahlon Williams and Company had a claim of $1,937.48 against Bell's estate, but Herndon paid the company only $54.30. The company and Bell's other creditors had to accept the small percentage. The only property that remained was Jane Bell's dower, which was not subject to creditors' claims. After Jane Bell's death her dower would descend to James Bell's heirs.[28] After Herndon finished his work, Probate Justice of the Peace Moffett declared James Bell's estate insolvent and barred anyone from filing further claims against it.[29]

If an estate had a surplus after the final settlement, statutory provisions again dictated how the excess land and money would be divided. Samuel Anno died intestate in Menard County in 1838 and left twelve heirs. Anno Ritter, the administrator of Samuel Anno's estate, calculated the final settlement of the estate, which had $61.94 and two hundred acres of land for distribution. In a friendly lawsuit in 1849 Pollard Anno and other heirs sued John Anno and other heirs to partition the land equally among them. In the evolution of inheritance laws, western states abandoned the idea of partible inheritance, which New England colonies had adopted. Partible inheritance distributed two shares of an estate to the oldest son, while the remaining heirs received equal shares.[30] Illinois statutes required that all property, both real and personal, descend to the heirs in equal parts regardless of birth order or gender.[31] The widow was not involved in the lawsuit because she had already received one-third of the property as her dower before the final settlement of the estate. The court granted the partition and appointed three commissioners to divide the land equally. The commissioners reported that they were unable to divide the land into twelve equal parts with equal value. The court appointed another commissioner to sell the land, according to the statute, and divide the proceeds equally among the heirs. The commissioner sold the land for $1,070. After subtracting expenses, court costs, and taxes, and adding the $61.94 from the personal property, the commissioner divided $778.19 among the twelve heirs.[32]

Intestate deaths and indebted estates like that of James Bell were common in antebellum Illinois and were typical of the settlement process. Widows possessed important rights and access to the legal system. Jane Bell had the first right to administer her husband's estate but chose not to do so. The statutes and the court allowed Jane Bell to maintain possession of their house and lots in Springfield even though her husband was insolvent at the time of his death. Finally, courts had the power to appoint temporary guardians so that children's rights and interests would be protected during the process. The courts maintained strict control over intestate succession.

Some men wrote wills to eliminate the problems that may have arisen with intestate succession. Wills allowed people to direct their real and personal possessions to whomever they wished. Historically, in England men were able to will personal property but did not gain the power to will real property until the passage of the Statute of Wills in 1540.[33] Generally, the English laws of inheritance migrated to the colonies. Individual colonies modified laws to suit their own needs, but the process remained substantially the same.[34] This general body of inheritance law went west with settlers as they traveled to Illinois.[35] Landowners had absolute control over the disposition of their lands as long as they left a will. Courts were reluctant to accept challenges to wills and even accepted oral wills in order to avoid the mechanical statutory distribution of property through intestacy laws.[36]

Wills reveal much about familial relationships.[37] In his will John Lucas gave his wife, Sarah Lucas, the option to take 253 acres of land in Logan County or to live with and be supported by their son. Sarah Lucas chose the land.[38] David Batterton wanted his wife to remain a widow and not to remarry after his death. In his will Batterton left all his personal property and real property, 160 acres of land, to his wife, Nancy Batterton. If she remarried, then David Batterton wanted all his property to be divided equally among his children.[39]

Men generally wanted their possessions to be divided equally among their heirs. Richard Bennett died in Halifax County, Virginia, in 1834. In his will he directed that all his real and personal property go to his wife, Ann Bennett. After her death he wanted all his property sold, with the proceeds to be divided equally among his children. Ann Bennett moved her family to Menard County and purchased 105 acres of land. When she died in 1842, John Bennett, the executor of Richard Bennett's estate, retained Abraham Lincoln and sued the remaining heirs to sell the property for equal distribution among the heirs.[40]

However, some men favored certain children over others. Wills and the distribution of property upon death reflected this favoritism. In his will James Adams left $3,000 each for his two daughters and $5,000 for his son. However, he protected his daughters by not allowing their future husbands to have any interest in their money and land.[41] Some men believed that their daughters would be provided for by their husbands. In the antebellum South many daughters discovered that unequal distribution in wills was common.[42] In the case of William McDaniel's daughters this tradition also extended into the North.[43]

William McDaniel was born in Kentucky in 1786. He married Margaret McDonald, and they had twelve children. In 1833 the family moved to Mechanicsburg in Sangamon County, where William McDaniel continued to farm. After twenty years in Illinois he had acquired 442 acres of land. The extended family, the McDaniels and their children and spouses, all lived in the same rural neighborhood. Also, several of McDaniel's brothers moved their families to the area, thus preserving the entire family unit.[44]

While on his deathbed in January 1853, William McDaniel wanted to dictate his will.[45] Joseph McDaniel and James McDaniel, William McDaniel's two sons, asked the attending physician, Alphonso Randall, to write their father's last will and testament. McDaniel left all his real and personal property to his wife, Margaret McDaniel.[46] After the death of Margaret, William McDaniel's land was to go to his sons and grandsons. William Sutcliff, a grandson and child of a deceased daughter, would receive eighty acres of land until his two sisters, Mary and Emeline, reached the age of twenty-one. At that time Sutcliff was to divide the eighty acres equally with his sisters. However, if Sutcliff agreed to take care of his grandmother, he could keep all eighty acres. Sutcliff was also to receive one-fourth of a large tract of timberland. William McDaniel's son James would receive eighty acres of land and another one-fourth share of the timberland. Joseph McDaniel would receive eighty-two acres and a one-fourth share of the timberland. Rufus and Robert McDaniel, two grandsons and children of a deceased son, would receive forty acres and the last quarter share of the timberland. Finally, William McDaniel's daughters and grandchildren—daughter Luanna Sparks; daughter Mary Ann Herrin; the female children of deceased daughter Elizabeth Langley; and the children of Sally (Sarah) Correll and of Martha McIntyre, the daughters he disinherited—would receive all the personal property that might be left after Margaret McDaniel's death.[47] William McDaniel apparently purposefully disinherited Correll and McIntyre because he did not like them.[48]

William McDaniel articulated a sharp division between his sons and his daughters. He wanted to perpetuate the family real estate through his male heirs and gave only personal property to his daughters. His level of inequity went deeper than a simple desire to keep the land in his family name; he wished to exclude his daughters Sally Correll and Martha McIntyre completely. McDaniel wrote his will to provide for his wife first, his sons second, and his daughters third. Both James and Joseph McDaniel were to pay rent to their

The Sangamon County homestead of Thomas and Sarah Correll, plaintiffs and appellees in *McDaniel et al. v. Correll et al.*, the legal contest about

mother on part of the land until she died, and grandson Sutcliff had to provide for his grandmother or divide his eighty-acre bequest with his sisters. Sally Correll, Mary Ann Herrin, and Martha McIntyre had a different view of why their father had divided his estate so inequitably. The daughters claimed that Joseph and James McDaniel actually dictated their father's last will.

William McDaniel died on January 10, 1853. Margaret McDaniel could accept or refuse the bequest "according to her judgment of her best interest."[49] Generally, a widow would relinquish a bequest because the dower was larger.[50] For example, John Bevans died in 1838 and left only bed and bedding to his wife in his will. In order to receive a larger amount of property Margaret Bevans relinquished her right to her bequest and sued for dower to receive one-third of the two hundred acres of land that John Bevans owned.[51] Margaret McDaniel, however, received a large and valuable bequest from her husband but relinquished her interest and accepted a smaller portion in the form of dower so that her children could immediately have possession of the land. In lieu of her bequest the court assigned 143 acres of land to her as her dower in December 1853, and court-appointed commissioners assigned her the property in December 1854.[52]

In March 1855 Thomas and Sarah Correll, James and Mary Ann Herrin, and Aaron and Martha McIntyre sued James McDaniel, Joseph McDaniel, and William McDaniel's remaining heirs to set aside the will. To sue their brothers the three daughters had to obtain their husbands' consent. Like all other states, the common law system in Illinois denied married women the right to sue, sell, or contract without their husband's consent.[53] A husband had to approve of the lawsuit. If their wives won their case to set aside the will, Thomas Correll, James Herrin, and Aaron McIntyre would have a financial interest in their father-in-law's real property, valued at $15,000 to $20,000. Not surprisingly, they supported the lawsuit.

The daughters claimed that William McDaniel dictated his will while he was extremely ill. Their brothers, Joseph and James McDaniel, gave their father wine to stimulate him, but according to the daughters, the sons took advantage of his inebriated and sick state and misled him into giving all his land to the sons only. The daughters believed that William McDaniel wanted all his children to share his property equally. The Corrells and others charged that William McDaniel was incompetent at the time he made his will. James McDaniel and the other defendants retained Abraham Lincoln to argue that William McDaniel's will was valid.[54]

In a case concerning the validity of a will, the statute provided that a jury should hear the evidence and determine whether the testator was competent at the time he made his will.[55] At the June 1855 term of the Sangamon Coun-

ty Circuit Court, Stephen T. Logan, who had been Lincoln's second law partner a decade earlier, argued the case for the Corrells. Logan defined what
constituted a sound memory, noted that witnesses heard William McDaniel
make bizarre statements, and argued that McDaniel was not competent when
he dictated his will. Logan discussed at length the real inequality of the distribution of the property. He appealed to the jury on the moral ground that
all the children should inherit equally. Finally, he warned the jury to "watch
[Lincoln] *very carefully.*"[56] Logan probably made this statement because he
knew how well Lincoln performed in front of juries.[57]

Lincoln then made his argument before the jury. Lincoln gave fourteen
reasons why McDaniel had a sound mind. For example, Lincoln stated that
William McDaniel wanted James McDaniel to pay rent to Margaret McDaniel
and, second, that William McDaniel remembered that he did not like Sally
Correll and Martha McIntyre. If James McDaniel had dictated the will as the
daughters claimed, then why would James McDaniel make himself pay rent?
Lincoln argued that the will was "unquestionably as it would have been, if it
had been made before his sickness." Lincoln called at least fourteen witnesses
to prove that William McDaniel had been competent during his last sickness.
Randall, the attending physician who wrote the will, testified that McDaniel
understood everything in it.[58] After the jurors heard arguments from both
sides, they were unable to agree on a verdict, and the court continued the case.

At the following term in November 1855 the attorneys made the same
arguments before a different jury. However, Dr. Randall testified that William McDaniel was not competent because of his diseased condition. The jury
found that the will was not valid because McDaniel was non compos men-
tis, or not of sound mind.[59] Lincoln quickly filed for a new trial on the ground
that Dr. Randall had testified differently at the June trial than at the November trial. Lincoln procured the testimony of jurors from the earlier trial to
prove Randall's inconsistent testimony. The earlier jurors believed that Randall did not give the opinion that the "old man's mind was impaired."[60] After a year the court finally ruled on Lincoln's motion and refused to grant a
new trial. In April 1857 Lincoln appealed the case to the Illinois Supreme
Court because of three errors that occurred during the case. First, the court
did not notify some of the adult defendants of the trial; second, two of the
named defendants were actually plaintiffs; and third, the court did not summon five of the minor defendants.[61]

The Illinois Supreme Court met in Springfield for its January 1858 term.
Lincoln argued the case for James McDaniel, Joseph McDaniel, and William
Sutcliff. Lincoln wanted the Illinois Supreme Court both to rule on the va-
lidity of the will and to reverse the lower court's decision because the Cor-

rells' attorneys had failed to proceed according to the statutes. Chief Justice John D. Caton overturned the judgment because of irregularities, as Lincoln had urged. Defendants had to be summoned, Caton ruled, or the proceedings against them were void. Equally important, Caton continued, the interests of the minors had to be protected by the guardian *ad litem*. The laws of the state provided this protection, and it "was indispensable." Caton considered ruling on the validity of the will and the equitable distribution of the real property but felt that because the court had reversed the decree on other technical matters, the jury at the remanded trial would be better able to reach a verdict.[62]

In the April 1858 term of the Sangamon County Circuit Court, the *McDaniel* case returned from the supreme court. The Corrells' attorneys corrected the irregularities from the earlier trial by summoning the defendants who had not been served. Randall, the attending physician who wrote the will, again testified that William McDaniel was not competent at the time he wrote his will. Other witnesses claimed that McDaniel was in a stupor most of the time and could not write a will.[63] The court continued the case for several years. During these continuances Lincoln was elected president of the United States and turned his practice over to his partner, William H. Herndon. Herndon had a particular expertise with family-related litigation and argued this case before a jury in April 1863. The jury found that William McDaniel was of sound mind and that a will did not have to be equitable to be valid.

The *McDaniel* case illustrates several important points in inheritance law in antebellum Illinois. Courts strongly protected the interests of minors through the guardian *ad litem*. A case would not be considered binding until the minors had a voice. As married women, the daughters had access to the law only through their husbands. Some women might have accepted the inequalities in the will, but Sally Correll, Martha McIntyre, and Mary Ann Herrin did not and, although they ultimately lost, they made a vigorous eight-year attempt to assert their interests.[64]

Wills were often inequitable, and courts rarely overturned them. In another inequitable will case Parmilla Marquis left all her real and personal property to her brother, Abraham Marquis. Their nephew, John Barnes, claimed that Abraham Marquis had coaxed his sister into giving him everything; Barnes sued to set aside the will. The jury found that the will was valid.[65] Women also had favorites when writing their wills.

Unequal treatment, however, was probably less common than equal treatment in Illinois. Generally, most testators, men and women, tried to divide their estates as evenly as possible. In the majority of the wills in cases in which Lincoln was involved, the testator left his wife all his real and personal property, which would be sold or distributed equally to his heirs after his widow's death. William McDaniel was an exception to the rule in the distribution of his estate. Apparently, a dispute between McDaniel and his daughters Correll and McIntyre must have angered him enough for him to disinherit them. McDaniel had to write a will to exclude his daughters because the equitable inheritance laws of Illinois provided for equal distribution among the heirs if McDaniel had died intestate.

Courts and juries did not always uphold the validity of wills. The court set aside Oliver Hillman's will because of its impossible conditions. Oliver Hillman was born in Philadelphia in 1785, married Rachel Smith in 1807, and had six children in Philadelphia and New Jersey. In 1839 the Hillman family emigrated to Springfield, Illinois. Rachel Hillman died in Springfield in 1842, and Oliver Hillman later married Mary Ann Short.[66] During his time in Illinois, Hillman acquired 597 acres of land in Sangamon County, and eighty acres of land in Morgan County. Because he owned a significant amount of property, Hillman wished to distribute his land after his death with a will. Hillman, like William McDaniel, dictated his will shortly before his death.

Oliver Hillman authored his will on February 21, 1856. He left $500 and some personal effects to his wife, Mary Ann Hillman. In the will he left all his land to his executors, his son John Hillman and his friend Jonathan Saunders, to hold in trust for his children and grandchildren. John Hillman and Saunders could sell the land within five years after Oliver Hillman's death, provided that it could be sold for at least $12,000. The proceeds from the sale would be divided into five parts: one share to his son John and his family; one share to his son Richard and his family; one share to his son Allen and his family; one share to be divided between two grandchildren, the children of a deceased daughter; and one share to his grandson William Unsworth, the son of another deceased daughter.

Oliver Hillman died on February 28, 1856. Two years later Hillman's property had fallen into disrepair. No one had maintained the land or fixed broken fences. Unknown people stole timber, and others squatted on the land. As a result of the misuse of the land and national economic problems in 1857, the value of the land plummeted. John Hillman and Saunders knew that they would never receive $12,000 for the land if they tried to sell it. The sons wanted the land rather than cash from a sale. In fact, the executors both refused to act in their capacity because of the impossibility of implementing the will. Saunders claimed that he could not execute the will in his lifetime or in the lifetime of Oliver Hillman's children.[67]

As a result, in September 1858 John Hillman, Richard Hillman, and William Unsworth sued Oliver Hillman's widow, Mary Ann Hillman, and the remaining heirs to set aside the will, to set off dower for Mary Ann Hillman, and to partition the land among the heirs. The three plaintiffs claimed that "the will is and must ever remain a useless thing for the reasons that the intention of the testator has been wholly defeated . . . because no safe and responsible person can be found who will under any circumstances undertake to carry out the provisions of the will."[68] The case continued for several terms in the Sangamon County Circuit Court. On August 27, 1859, the court appointed Herndon as guardian *ad litem* for the minor defendants. Herndon answered that he did not know whether the allegations in the bill of complaint were true, but he asked the court to demand full proof. Herndon's response protected the interests of the minor heirs. Herndon was unsure that the invalidation of the will would be beneficial and wanted John Hillman and others to prove to the court that it would be beneficial for the minor heirs.

Stephen T. Logan, Lincoln's law partner from 1841 to 1844, testified that he went to Oliver Hillman's house several miles outside of Springfield to write Hillman's will for him. When Hillman told Logan the provisions of his will, Logan debated whether to write it for him. Hillman urged Logan to write it, and Logan did. Logan stated that the children's and grandchildren's interest in the land would be ruined if the will was executed accordingly.

When the court called the case to be tried on February 24, 1860, the adult defendants defaulted. Mary Ann Hillman had married Joseph Hesser and moved to Jefferson County, Missouri. The court ruled for John Hillman, Richard Hillman, and William Unsworth and ordered the last will and testament of Oliver Hillman to be set aside. The court also appointed three commissioners to allot dower to Mary Ann Hesser and to divide the land in five equal shares to be distributed among the heirs. John Hillman, Richard Hillman, and William Unsworth each received one share. Allen and Martha Hillman, the children of Allen Hillman, deceased, received one-half of one share each. Finally, the unknown heirs of Margaret Hardin, a deceased daughter, received one share. Three months later the commissioners reported that they had set off 161 acres for Mary Ann Hesser and divided the land equitably among the heirs. Each share equaled about 120 acres.

On July 30, 1862, Charles Arnold, the administrator of Oliver Hillman's estate, made the final settlement. After receiving $1,560.08 owed to the estate, and paying out claims totaling $1,420, Arnold calculated that $140.08 remained for distribution among the heirs. Mary Ann Hesser received one-third of the amount, $46.69. Arnold divided the remaining amount of money into five equal parts. John Hillman, Richard Hillman, William Unsworth, and the legal heirs of Margaret Hardin each received $18.67, as did Allen Hillman's children.[69]

Courts were willing to invalidate a will if its objective was impossible to attain. Hillman had set a completely unreasonable price on his land. As a result, after his death the children were unable to receive clear title to the land. Rather than wait for the land to appreciate, the children successfully invalidated Oliver Hillman's will, partitioned the land equally as if Hillman had died intestate, and acquired the proper ownership of the land. In his will, however, Hillman treated all his heirs equally. Hillman probably wanted to provide for all his children and established the high price so that it would support his family after his death. Hillman differed substantially from McDaniel in his views on providing equally for his family. The irony, of course, is that the court found McDaniel's will valid and Hillman's will invalid.

Inequality between sons and daughters took other forms besides making a will. Rather than write a will, Justus Hinkle wanted to distribute his possessions during his lifetime. Advancements allowed people to save the expense of writing a will, to know that the recipients appreciated the gifts, and to eliminate some of the potential problems of inequitable distributions. However, problems did arise. In a different example of unequal treatment of sons and daughters, Hinkle gave money to his five sons and one of his daughters but not to his other three daughters.

Justus Hinkle was born in 1775 in Virginia. He married Elizabeth Judy in Randolph County, Virginia, and had eleven children. In 1817 the Hinkle family moved to Belleville, Illinois, then to Sangamon County one year later. Elizabeth Hinkle died in Sangamon County in 1836.[70] After his wife's death Justus Hinkle gave his surviving children their inheritance. Martin Hinkle, Elijah Hinkle, Levi Hinkle, Jesse Hinkle, and Jacob Hinkle each received $100, a horse, a bridle, and a saddle. Hannah Hinkle, Justus Hinkle's daughter, received $100, a bridle, a saddle, and a bed and bedding. Justus Hinkle's three other daughters—Sally Mycenhammer, Catherine Hinkle, and Abigail Hinkle—each received a bed and bedding but no money.[71]

Justus Hinkle died on November 27, 1842. Sally Mycenhammer believed that her father should have divided the money equally among his sons and daughters. She sued her brother Jesse Hinkle in an action of hotchpot in the Sangamon County Probate Justice of the Peace Court. Hotchpot was a legal action to bring together and redistribute property equally after a person's death when some of the property had been distributed by advance before the person's death.[72] Jesse Hinkle retained Lincoln and Herndon to defend him against his sister's suit. Thomas Moffett, the probate justice of the peace, heard the case on June 27, 1845. Sally Mycenhammer appeared before the probate justice of the peace, as did Levi Hinkle, Jacob Hinkle, and Aaron Vandeveer, who was the administrator of Justus Hinkle's estate. Moffett heard the testimony of Levi and Jacob Hinkle, who agreed that their sisters were entitled to their fair share from the money remaining in the estate. Jesse Hinkle decided not to contest the case and defaulted. Moffett ruled for Sally Mycenhammer and ordered that when Vandeveer settled the estate and distributed the money, Jesse Hinkle would not receive any disbursement.[73]

Vandeveer calculated the debts and assets of the estate and found that the estate had $105.74 for distribution. He divided the money three ways for the three neglected daughters. On September 17, 1845, Mycenhammer received $35.25. Catherine Hinkle had become insane, and a court appointed Jacob Hinkle as her conservator. Jacob Hinkle received $35.25 for his sister Catherine. The third sister, Abigail Hinkle, had died during the administration of her father's estate. Abigail's legal heirs were her brothers and sisters. Since Abigail's share of the money was an inheritance from her father, the siblings who had received $100 were not entitled to receive a disbursement of the money because of the hotchpot judgment. Nearly half the money went to funeral expenses, but Mycenhammer and Catherine Hinkle each received $6.67 and agreed to allow Jesse Hinkle $1.66.[74]

Justus Hinkle had failed to advance the same inheritance to all his children but was not as gender exclusive as McDaniel. Hinkle may have had favorites among his children, but a lack of time probably led to the inequitable advancement of money. Hinkle could have been saving his money and when he had set aside $100, he would give that amount to one of his children. He died before earning the remaining $300 for his three remaining children. However, if that was what he was doing, Hinkle ensured that his sons would receive the money before his daughters. Hinkle did not maintain the same attitude toward his daughters as McDaniel, who wanted to keep the family name attached to his real property. Hinkle owned land, but it had been sold to pay the debts of his estate.[75] Hotchpot was an uncommon proceeding. If men were advancing property before their deaths, they generally did so equitably. If not, there would have been more hotchpot cases in the courts. Of the nine hundred inheritance-related lawsuits in which Lincoln was involved, Mycenhammer's case was the only hotchpot suit.

Mycenhammer's siblings realized the inequity of their father's failing to give any amount of money to his three daughters. Jesse Hinkle refused to contest the case brought by his sister and still had to pay Lincoln and Herndon $5 for their legal services. Although Mycenhammer won her lawsuit for equitable distribution, she did not receive an equal amount. Her share totaled $41.92 from her father's estate, not even half of what her brothers had received. The law provided relief for the inequity, but Mycenhammer could not gain total equity because of the lack of money in her father's estate.

Although she was a married woman, Mycenhammer had access to the law. Rather than sue in her own name or in the name of her husband, she informed the attorney general and took the case to the courts by an *ex relatione* proceeding.[76] The attorney general brought the case but at the instigation of Mycenhammer, who had a personal interest in the matter. Mycenhammer had used another avenue available to women. Resourceful women found ways to gain what rightfully belonged to them.

In another example of a resourceful woman's suing to recover her rightful property, Catherine Glynn claimed some property that she believed was hers and had the law of inheritance on her side. The Glynn family of Sangamon County experienced several inheritance-related problems after Michael Glynn, the head of the household, died in 1848. Michael Glynn owned two lots in Springfield and six acres of land outside the city. Like McDaniel and Hillman, he wrote his will shortly before his death. He left a widow, Margaret Glynn, and two children, William Glynn and Margaret Glynn Jr. (Daughters with the same name as their mother often used "junior.") Shortly afterward, the widow Margaret Glynn married Matthew Murray. The family members soon learned more about Michael Glynn's earlier life than they wanted to know.

In March 1850 Catherine Glynn of Boston, Massachusetts, filed a petition for dower in the Sangamon County Circuit Court. Catherine Glynn sued Margaret Murray and the two children and claimed to be the true and legal wife of Michael Glynn. As his wife, Catherine Glynn did not consent to any transfer of land and had the right to sue for her dower.[77] She claimed that she and Michael had married in Massachusetts in 1825 and had lived as husband and wife for five years before Michael deserted her. Michael Glynn eventually settled in Sangamon County, married another woman—Margaret— and had children with her.[78] Catherine Glynn requested that the court appoint commissioners to assign her dower from the two lots, the six acres, and Michael Glynn's personal property.[79]

Lincoln's partner, Herndon, represented Margaret Glynn Murray, who denied Catherine Glynn's right to dower in the personal property because it had come from her second husband, Matthew Murray, who had since died. Herndon answered for the children, William Glynn and Margaret Glynn Jr. and denied that Catherine Glynn had married their father. Herndon claimed that William Glynn owned the real property because his grandmother had deeded it to him. Margaret Glynn Jr. reported that her parents were married in Ireland in 1828. She denied Catherine Glynn's right to dower from the personal property because it came from Margaret Glynn Murray, not Michael Glynn.[80]

Catherine Glynn had strong evidence of her marriage to Michael Glynn. Several depositions arrived in Springfield from Boston. Patrick Dennis, who had married Catherine Glynn's sister, testified that he had attended the wedding between Michael Glynn and Catherine McGarr. The Reverend William Taylor had married them at the Catholic church in Boston. Catherine Glynn submitted a marriage certificate supporting Dennis's statement. Margaret Glynn, Michael Glynn's mother, who still lived in Boston, testified that she was not present at the wedding between Michael Glynn and Catherine McGarr, but she reported that the couple had lived together as man and wife before Michael went west. She also testified that she had lived in Springfield with her son for nearly three years and that his wife in Springfield was not the same as his wife in Boston.[81]

The court continued the case for two years. During the interim Margaret Murray had remarried again, this time to James Hailey, but she died a short time later. After Margaret Glynn Jr. married Edward Todd, Catherine Glynn dismissed the case against Margaret Glynn (Jr.) Todd and instituted a new dower case against Edward and Margaret Todd.[82] In the March 1852 term the court heard the evidence of both parties and ruled that Catherine Glynn had indeed married Michael Glynn and had never relinquished her right to dower on the property. According to Marylynn Salmon, courts consistently found for women who had not consented to land transfers during their marriage.[83] The court appointed three commissioners to assess the value of the property and to assign dower for Catherine Glynn. Shortly afterward, the commissioners reported that they could not divide the property because the layout of the lots made it impossible to divide the land equitably.

Before the court ordered the master in chancery to sell the land, the parties reached an agreement. Strangely, the opposing sides divided the house itself. Catherine Glynn received her dower as the two east rooms in Michael Glynn's former house, now owned by William Glynn, and she had free use of the hallways. Catherine also received dower rights to part of the garden around the house. In return, Catherine gave up her rights to the west side of the house.[84]

Herndon took an interest in the well-being of the family, particularly the eight-year-old son, William Glynn. Herndon spoke for the child in the dower suit and in another legal battle against Michael Glynn's creditors, who wanted to take all of William Glynn's land from him. While Catherine Glynn's dower suit was still pending, Thomas Henderson sued William Glynn and other members of the family to set aside the fraudulent land transactions. Henderson had previously recovered a judgment against Michael Glynn for $483.72 and claimed that Michael Glynn had fraudulently sold the two lots to an Edmund Taylor to escape Henderson and other creditors. William Glynn later ended up with possession of the two lots, of which he gave a part to Catherine Glynn for her dower. William Glynn claimed title to the land in two ways. First, he claimed the lots by virtue of a deed from his grandmother to him. Second, he claimed that Michael Glynn had bequeathed the lots to him in his will.[85]

According to Herndon, William Glynn was embarrassed about the whole situation. His father had died, and he had discovered that his father had been married before. His mother died, and he had to live with his father's first wife. Herndon's answer to Henderson's bill of complaint showed his anger during the lawsuits. Herndon, in speaking for William Glynn, claimed that "Michael had an other wife living at the time of the marriage of [my mother] to Michael and that said Michael's lawful wife is now in the city of Springfield Ills., which facts make [me] the illegitimate child of said Michael and the said Michael being bound in law and justice and in the sight of heaven to provide for the innocent offspring of his infamy." Herndon was angry that Henderson now attempted to take William Glynn's land. Henderson and the other creditors think "that in addition to my disgrace and mortification they can religiously add the crime of poverty to my many unenviable titles and thus throw me a tender infant upon the cold charities of the chilling current of human exertion, whilst [Henderson] can smack his lips in praise of his maker." Realizing that this lawsuit probably favored Henderson as a creditor, Herndon exclaimed, "so be it if the law gives [the land] to him."[86] Herndon mainly wrote formulaic legal documents, but his arguments in this case show an impassioned plea for justice based upon the youth of the defendant.[87] Herndon also argued that if Henderson gained possession of the land, then society would have to provide for the education and support of William Glynn. Michael Glynn had made these arrangements so that his son would have a home, but the court would take that away. The court continued the case for four years. Finally, Henderson and Glynn reached an agreement, and the court dismissed the case, with each party paying half of the court costs. The contents of the agreement are unknown, but William Glynn did maintain possession of the lots.

The settlement benefited William Glynn and his family. Had the case reached trial, the court probably would have ruled for Henderson. The legal system frowned upon fraudulent land transactions to escape creditors, and courts generally voided them. Herndon realized this fact and attempted an emotional appeal to the court based on the best interests of the child. Herndon also argued that society would not have to care for the child because he possessed real and personal property for his support. However, the plea probably would have failed despite Herndon's rhetoric. Although courts and judges occasionally set aside the rigidity of the law for the best interests of victims, particularly children, they consistently ruled for creditors. Each of these families had different problems, which the antebellum Illinois legal system attempted to solve. In the *Bell* case the courts followed a structure of succession put in place by the legislature. As a result of legally protected interests, the widow was able to maintain possession of the homestead. In the *McDaniel* case the courts refused to alter a will to settle an inequitable distribution by the head of the household. Some daughters found that fathers treated them differently than sons; however, inequitable wills were not illegal. In the *Hillman* case the court set aside a will because it was impossible to execute. Courts would invalidate a will if it were bad, so long as all the heirs benefited equally. In the *Hinkle* case the court had a remedy for the inequitable advancements made before death, but the estate did not have enough money to redress the inequity completely. Finally, the *Glynn* case pitted a deserted widow against "newly illegitimate" children. The courts again demonstrated that dower was an important right, particularly when a woman did not consent to a land transfer.

The antebellum Illinois statutes provided a structure for inheritance from a person who did or did not leave a will. In intestate succession men benefited no more than women because laws dictated that all heirs inherited equally. This was a major change from English and some colonial inheritance laws. English law put many encumbrances on land, and some colonial laws allowed the eldest male heir to inherit two shares of an estate, while the remaining heirs inherited one share each.[88] Western states generally adopted a more equitable distribution of estate assets, and Illinois joined the newer states by not placing encumbrances on real property, except for dower. Dower protected women and at least provided a means for a widow to support herself after the death of her husband. In the case of wills descendants were at the mercy of the testator, who sometimes gave more property to favorite children. However, in most cases a testator wanted to provide for his widow first, then to distribute his property equally to his children after the death of his widow. Both men and women were capable of writing inequitable wills, and courts rarely overturned them. Although disinheritance was a disheartening experience, disinherited offspring had to accept fewer or no shares of an estate. The law provided a remedy to set aside wills, but unless the evidence was compelling that a testator was indeed incapable of writing a will, courts generally affirmed their validity.

Inheritance was a legal process, whether there were any disputes or not. The problems that arose in the court system in antebellum Illinois illustrate the average citizen's experience to inherit the earth. All interested parties—men, women, and children—had an opportunity to voice their interests. As a result, inheritance was a long process. The courts allowed the interests of women and children to be heard and gave them access to the legal system during the antebellum period in Illinois. The statutes provided remedies for a woman to receive dower, to administer her husband's estate, to relinquish her right to a bequest, and to sue to receive equitable inheritance. Children's interests in court were generally well protected by a temporary guardian. Courts rarely infringed on a child's right to an inheritance. Jurists respected and guarded inheritance laws over others because of their duty to protect all heirs, including women and children.

Notes

1. Elijah M. Haines, *The Probate Manual Being a Complete Guide for Executors, Administrators and Guardians under the Laws of Illinois, with Practical Forms* (Chicago: Keen and Lee, 1856), xiv; Stanley N. Katz, "Republicanism and the Law of Inheritance in the American Revolutionary Era," *Michigan Law Review* 76 (November 1977): 9.

2. Katz, "Republicanism and the Law of Inheritance," 11. Andrew Jackson's legal career in the 1790s is illustrative of the emerging American legal system. See James W. Ely Jr. and Theodore Brown Jr., *Legal Papers of Andrew Jackson* (Knoxville: University of Tennessee Press, 1987), xxvii–xxx; Carole Shammas, "English Inheritance Law and Its Transfer to the Colonies," *American Journal of Legal History* 31 (April 1987): 153–54.

3. Maurice G. Baxter, *Henry Clay the Lawyer* (Lexington: University Press of Kentucky, 2000), vii, 14, 80.

4. *Hall v. Irwin et al.,* 7 Ill. 176 (1845).

5. Ibid.

6. Susan E. Gray, *The Yankee West: Community Life on the Michigan Frontier* (Chapel Hill: University of North Carolina Press, 1996), 100.

7. Theda Skocpol, *Protecting Soldiers and Mothers: The Political Origins of Social Policy in the United States* (Cambridge, Mass.: Belknap, 1992), 67–101; Helena Znaniecka Lopata and Henry P. Brehm, *Widows and Dependent Wives: From Social Problem to Federal Program* (New York: Praeger, 1986), 25–35; Mimi Abramovitz, *Regulating the Lives of Women: Social Welfare Policy from Colonial Times to the Present* (Boston: South End, 1988), 137–71.

8. Peter Karsten, *Heart versus Head: Judge-Made Law in Nineteenth-Century America* (Chapel Hill: University of North Carolina Press, 1997), 4. Jurists who practiced "jurisprudence of the heart" listened to reason and changed established legal doctrines for the benefit of poor and disadvantaged litigants.

9. John Mack Faragher, *Sugar Creek: Life on the Illinois Prairie* (New Haven, Conn.: Yale University Press, 1986), 107.

10. Bill for Accounting, August 1860; Decree, 30 August 1861, *Snow et ux. v. Price et ux.,* in *The Law Practice of Abraham Lincoln: Complete Documentary Edition*, ed. Martha L. Benner and Cullom Davis et al. (DVD; Urbana: University of Illinois Press, 2000), hereafter cited as *LPAL.*

11. "An Act to Regulate Administrations and the Descent of Intestate Estates, and for

Other Purposes," 23 March 1819, *Laws of the State of Illinois* (1819), 223–33; "An Act Establishing Courts of Probate," 10 February 1821, *Laws of the State of Illinois* (1821), 119–26; "An Act to Provide for the Election of Probate Justices of the Peace," 4 March 1837, *Laws of the State of Illinois* (1837), 176–78; "An Act Establishing County Courts, and Providing for the Election of Justices of the Peace and Constables, and for Other Purposes," 13 April 1849, *Laws of the State of Illinois* (1849), 62–67.

For further discussion of the mechanics of probate court evolution in the western states, see Lewis M. Simes and Paul E. Basye, "The Organization of the Probate Court in America: I," *Michigan Law Review* 42 (June 1944): 965–1008; William Wirt Blume, "Probate and Administration on the American Frontier," *Michigan Law Review* 58 (November 1959): 209–46; Earl Finbar Murphy, "Laws of Inheritance in Indiana before 1816," *New York Law Forum* 2 (July 1956): 249–82; Rush H. Limbaugh, "The Sources and Development of Probate Law," *Washington University Law Quarterly* (December 1956): 419–47; and Cecil Bronston, "Jurisdiction of the Probate Courts of Illinois," *Chicago-Kent Law Review* 18 (1939–40): 257–65.

12. "James Bell," Biography, *LPAL*.

13. Affidavit of Decease, 2 September 1844, *Herndon served as administrator of Bell's estate, LPAL*.

14. Joan R. Gunderson and Gwen Victor Gampel, "Married Women's Legal Status in Eighteenth-Century New York and Virginia," *William and Mary Quarterly* 39 (January 1982): 119.

15. Probate Record, 2 September 1844, *Herndon served as administrator of Bell's estate, LPAL;* "An Act to Regulate Administrations," 224.

16. "An Act to Regulate Administrations," 226.

17. Appraisal, 7 November 1844; Bill of Sale, 24 January 1845, *Herndon served as administrator of Bell's estate, LPAL;* "An Act to Regulate Administrations," 226–27. Personal property consisted of furniture, clothes, kitchen utensils, and the like.

18. "An Act Relative to Wills and Testaments, Executors and Administrators, and the Settlement of Estates," 23 January 1829, *Revised Code of Laws of the State of Illinois* (1829), 229; Haines, *Probate Manual*, 57.

19. George L. Haskins, "The Beginnings of Partible Inheritance in the American Colonies," *Yale Law Journal* 51 (June 1942): 1290.

20. Eileen Spring, *Law, Land, and Family: Aristocratic Inheritance in England, 1300 to 1800* (Chapel Hill: University of North Carolina Press, 1993), 40; Marylynn Salmon, *Women and the Law of Property in Early America* (Chapel Hill: University of North Carolina Press, 1986), 141, 143.

21. "An Act for the Speedy Assignment of Dower," 12 February 1819, *Laws of the State of Illinois* (1819), 12.

22. "An Act for the Speedy Assignment of Dower, and Partition of Real Estate," 6 February 1827, *Revised Code of Laws of Illinois* (1827), 184; "An Act to Prevent Fraudulent Devises, and for Other Purposes," *Revised Laws of Illinois* (1833), 315–16; John Bouvier, *A Law Dictionary Adapted to the Constitution and Laws of the United States of America,* 7th ed., 2 vols. (Philadelphia: Childs and Peterson, 1857), 1:572; *Black's Law Dictionary*, 6th ed. (St. Paul, Minn.: West, 1990), 706.

23. Petition for Dower, 11 February 1845; Guardian *ad litem*'s Answer, 24 March 1845; Decree, 29 March 1845; Commissioners' Report, 23 July 1845, *Bell v. Bell et al., LPAL;* Haskins, "Beginnings of Partible Inheritance," 1290–91.

24. For additional information on Margaret Porter, see Christopher A. Schnell's essay, chapter 5 in this volume.
25. "An Act to Regulate Administrations," 226–29.
26. The petition did not identify Elizabeth Bell. She apparently died between the filing of the dower suit and the filing of the suit to sell land. See Petition to Sell Real Estate, 18 November 1844, *Herndon v. Bell et al., LPAL.*
27. Guardian *ad litem*'s Answer, [18] November 1844; Decree, 18 November 1844, *Herndon v. Bell et al., LPAL;* Probate Record, 7 July 1847, *Herndon served as administrator of Bell's estate, LPAL.*
28. Haines, *Probate Manual,* 73.
29. Probate Record, 7 July 1847, *Herndon served as administrator of Bell's estate, LPAL; Gale's Statutes,* 714–16.
30. Charles M. Andrews, *The Connecticut Intestacy Law* (New Haven, Conn.: Yale University Press, 1933), 5; William E. Nelson, *Americanization of the American Common Law: The Impact of Legal Change on Massachusetts Society, 1760–1830* (Athens: University of Georgia Press, 1994), 48; Haskins, "Beginnings of Partible Inheritance," 1281.
31. Haines, *Probate Manual,* 46; Faragher, *Sugar Creek,* 109.
32. Petition for Partition, 27 July 1849; Decree, 7 November 1849; Commissioners' report, [8 November 1849]; Commissioner's Report, 11 November 1849, *Anno et al. v. Anno et al., LPAL;* "An Act for the Partition of Lands," 20 February 1819, *Laws of the State of Illinois* (1819), 386.
33. Carole Shammas, Marylynn Salmon, and Michael Dahlin, *Inheritance in America From Colonial Times to the Present* (New Brunswick, N.J.: Rutgers University Press, 1987), 26; Katz, "Republicanism and the Law of Inheritance," 9; Ronald Chester, *Inheritance, Wealth, and Society* (Bloomington: Indiana University Press, 1982), 12.
34. Marylynn Salmon, "The Legal Status of Women in Early America: A Reappraisal," *Law and History Review* 1 (Spring 1983): 136.
35. For more on the migration of legal patterns see John Phillip Reid, *Law for the Elephant: Property and Social Behavior on the Overland Trail* (San Marino, Calif.: Huntington Library, 1980).
36. Haskins, "Beginnings of Partible Inheritance," 1288.
37. Trevor Burnard, "Inheritance and Independence: Women's Status in Early Colonial Jamaica," *William and Mary Quarterly* 48 (January 1991): 93; James W. Deen Jr., "Patterns of Testation: Four Tidewater Counties in Colonial Virginia," *American Journal of Legal History* 16 (April 1972): 155; John J. Waters, "Family, Inheritance, and Migration in Colonial New England: The Evidence from Guilford, Connecticut," *William and Mary Quarterly* 39 (January 1982): 75; Spring, *Law, Land, and Family,* 146.
38. Bill for Dower, 17 February 1859, *Mann et ux. v. Lucas, LPAL.*
39. Opinion, December term 1855, *Batterton et al. v. Yoakum, LPAL; Batterton et al. v. Yoakum,* 17 Ill. 288 (1855).
40. Petition to Sell Real Estate, 16 May 1846, *Bennett v. Bennett et al., LPAL.*
41. Will, 5 May 1838, *McGraw v. Adams et al., LPAL.*
42. Joan E. Cashin, "According to His Wish and Desire: Female Kin and Female Slaves in Planter Wills," in *Women of the American South: A Multicultural Reader,* ed. Christie Anne Farnham (New York: New York University Press, 1997), 100–1.
43. John Mack Faragher also found inequitable distribution on the Illinois prairie (*Sugar Creek,* 108–9).

44. Deen, "Patterns of Testation," 172; John Carroll Power, *History of the Early Settlers, Sangamon County, Illinois* (1876; rpt., Springfield, Ill.: Phillips Brothers, 1970), 496–97.

45. A testator often made his will while on his deathbed. See Haskins, "Beginnings of Partible Inheritance," 1289.

46. In colonial Virginia men gave preference to male heirs over wives and daughters to perpetuate wealth within the family. In colonial Maryland men rarely left their wives more than dower. South Carolina was an exception because dissatisfaction with laws of intestacy may have caused men to be more generous to their wives. In colonial New York men tended to be generous. Marlene Stein Wortman claims that will-making practices evolved from the seventeenth to the nineteenth centuries. In earlier, less-populated periods men gave wives large bequests, but as population increased, men gave wives less and male children more. See Deen, "Patterns of Testation," 158–59; Lois Green Carr and Lorena S. Walsh, "The Planter's Wife: The Experience of White Women in Seventeenth-Century Maryland," *William and Mary Quarterly* 34 (October 1977): 555; Salmon, *Women and the Law of Property*, 158; Gunderson and Gampel, "Married Women's Legal Status," 127; Marlene Stein Wortman, ed., *Women in American Law*, 2 vols. (New York: Holmes and Meier, 1985), 1:18.

47. Will, 7 January 1853, *McDaniel et al. v. Correll et al., LPAL*.

48. Judge's Notes, [June 1855]; Brief, [June 1855], *McDaniel et al. v. Correll et al., LPAL*.

49. "An Act Relative to Wills and Testaments," 205; Salmon, *Women and the Law of Property*, 143.

50. Gunderson and Gampel, "Married Women's Legal Status," 121.

51. Widow's Relinquishment, 26 December 1838, *Bevans v. Brown et al., LPAL*.

52. Decree, 3 December 1853; Commissioners' Report, 1 December 1854, *McDaniel et al. v. McDaniel, LPAL*.

53. Joan Hoff, *Law, Gender, and Injustice: A Legal History of Women* (New York: New York University Press, 1991), 128; Dianne Avery and Alfred S. Konefsky, "The Daughters of Job: Property Rights and Women's Lives in Mid-Nineteenth-Century Massachusetts," *Law and History Review* 10 (Fall 1992): 326; Norma Basch, "The Emerging Legal History of Women in the United States: Property, Divorce, and the Constitution," *Signs: Journal of Women in Culture and Society* 12 (Autumn 1986): 99.

54. Bill to Set Aside Will, 8 March 1855, *McDaniel et al. v. Correll et al., LPAL*.

55. "An Act Relative to Wills and Testaments," 193.

56. Brief, [June 1855], *McDaniel et al. v. Correll et al., LPAL*.

57. Several of Lincoln's contemporaries claimed that Lincoln was at his best in a courtroom in front of a jury. See Isaac N. Arnold, *The Life of Abraham Lincoln* (Chicago: Jansen, McClurg, 1885), 84.

58. Brief, [June 1855], *McDaniel et al. v. Correll et al., LPAL*.

59. *(Springfield) Illinois State Journal*, 12 December 1855, p. 4, col. 1.

60. Affidavit, 7 December 1855, *McDaniel et al. v. Correll et al., LPAL*.

61. Motion for new trial, 12 December 1855; Decree, 22 December 1856; Bill of Exceptions, 25 April 1857; Assignment of Errors, 5 January 1858, *McDaniel et al. v. Correll et al., LPAL*.

62. *McDaniel et al. v. Correll et al.*, 19 Ill. 226 (1857).

63. Affidavit for Continuance, 12 November 1860; Deposition of Uriah Ham, 12 October 1861, *McDaniel et al. v. Correll et al., LPAL*.

64. Cashin, "According to His Wish and Desire," 110.

65. Bill to Set Aside Will, 20 August 1849, *Barnes v. Marquis, LPAL.*

66. Power, *History of the Early Settlers,* 379–80.

67. Will, 21 February 1856; Testimony, [24 February 1860], *Hillman et al. v. Hillman et al., LPAL.*

68. Bill of Complaint, 20 September 1858, *Hillman et al. v. Hillman et al., LPAL.*

69. Sangamon County Probate Record 5 (1861–63), 279–80, Illinois Regional Archives Depository, University of Illinois at Springfield.

70. Power, *History of the Early Settlers,* 368–69.

71. Citation for Hotchpot, 13 June 1845, *People ex rel. Mycenhammer v. Hinkle, LPAL.*

72. Bouvier, *Law Dictionary,* 590; *Black's Law Dictionary,* 738–39.

73. Citation for Hotchpot, 13 June 1845; Decree, 27 June 1845, *People ex rel. Mycenhammer v. Hinkle, LPAL.*

74. Decree, 9 February 1846, *People ex rel. Mycenhammer v. Hinkle, LPAL.*

75. Decree, 1 April 1844, *Vandeveer v. Hinkle et al., LPAL.*

76. *Black's Law Dictionary,* 582.

77. Salmon, *Women and the Law of Property,* 7; Gunderson and Gampel, "Married Women's Legal Status," 119–20.

78. Norma Basch and Richard H. Chused have both shown that eastern men found it easier to desert their wives and begin a new life in the western states with new families and new business pursuits rather than go through legal divorce proceedings. See Basch, *Framing American Divorce from the Revolutionary Generation to the Victorians* (Berkeley: University of California Press, 1999), 91, 107, 119, and Chused, *Private Acts in Public Places: A Social History of Divorce in the Formative Era of American Family Law* (Philadelphia: University of Pennsylvania Press, 1994), 87.

79. Petition for Dower, 25 December 1849, *Glynn v. Hailey et al., LPAL.*

80. Guardian *ad litem*'s Answer, 26 March 1850; Guardian *ad litem*'s Answer, 27 March 1850; Separate Answer, 27 March 1850, *Glynn v. Hailey et al., LPAL.*

81. Deposition, 13 May 1850, *Glynn v. Hailey et al., LPAL.*

82. Petition for Dower, 10 August 1851, *Glynn v. Todd et ux., LPAL.* This case continued without a judgment until the August 1858 term, when the court struck the case from the docket with leave to reinstate, but neither litigant reinstated the case.

83. Salmon, *Women and the Law of Property,* 7, 145.

84. Agreement, 2 April 1853, *Glynn v. Hailey et al., LPAL.*

85. Bill to Set Aside Deed, 26 June 1850, *Henderson v. Glynn et al., LPAL.*

86. Answer, 22 September 1852; Cross-bill, 22 September 1852, *Henderson v. Glynn et al., LPAL.*

87. Karsten, *Heart versus Head,* 303–4.

88. Andrews, *Connecticut Intestacy Law,* 5; Haskins, "Beginnings of Partible Inheritance," 1281.

5

Wives, Widows, and Will Makers:
Women and the Law of Property

CHRISTOPHER A. SCHNELL

The legal status of a woman in antebellum Illinois varied greatly during the course of her lifetime. As a girl, she shared equal status with her brothers, as minors had few rights generally. Typically, a young woman went from being a minor to being a *feme covert* in marriage, when her legal presence was subsumed by her husband's legal personality. At her marriage an Illinois woman, and to varying degrees women throughout the United States, forfeited her right to own, manage, or sell property. In many states, including Illinois, this restriction included property that women owned before marriage. A woman's status as a *feme covert* ended only with widowhood or divorce. With certain limitations a widow had many of the same property rights afforded men. The few women who never married or obtained a divorce retained the same legal status as men when it came to property ownership.

An examination of the property rights of married women and widows in antebellum Illinois (1820–60) reveals much about the legal status of women. Legally invisible during her marriage yet suddenly visible at the end of her marriage, the antebellum widow used her right to dower to maintain a degree of financial security. During marriage women used their right to dower to influence family (male) decisions about property, and during widowhood dower afforded them some financial protection from creditors and unscrupulous heirs. As widows, women were active managers of property they did not own but held for life. Dower was the minimum right of the widow to hold and manage one-third of her deceased husband's estate during her lifetime, and the statutory codes that enacted dower also defined the few property rights that a married woman possessed in antebellum Illinois. An examination of dower, its use and interpretation by women, illuminates the property rights of women in antebellum Illinois. Furthermore, a close examination of the estates of women—most of whom were widows—reveals the status that many women held as managers of property that they did not own.

During the 1820s Sangamon County, Illinois, witnessed no dower suits before the circuit court. Indeed, few actions in equity are recorded in county records during the 1820s, and the first dower suits were docketed in 1831, ten years after the county's first court term. As immigrants entered and settled county lands, county and circuit court dockets became filled with legal problems arising from dower claims and estate partitions. Fifteen dower cases occurred during the 1830s, and the number of cases increased to twenty-five and sixty-six during the 1840s and 1850s, respectively. Taking into account population growth during the period, according to the 1840, 1850, and 1860 U.S. censuses, one dower case came to court for every 981 Sangamon County residents during the 1830s; one case for every 769 residents during the 1840s; and one case for every 489 residents during the 1850s. The substantial rise in the number of cases and the per capita use of dower illustrate the continued presence of the ancient remedy in everyday legal use throughout Illinois's frontier period and early settlement.

Women continued to use dower in Illinois as a way of obtaining some semblance of equity in marriage. Often women were not alone in trying to remedy the strictures of marriage at common law. In at least nine of the 107 dower cases in Sangamon County during the period, husbands sued on behalf of their wives who were widows from an earlier marriage. Widows initiated the vast majority of dower suits; heirs interested in having their father's estate partitioned brought the remainder. Dower remained the dominant method for women to obtain financial security during widowhood, while trusts were an option for wealthier women.

At the end of this period and by the onset of the Civil War, Illinois women shared many of the same property rights that their counterparts already had in other parts of the country.[1] With the codification of separate property rights for married women in February 1861, Illinois took the first small step toward equity in property rights and overall equality of status for women before the law. After 1861 Illinois women shared with their husbands the ability to own outright any property they brought into their marriages or acquired during coverture. Increasingly, women were entering the market as property owners or managers. As reforms gave women new rights during marriage, the need for remedies in chancery court (such as dower) faded away. Dower petitions began to disappear from Illinois courts as more and more women held the rights to their own property, whether the land was acquired, inherited, or received in trust. An examination of the legal status of women during the period before reforms illustrates, however, that women were already participating in the market economy, especially during widowhood, through the use of dower.

LUCY DAVENPORT

In March 1857 Peter Doty, the clerk of the Woodford County Circuit Court in Illinois, received a frantic letter from the widow Lucy Davenport, the plaintiff in a chancery suit docketed for the next term of court. Davenport's letter was an informal motion to dismiss her petition for dower, which she had brought two years earlier against the heirs of the estate of her deceased husband, John Davenport. The short letter poignantly emphasized Davenport's desire to end the suit: "I do not want it to go on at all. I want it to stop and not to go on. This must stop, I want it to stop."[2]

The frustration apparent in this letter was the result of the long court battle over John Davenport's estate. Aside from the strain and cost of the suit, Davenport had to sense, at that point in the case, that she was going to lose her right to any claim to the farm that she and her husband had worked during their marriage. She was having a hard time producing evidence of her husband's ownership of the real estate they farmed and thus of her dower right to it. Lucy Davenport, a young woman, faced the remainder of her life with no means of financial independence and certain dependence upon her in-laws for support.[3]

Unfortunately for women like Lucy Davenport, the law and the society in which they lived held little regard for the value of their household labor as a contribution to the success of a farming enterprise. Women made valuable contributions to household production and maintenance on farmsteads across Illinois. While women were producing marketable products for the profit of their families, their household work also sustained their families; all this work went uncounted in the eyes of Illinois law. Women's contributions to the farm economy held less importance than crop profits and land improvements. As women began to demand attention for these labors in eastern states during the 1840s and 1850s, rural Illinois women continued their household labor and silently contributed to the growing market economy.[4] Illinois did not allow wives to maintain separate earnings until 1869, when new legislation allowed a married woman to "possess her own earnings, and sue for the same in her own name, free from interference of her husband." Those earnings did not include "any right to compensation for any labor performed" for her family.[5]

Throughout her marriage Lucy Davenport held few discernible property rights, and during her widowhood she could have expected little improvement under the common law. Chancery courts handled petitions for dower, because the common law had little to say about married women or their property rights. Both James Kent's *Commentaries on American Law* and St. George Tucker's edition of *Blackstone's Commentaries* were famous antebellum treatises on the common law, and they maintained the principle of marital unity.[6] In marriage the husband and wife became "one person in law"; the wife's "legal existence" was "suspended," and she was subsumed in her husband, under his protection and influence.[7] Despite this verbal patina of unity, the law clearly made the husband the master: "The husband, by marriage, acquires a right to the use of the real estate of his wife . . . he acquires an absolute right to her chattels real and may dispose of them . . . he acquires an absolute property in her chattels personal in possession."[8] The husband was *baron* and the wife was *feme-covert;* she was responsible to her "lord" "under whose wing, protection, and cover, she performs every thing."[9]

Property brought to the marriage by the wife became the husband's entitlement, and he garnered "the profits during the marriage" while he lived. If a legal dispute arose involving land that his wife brought into the marriage, the husband sued in his name only. The husband became responsible for his wife's debts and came to court as sole defendant when those debts went unpaid. The wife joined her husband in issues involving her inheritance. When he committed waste upon her estate, marital unity protected the husband. The wife could not sue her husband during coverture to recover for damages he had inflicted upon property that she brought into the marriage.[10]

Davenport's situation was an aberration compared to that of other antebellum widows who sought dower through the courts. During the decades before the Civil War married women in Illinois shared a measure of financial protection and security by virtue of their statutory right to dower.[11] Historians have maintained that the development of protections for married women during the first half of the nineteenth century were a result of economic volatility born of speculation. Legislatures throughout the United States supported and strengthened married women's property rights during the early decades of the nineteenth century. Dower, an early modern English convention, along with newly created laws, protected women from their husband's losses and ensured some measure of inheritance for the next generation.[12] Communities also held a common interest in the private support or maintenance of widows, during a vulnerable time in family financial security after the death of the patriarch. Neighbors and community leaders saw widows as potential paupers and burdens to the county. Public agencies for supporting widows and their children were nonexistent in early Illinois, and the burden of support for paupers fell to the local citizenry.[13] To minimize the public cost of supporting penniless widows, lawyers and judges maintained laws to promote some financial protection for women at the end of coverture.

One of the first acts of the new Illinois General Assembly, approved on February 12, 1819, was to give widows the right to a "speedy assignment of dower."[14] Illinois statutes held that a married woman was entitled to dower upon the death of her husband. Dower was a life interest in one-third of all lands and personal property held or acquired during marriage. Because her claim was a life interest, she could not sell or assign the property (without petitioning the court), because upon her death the land reverted to the heirs of her husband's estate. A widow could profit from dower land, rents, and harvest, but she could not alter the property. When an estate was indivisible, the court gave the widow an annual allowance based upon one-third of the yearly value of the property. Unless she relinquished her dower rights during her marriage, the widow was to receive her "thirds" within one month of her husband's death. When the estate's administrator, heirs, or current owner of the property in question failed to meet this requirement, the widow could petition the court for her dower. If the court allowed the widow's petition, it appointed three impartial commissioners to assign dower in each parcel of estate land while reserving the homestead for the widow.[15]

Just as a widow could not convey dower property, a husband could not convey property without the consent of his wife because of her claim to dower, and she had to give her consent with full knowledge of the consequences and without coercion.[16] The long-established principle of separate examination of widows by county clerks or probate officials was enforced to varying degrees throughout the United States. Marylynn Salmon illustrates the diversity of law in colonial and early national America by looking at how different regions enforced the procedures for private examinations of married women during land conveyances. English antecedents established the examinations for the protection of women who faced widowhood with dependent families, and the courts wanted to be certain that a woman entered into the agreement willingly and not under the influence of her husband. Salmon found, for instance, that colonies with the provisions for private examinations enforced them with varying degrees of effectiveness, whereas some colonies (and later states) did not even recognize the rights of women to participate in conveyances. In Illinois the private examination was, with some exceptions, strictly enforced. For one instant during married life women in Illinois shared some measure of equality with their husbands when it came to family property. Land conveyed without the wife's consent was a risky investment because the purchaser, and subsequent purchasers, faced the possibility that a widow would one day come seeking her dower. This power represented the extent of a married woman's influence over marriage property.[17]

Occasionally, married women benefited from trusts established before marriage or by marriage settlements. Typically, these were agreements that allowed a woman to maintain control of land she brought into a marriage. The grantor placed the property, usually an inheritance or parental gift, in the trust of a third party. The trustee then held the property according to the instructions of the agreement. If she entered into a trust willingly, she gave up all right to dower upon land accumulated during marriage. If she did not consent to a trust or if her husband left her property by his will, the widow could then choose between dower and the allowance made in the trust or will. Wealthy urban families used prenuptial agreements when both the man and the woman brought substantial wealth to the marriage; she put her property into a trust for security during widowhood. In other instances husbands established trusts during marriage to avoid creditors; he conveyed property in his wife's name to a trustee, and the property was protected from debt collectors. Thus, to mitigate the "harshness" of marriage under the common law, the chancery court—which enforced dower claims and trusts—in Illinois provided women with means to circumvent some of the obstacles barring them from self-sustenance during widowhood.[18]

Toward the middle of the nineteenth century statutory reforms gained momentum. In 1850 a Springfield newspaper reprinted the Wisconsin act that allowed separate equitable estates for married women and made mention of its significance "in the rights of property and the credit system."[19] The act allowed a married woman to own land she brought into a marriage and to acquire land during marriage. This property was exempt from liquidation to pay her husband's debts. However, creditors could execute judgments upon property conveyed from husband to wife under this act. Not until 1861 did Illinois lawmakers pass a similar act.[20] The market economy, coupled with changing attitudes toward women's roles in the family, brought about wholesale changes in married women's property rights in most states between 1840 and the Civil War.[21] While far from equal, the status of women "in the eyes of the common law" improved during the decades before the Civil War more than during any other period in American history.[22]

The English system of land law was a burden to the American land market. A working middle class dominated the land market, and it had little patience for the complex traditions of the English system. Among the elements of the English system that slowed the growing market economy were dower and the common law institution of marital unity. By liberalizing statutes on the property rights of women, state legislatures made it easier to convey property.[23] Creditors in turn benefited from property reform because they were better able to locate the husband's property and collect from his estate. These reforms cleared debt collection of the encumbrances that coverture placed upon land conveyances.[24]

The Illinois legislature added a statute that allowed a married woman to maintain a separate equitable estate, free from the influence and interference of her husband.[25] When those changes occurred in 1861, they brought to an end the principle of marital unity and thus ended the reliance of women in Illinois upon dower as their sole protection against financial ruin. The fundamental legal changes in women's property rights during this period permitted a substantial step toward the equality of women in society as a whole.

In November 1855 Lucy Davenport's attorney, Norman H. Purple, drafted and filed her petition for dower in the Woodford County Circuit Court. At stake was Davenport's dower interest in the ninety-two-acre farm that she and her husband had worked until he died, and she intended to continue farming at least part of that farm to support her family. In the petition Purple established that John Davenport had died intestate, or without a will, on May 31, 1852, and that his widow was "entitled to Dower of the third part of all lands whereof her said husband was seized of or possessed or had any equitable claim to during Coverture." Later in the petition Purple showed that John Davenport had obtained the real estate from William H. Davenport and William Davenport—his brother and father, respectively—both of whom were listed among the defendants in the suit. John Davenport had obtained the property by "parole purchase [oral agreement] from William Davenport . . . by possession cultivation and large and valuable improvements" and finally by virtue of a contract between John Davenport and his brother and father.[26] Several witnesses testified to the validity of a written instrument that secured title in the name of John, but the parole agreement and contract were never entered into evidence during the suit.[27]

ABRAHAM LINCOLN

The defendants' attorney, Abraham Lincoln, filed a deed of trust during the next term of court as evidence that neither John Davenport nor Lucy Davenport held a legal claim, through dower or other means. Lincoln contended that John Davenport held only a life interest in the land and that upon his death the land reverted to his father, who was the administrator of his son's estate. The trust, Lincoln insisted, was the best support available to Lucy Davenport and her young family. William Davenport, John Davenport's father, had established a trust with his other son, William H. Davenport, to manage the property and use the profits to provide for John's infant heirs. Lucy Davenport was provided for but not included in the trust. William and William H. Davenport gave Lucy Davenport the right to look after her children and no more. Once the infant heirs reached the age of majority, the land descended to each of them equally.[28] Lucy Davenport did receive a portion of her husband's personal property and part of the profits from the sale of the remaining personal property. Lincoln's defense held that John Davenport never actually owned the property in fee simple, or entirely and without condition. Lincoln questioned the reliability of the parole agreement when the complainant was unable to produce witnesses to prove that such an agreement actually occurred between the parties.[29]

After Lucy Davenport's emotional dismissal in March 1857, she reinstated her suit during the same court term. The reasons for her ambivalent handling of the case at this point are not evident from the case record; however, the difficulty she faced in getting witnesses to testify on her behalf may explain her reversal. The case languished as Lincoln asked for and received several continuances until the fall 1858 term of court, when Judge James Harriott dismissed the case at the cost of the petitioner, which amounted to about $88.[30]

Abraham Lincoln had many encounters with the various laws governing married women's property during his twenty-five-year practice. Along with many other members of the Illinois bench and bar, Lincoln saw women clients as legally vulnerable to the extremes of coverture. These lawyers identified opportunities for their female clients to take advantage of the few protections coverture did offer. With the bar's paternal guidance a woman could protect herself from financial ruin at the end of coverture.

Like other members of the Illinois bar, Lincoln had a strong sense of community, and this often meant special treatment for those community members who were economically and legally vulnerable. A pragmatic lawyer, Lincoln generally took only cases in which widowed clients held serious claims, and he was quick to advise clients against litigation when they did not have a chance in court. Remuneration was minimal, and the litigation was not the prestigious sort, but Lincoln, and other attorneys like him, helped to lessen the difficulties that widows faced and in turn minimized the public burden of pauperism.

In his writings Lincoln remained silent on women's property rights throughout his life, yet according to his third law partner, William H. Herndon, Lincoln "always advocated" women's "rights." Herndon was speaking about suffrage when he reminisced about how Lincoln saw "that Woman was denied in *free* America her right to franchise, being the equal but the other side—the other better half of man."[31] Herndon was less reticent than Lincoln on the subject and wrote Caroline Dall a triumphant letter after the passage of the 1861 reforms: "Our Illinois Legislature has this winter (1860–61) enacted a law, allowing women (married women) all their property—real, personal, mixed—free from all debt, contract, obligation, and control of their husbands." Herndon now saw men and women as equals when it came to property ownership: "For my life, I cannot see why there should be any distinction between men and women, when we speak of rights under government."[32]

A better view of Lincoln's paternal attitude toward women emerges from a look at Lincoln's law practice. In a March 1850 letter to a fellow attorney, Lincoln wrote about his neighbor, a woman who had "convinced me, that I strongly sympathize with her, and intend to not drop the case till I learn more about it." Lincoln's client, Huldah Stout, had prevailed upon him to look into whether her relatives had withheld a substantial inheritance from her, an equal share of her grandmother's estate. Motivated by his neighbor's entreaties, Lincoln wrote to several contacts in the area in which the disputed property was located. This case and numerous others like it illustrate how an antebellum lawyer represented the interests of women in court.[33]

When Matilda Moor found that her late husband had "fixed all of his property" so that she was "left to shift for her self," she sought Lincoln's help in court. Moor hired a local attorney to bring suit in the Coles County Circuit Court, but they contacted Lincoln to improve their chances of success.[34] In another instance Joseph Means, a Woodford County farmer, wrote Lincoln concerning his widowed daughter's property. Lincoln answered by return mail, briefly stating his opinion. The executor of the son-in-law's estate had sold property fraudulently, and, given the evidence, Lincoln saw room for legal action to nullify the sale.[35]

On occasion Lincoln had to broker peaceful resolutions to difficult legal problems that a widow may have inherited from her husband. Harriet B. Neale sought Lincoln's help in identifying some property that her deceased husband had conveyed during his life. The owner had never allowed her to take possession of her dower assignment, and the dispute required a new survey to establish the exact boundaries of the Springfield lot. In a written request to the county surveyor Lincoln described Neale as "for ten years a widow, and very necessitous," and in exchange for the free survey, Lincoln offered future professional services. Lincoln was "not expecting any compensation from Mrs. Neale." The litigants settled the issue out of court.[36]

Some of Lincoln's busiest clients were widows who owned or managed property. Mary Welles, the widow of a Springfield lawyer and a friend of the Lincolns, hired Lincoln during the 1850s to handle several suits in Sangamon County Circuit Court. When Charles Welles died, he left several land sales in various stages of completion. Purchasers sued Mary Welles and her children as heirs to the Welles estate, and they in turn sued other purchasers in friendly suits to complete the land transactions. Welles gave Lincoln her authority to confess judgment in the cases in which she and her children were defendants, and she gave Lincoln instructions to give deeds to purchasers when they had paid their debts.[37]

Lincoln exhibited a lawyer's paternalism most clearly with his own family. After his father's death in 1851 Lincoln assumed a watchful interest in his stepmother's property in Coles County. In letters to his stepbrother, John D. Johnston, Lincoln showed concern about Johnston's mismanagement of the farmland. Johnston, who had also inherited some of Thomas Lincoln's property—farmland adjacent to Sarah Lincoln's dower land—failed to cultivate much of it or make a profit from the land. Lincoln's concern became acute when Johnston convinced Sarah Lincoln to allow him to sell some of her dower property and manage her finances. Lincoln bitterly censured Johnston for prevailing upon the widow to relinquish half her dower "hook and line." Johnston then wanted to sell Sarah Lincoln's main forty-acre tract, use the profits to make loans, and support the widow with the interest. Lincoln in-

Abraham Lincoln's stepmother, Sarah Bush Johnston Lincoln (1788–1869), in Charleston, Illinois, c. 1864. When Thomas Lincoln died in 1851, she became a widow for the second time. Courtesy of the Illinois State Historical Library, Springfield.

sisted that Johnston "go to work" and cultivate the land, and if he would not do that for Sarah, then rent the land to support her. "The Eastern forty acres I intend to keep for Mother while she lives," Lincoln wrote, and later after hearing another one of his stepbrother's schemes, "I am confident that land can be made to produce for Mother, at least $30 a year." Again Johnston wanted to sell the land and use the profits to support her, a plan that would allow her $16 in annual support, with a portion of the sale profits going directly into Johnston's pocket. "Now, if you are satisfied with treating her in that way, I am not," came Lincoln's response after making sarcastic comments about the amount of the planned annual support.[38]

DOWER IN SANGAMON COUNTY

The statutory maintenance of dower in Illinois law was one method of mitigating the strict conditions of marriage. Trusts also gave women greater equity in marriage and some say in family property management. Unfortunately for Lucy Davenport, the trust written by her in-laws to govern the title to her husband's farm was not drawn to include all her interests. The nature of the trust denied John Davenport's interest in the estate and thus denied her access to dower. Her in-laws used the trust to influence the descent of the property and in effect to keep the whole within the patrilineal family. This arrangement denied Lucy Davenport even a life estate in the family farm, but William H. Davenport, a successful farmer and landowner, took over his brother's farm, cared for his brother's children, and extended care to his brother's widow.[39]

Unlike Lucy Davenport, most women in Sangamon County who sued for dower received their claims despite resistance from creditors or heirs. Overall, the Sangamon County Circuit Court granted 58 percent of all petitions for dower, and widows initiated most of those cases. The same pattern existed throughout central Illinois during the antebellum years. Many women were not adverse to using dower as a protection against their husband's debts. Dower represented a minimum of what a widow could expect from her husband's estate, a minimum for a lifetime of labor during marriage. While the widow's ownership was conditional under dower or trust, for most women widowhood was the first and only period of limited financial independence.[40]

Married women in Sangamon County held few codified property rights during marriage; however, widowhood offered them the opportunity to manage property until the heirs reached the age of majority. Before the reform of 1861 women relied on dower to safeguard real estate garnered during marriage and to ensure support during widowhood. Most Sangamon

County men did not leave a will, and even fewer women had prenuptial agreements to ensure support after their husband's death. Thus the main recourse for a widow was her right to dower. A widow sued in circuit court to obtain her thirds when heirs could not reach an agreement or when the heirs were minors. At the same time that it awarded dower, the court assigned three independent commissioners the task of partitioning the estate equally among all living heirs. The widow received her dower by "metes and bounds," or one-third of each individual parcel, and was given the homestead property so as to maintain a household for the youngest heirs.

Many Sangamon County widows were like Lucy Davenport in two respects: they had a family to support and they were themselves young. These circumstances forced women to become the provider and the guardian for the family, roles that had been shared with their husband. Many widows did not remarry and remained the head of the family until the children reached maturity. In his study of Sugar Creek, a Sangamon County community, John Mack Faragher maintains that women tended to outlive their husbands, and because of a propensity not to remarry, headed a substantial number of families in the community.[41] Even when widows did remarry, they maintained strong ties to the children from their earlier marriage and often continued as the provider for those children. When, for example, Paulina Fobes's second husband threatened divorce if she did not join him in the Wisconsin Territory and leave her children with her first husband's family, she chose to remain in Sangamon County and support her children.[42]

DOWER AGAINST DEBT: THE CASE OF BARBARA KIRSCH

The Sangamon County widow Barbara Kirsch faced the same problems of supporting a young family as did Lucy Davenport, but Barbara Kirsch was better able to use the courts to maintain support for her family. During the mid- and late 1850s Kirsch brought several suits before the Sangamon County courts to ensure independent care for her family. Louis Kirsch died intestate in October 1853, and Barbara Kirsch assumed administration of his estate that December. Twice during her administration Kirsch had to sell real estate to keep the estate solvent. First, she raised $176 at an auction in 1855; in 1856 she raised $390 at another auction to satisfy creditors. In both cases Kirsch had to sue the minor heirs of Louis Kirsch—her own children—and provide evidence of the debts. The court reviewed the petitions and allowed the sale of land in each case.[43]

In 1858 Kirsch petitioned the court to obtain her dower from the remaining property in the estate, including ten acres of land adjacent to a railroad right-of-way. While Kirsch had previously released her claim to dower in the land that she had sold to pay debts, she maintained a right to her thirds in the remaining unsold property. Commissioners appointed by the court set off the three-acre homestead lot as Kirsch's dower.[44]

Two years later Kirsch submitted to William H. Herndon, her children's court guardian, an account listing $1,050 in expenses that she had incurred in supporting and educating her seven children. Herndon brought a friendly suit against Kirsch and her children to obtain a decree to sell the remaining real estate and to apply the funds from that sale toward the costs of family maintenance. Kirsch did not challenge the guardian's petition, and the court ordered the guardian to sell the remaining nondower property to the highest bidder. In 1864 the guardian sold the three parcels for a total of $1,300 and applied the amount to Kirsch's family support.[45]

Barbara Kirsch's administration allowed her to pay off the debts of her husband's estate and to enjoy financial independence during widowhood. Kirsch relinquished her right to dower on the entire estate by selling land— after gaining the court's permission—to pay debts or to maintain her family; she received a limited dower based on a fraction of what was in the estate at the time of Louis Kirsch's death. In taking an abbreviated dower, Kirsch was able to sell land she would not have been able to sell had she received her complete dower at her husband's death. Illinois statutes prohibited the assignment or conveyance of land obtained by dower.[46]

Many other widows found protection from insolvency in Illinois dower statutes. Lucetta West was left with a $4,272 debt when her husband died in 1839 without leaving a will. West petitioned the Sangamon County Circuit Court for her thirds, and the court appointed commissioners to assign her dower. The commissioners gave Lucetta West one-third of the estate for maintenance during her life, before the court sold the remainder of the estate to satisfy creditors.[47] Similarly, Sarah McNutt petitioned for dower upon her husband's indebted estate. The administrator of her husband's estate had sold some estate property before McNutt filed her petition in the Cass County Circuit Court. She claimed her right to dower upon the sold land. The profits from the administrator's sale had already been applied toward the debt on the estate, yet the court awarded McNutt a life interest in one-third of both the sold and unsold real estate.[48]

AGGRESSIVE USE OF DOWER: THE CASE
OF MARGARET PORTER

Many Sangamon County widows managed their husband's estates with success. Margaret Porter initiated twenty-four petitions for dower against various Springfield-area landowners between 1851 and 1858. In every case Porter claimed dower in lands that at one time during her marriage her husband, William Porter, had conveyed to a purchaser. In some instances the property had been conveyed again after Porter sold it. Despite having an interest twice or thrice removed, Margaret Porter, unless she had relinquished her right to dower during the original conveyance, still held a claim. Because of her claims to a widow's third, Margaret Porter sued all the grantees of property in which her deceased husband had had some interest during his life.

Porter filed nine suits for dower during 1851 in the Sangamon County Circuit Court. The court assigned Porter her dower in only two of the suits, but she obtained out-of-court monetary settlements in five other cases after dismissing her petitions against those defendants. In those five suits Porter authorized quitclaim deeds that relinquished her claim to dower in exchange for a one-time payment, and in so doing she collected a total of $1,100.[49] By using her legal claim to dower as leverage, Porter provided support for her family.

The pleadings from *Porter v. Sangamon County, Illinois,* illustrate the technical side of Porter's claim. In its answer to Porter's petition the county acknowledged that it had purchased land from William Porter but insisted that Margaret Porter had relinquished her dower in front of a justice of the peace, according to the statutory requirement. The county then conceded that the justice had neglected to include the signed relinquishment with his certificate on the original deed, causing the deed to be recorded without proper relinquishment. By asserting that Porter had willingly and knowingly released her claim at the time of conveyance, the county also had to concede irregularity in the recording of the deed, and on that technicality the county was open to Porter's claim. The defendant was especially vulnerable because the property at stake had become the site of the Sangamon County courthouse. The county commissioners pleaded for exclusion from the claim because of the absurd possibility of the widow Porter's owning one-third of the land upon which the courthouse stood, but the county was eventually forced to settle with her. The good widow's quitclaim deed cost Sangamon County $350.[50]

In the similar case of *Porter v. Hoffman et al.* Margaret Porter filed suit for dower on property that had been developed into a commercial block known in Springfield as Hoffman's Row (at one time the site of the Stuart and Lincoln law office). The court decided for Porter and appointed commissioners to assign Porter's dower. They, in turn, reported that the property was not equitably divisible. The court then called a jury to assign an annual payment due to Porter by Hoffman and others in lieu of her one-third interest. The jury assigned to Porter a lifetime payment of $10 per year. Later Porter executed a deed transferring her interest in the property to St. Louis investors for $200.[51]

A Bill of appraisment of the specific property allowed by law to

Margaret M. Porter .... **Widow of**

William Porter .... **deceased for herself**

and ——— children.

	$	
Necessary House hold and Kitchen Furniture for self and family	300	
Necessary beds bedstead and bedding	117	
One Spinning Wheel	5	
One Loom with its appendages	15	
One pair of Cards	1	
One Stove & the necessary pipe therefor	28	
The Wearing apparel of herself & Family, (need not value this)		
One milk Cow & Calf for every 4 in the family,	40	
One Horse of the value of 40 Dollars	40	00
One Womans saddle & Bridle of the value of	15	00
Provision for herself & family for 1 year	500	
Two Sheep for each member of the family & the fleeces,	20	
Food for the above discribed stock for 6 Months	75	
Fuel for herself and family for 3 months,	30	
And Sixty Dollars worth of other property	60	00
	$1329 -	

We the undersigned Appraisers of the personal property of William Porter Deceased, do hereby certify that the above is a correct Bill of Appraisement of the specific property allowed by law to Margaret McPorter Widow of William Porter Deceased, for herself and children, made out by us according to the best of our skill and judgment. Given under our hands and Seals this .... day of ....

A. D. 183_.

Charles W. Chesterson (SEAL)

James Wilkins (SEAL)

D. R. Williams (SEAL)

JOHNSON & BRADFORD, Dealers in Blanks, Springfield Ill.

Widow's assignment for Margaret Porter, May 9, 1856, providing her with personal property from her husband's estate. Reprinted from the William Porter estate file, Illinois Regional Archives Depository, University of Illinois at Springfield.

In 1855 Porter initiated fifteen new petitions for dower in the Sangamon County Circuit Court. With nearly identically written petitions Porter's attorney laid down his arguments for why his client had a right to dower in property that William Porter had sold during his lifetime. As in the first series of cases in 1851, the defendants in the 1855 cases were all purchasers of land that William Porter had owned at one time during his marriage to Margaret Porter. During a period of three years each case was dismissed, either voluntarily by Porter or by the court. The defendants were better able to provide proof of dower relinquishment in this second generation of cases, and Porter was able to garner only four small settlements. In three additional quitclaim deeds that were not a result of litigation, she was able to finesse settlements from three men who had purchased property from William Porter.[52]

While the record shows Margaret Porter's aggressive use of her dower right, it also reveals the disposition of the William Porter estate. Margaret Porter received $1,329 in personal property from the estate, yet at least one defendant from the dower cases characterized the estate as insolvent. Although William Porter's estate was indeed insolvent, the probate court assigned Margaret Porter a list of personal property allowed by statute: goods and household items necessary for basic family maintenance. These few necessities, along with the minimal assignment of dower, were all that Porter had to support her family.[53] Illinois widows were allowed a specific list of household articles to be set off by the probate court before the liquidation of personal property to pay debts. These articles included the necessities for everyday life: clothing, a stove, fuel, bed and bedding, and a horse with saddle, among other items.

Married women in Illinois shared the statutory protection of dower. Since colonial times the trend in the United States, however, had been to weaken the constraints of dower to streamline the process of property conveyance.[54] By the early decades of the nineteenth century, women relied less upon dower than upon establishing a separate equitable estate as a primary means of ensuring protection against poverty during widowhood. In frontier Illinois these trends are less noticeable. Compared to eastern and southern neighbors, Illinois lagged behind in enacting women's property reforms.

According to Richard Chused, married women's property acts slowly began to emerge in the 1840s. As early as 1835 southern states passed acts protecting married women's personal and real property from creditors seeking to collect on debts incurred by the family. Having mostly to do with protecting slaves brought into the family by the wife, the first reforms were mostly economic in nature, a reaction to the poor national economy of the late 1830s. New York's 1848 reforms allowed women separate use of property brought into or acquired during a marriage. These broader reforms reflected the efforts of women and men seeking to mitigate the harshness of coverture in regard to women's status.[55] Thus the Illinois reforms occurred a full decade after most neighboring states had seen fit to give married women at least limited control of property they brought into a marriage. While Illinois was not a conservative state in other aspects of family law, namely, divorce, it did not expand property rights. Women toiled within the common law constraints of property rights until 1861, but during that time they took advantage of the few age-old protections, especially dower. An examination of Sangamon County dower actions and the increasing use of that action during the four decades of the county's existence before the Civil War confirm this development.

WOMEN'S ESTATES IN SANGAMON COUNTY

Throughout the antebellum era Sangamon County women inherited, bequeathed, and managed real and personal property. The restrictions of marital unity and the common law traditions that Illinois continued to observe in its statutes hid these activities. In reality Sangamon County women made important contributions to the growing market economy of the county, and although they may not have owned real estate in fee simple, they managed land that yielded profitable agricultural produce. A close examination of women's estates illustrates the reality that many widows and single women faced in dealing with limited property rights. Looking at dower cases provides an illustration of the active participation of women in the legal system and of their efforts to obtain a meager financial standing during widowhood. Their management of estates clarifies, retrospectively, what women did with their property rights during their lives. What did Sangamon County women do with their property once they became managers of their dower property? In rare instances the estates of Sangamon County's few *feme sole* residents, and the wills they left, illuminate the legal condition of wealthier women. Women's estate records provide a better view of the financial standing, and thus the real legal standing, they held in their community. Many women were leaders of extensive family units, and not only served as matriarchal leaders but also actively took part in everyday work and farm management.

The heirs of 111 women opened estate files in Sangamon County courts from 1821 to 1860. The 111 estates represent more than 7 percent of the 1,501 estates filed during the same period, and a survey of the estate files reveals the financial standing that women held in their community during the antebellum period. Typically, a file contains a set of required documentation—an affidavit asserting the death of the subject, administration papers, inventories and appraisals of property, claims against the estate, and documentation of estate sales—that provide an outline of a particular woman's holdings at the time of her death. Most revealing are the inventories and sale bills; these documents list items of personal property owned by the deceased individual.

Nearly all the estates hold some record of household-related personalty. The court required an administrator to pay the debts of the estate, and payment was made once enough of the estate had been liquidated to garner enough cash to pay the creditors. If there was not enough cash in the estate, as was the case for most estates, the administrator inventoried the deceased woman's personal property, and the court appointed appraisers to assign a value to the estate. The administrator then held an estate sale to raise the funds necessary to pay off the debts. If the sale of personal property was insufficient to pay all debts, the administrator had to sell real estate in the same manner. Often the heirs of the estate bought items from their mother's estate, or the creditor would balance his books by obtaining personal property from the estate to offset the debt. With the personal and real property in the estate inventoried, the administrator then divided the unsold property among the heirs. Most often, however, the administrator inventoried and sold personal property and real estate to divide the estate equitably among all the heirs.

Of the Sangamon County women whose estates were probated, 84 percent were widows, or *femes sole,* at the time of their death. These women owned or held for life both real and personal property as accounted for in estate records. Many of these women productively managed farms or businesses for several years after their husband's death. Often the assets left for the administrator were sizable and rivaled men's estates in terms of wealth. Among the remaining estates are those of women who owned property in trust and were survived by their husbands or who were minors who died with an inheritance.

Estate inventories included household items like bedding, kitchenware, clothing, foodstuffs, and the day-to-day tools required for basic household production, from butter churning to wool carding. Administrators also inventoried the horses, cows, hogs, and other common farmyard animals that made up average household property. Nearly 41 percent of women's estates in Sangamon County had personal property related to farming or produce ready for market. These exceptional estates included inventories of farming implements—plows, harnesses, oxen, and tools—as well as a large number of farm animals. Large quantities of stacked or busheled produce also indicated farm production in a woman's estate. While most households included the usual assortment of necessities for rural living, a substantial subset also included material culture commonly associated with working farms. Widows managed their husband's farm or their dower estates in Sangamon County as early as 1830. Catherine Mischler's 1830 estate inventory includes a separate section devoted to farm implements and stock. Approximately half the value in Mischler's estate was derived from "ploughs, cattle and horses."[56] While the husband accumulated this equipment and stock during his life, the widow continued to manage the farm and its resources for several years after his death. Catherine Mischler's estate includes records of her business dealings, among them, unpaid accounts and money owed her by men who purchased her farm's produce. The administrator of Nancy Sayles's estate sold off her personal property within a month of her death in August 1836, but the following spring he sold an additional 109.5 bushels of corn from the previous fall's harvest.[57] Jane Davis's administrator paid carpenters and laborers for work done on her farm before her death in August 1840. Davis's estate included farmland parcels in excess of 140 acres and a large accumulation of produce harvested during the fall of 1840.[58] Margaret Renshaw's 1842 will left instructions to her executor about raising and fattening the family hogs to obtain the best profit from their sale at market. The hogs were to be sold to pay the merchandise credit account that Renshaw had accumulated while managing the family farm. Renshaw bequeathed specific allotments of surplus wheat to her son and daughter to assist them in starting their own farms.[59] Elizabeth Morgan's estate was primarily a $92 credit with a local merchant who had purchased Morgan's hogs just before her death in 1852.[60] Mary Ellen Greenwalt's 1851 estate contained produce, including sixteen bushels of wheat and 210 bushels of corn harvested from three parcels of farmland in Sangamon County. During the antebellum period estate administrators probated several modest farms that Sangamon County women managed, and their estates included the typical farm implements, stock, and produce, indicating that they played an active role in managing property.

Elizabeth Mathews died during harvest time in October 1850, leaving her farm business to be probated in the Sangamon County Court. Appraisers valued both her harvested produce and that still in the field. Mathews also had a store credit for hogs she had sold to a local merchant before she died. The line of credit was already diminished by products that Mathews had purchased for her farm and household. In all, her personal property was worth $736.90, yet household-related assets accounted for only $81.50 of that total. The majority of Mathews's estate was her farm implements, stock, and produce. Mathews's substantial farm included "thirty fat hogs," "twenty-four shoats," one horse, one mare, three colts, two cows, one steer, one bull, three heifers, and eighteen sheep. Evidence of Mathews's management becomes clear from the creditors who filed their claims against the estate; hired hands filed for labor that they performed on the farm before Mathews's death, including bills for plowing and "work around house." Despite the work she put into managing her farm, Mathews did not own her land. She labored on her deceased husband's farm, and when she died, her farm went to his heirs.[61]

Paulina Fobes died in 1853, leaving an eighty-acre farm and a personal estate that included farm implements, stock, and household goods for her children. Her second husband had left Fobes and her seven children by her first husband to run the farm on their own. Before Paulina Fobes died, Benjamin Fobes, her second husband, wrote to her from a logging camp in the Wisconsin Territory. He suggested that they were better off apart and that unless she left her children and joined him, their marriage was over. Benjamin Fobes could not realize a profit from farming land that was not his to begin with, and in return for her keeping the stove and harnesses, he wanted his plow and bedding. Paulina Fobes died before she could answer, but her estate contains no further indication of Benjamin Fobes's claims. Paulina Fobes's seven children each received an equal distribution after the sale of property to pay their mother's debts.[62]

Many estates that included personal property related to farming also included real estate. Most women who managed a farm also held interest in the land that they farmed, whether it was dower land or land held in fee. From modest fourteen- and twenty-six-acre holdings to 360-acre farms, women in Sangamon County managed farmland. Tax receipts in estate files reveal that not only did women hold interest in real estate but they paid taxes on the land. Elizabeth Langley's 1847 estate included a twenty-acre farm and the equipment required to produce a living from the land. With personal property valued at $177 Langley was not wealthy; however, evidence that she paid taxes on her land and the presence of farming equipment among her inventoried possessions indicates an independent subsistence lifestyle.[63]

Women with property took active roles in managing their property and maintaining the financial solvency of their estates in the growing market economy of antebellum Illinois. Of the 111 estates, only 5 percent appeared to be insolvent after the sale of property. The solvency of the vast majority of their estates suggests that Sangamon County women did not speculate with their holdings. Instead, Sangamon County women labored to maintain solvent estates because many were widows who depended on their property to support their family. Widows who did not remarry were left to fend for their family, while those who did remarry still held an interest in providing for their children from the first marriage. These responsibilities ensured careful management of family property. In many instances women were restrained by statutes that prohibited waste on dower land or by a husband's will that restricted property use or limited inheritance if the widow remarried. Some widows became the matriarch of the family unit and owned the family farm worked by the heirs. While her husband's heirs worked the land that they inherited or would inherit upon her death, she maintained the homestead and oversaw the farm's operation as she had when her husband was alive. The widow owned the farm implements used by the sons and in-laws, the farm stock, and often the real estate, and when she did not own the land outright, she at least held a dower right to one-third of the family farm. All around the homestead the widow's family members worked their parcels broken off from the original settlement, yet she remained the central figure in the family until her death, when everything descended to the heirs.

John Mack Faragher's study of the Sangamon County community of Sugar Creek highlights Jane McElvain Fletcher's management of her husband's farm after he died shortly after they arrived in Illinois. At his estate sale in 1830 Jane Fletcher served as the administratrix of James Fletcher's estate and both sold and bought the personal property of her late husband. She bought $75 worth of farm equipment and stock for the farm.[64] Jane Fletcher never owned her farmland but managed it until her death in 1853. The real estate was valued at $1,600, and her personal property, which included household wares and farm stock, eventually amounted to $1,021 after sale. Jane Fletcher's debts, most of which were for merchandise she purchased on credit for the support of her household and farm, were paid by the administrator of her estate after he sold her personal property at auction. The administrator then distributed the remaining personal assets among Jane Fletcher's heirs. For more than twenty years Jane Fletcher carefully managed her farm so that her family would remain financially independent. Her sons continued working the prosperous family farm, one that had become successful under the management of their mother.[65]

Faragher estimates that as many as 10 to 15 percent of married Sugar Creek women became widowed and managed the family farm during widowhood.[66] An examination of the estates of Sangamon County women suggests widespread management of property by women during the decades before the Civil War. Of the 111 estates, 41 percent include the ownership of farming tools and stock. Listed among the inventories of household property, appraised and sold to pay debts or to divide the estate equitably, is the material evidence of farm labor. Plows, harnesses, chains, tools, scythes, and produce, along with horses, cows, cattle, swine, sheep, and fowl, are evidence of a working farm.

Administrators inventoried land as an asset in 30 percent of the women's estates in Sangamon County, and in most instances those inventories describe developed farmland.

During the 1850s increasing numbers of women in Sangamon County owned town lots and maintained developed homesteads thereon. Instead of farming, these women owned property as an investment or as a homestead. Elizabeth Snodgrass and Eliza Rape, both widowed, contracted with a carpenter in 1854 to build a house for the two of them on Snodgrass's Springfield town lot. When Rape died a month later, the carpenter filed his account for labor with her administrator.[67] Elizabeth Trainer of Hamilton County, Ohio, owned a Springfield lot, which was sold after her death in 1850. Her administrator sold the property at auction to pay Trainer's property taxes and the labor that a Springfield man had put into maintaining the property.[68]

The wealthiest woman in Sangamon County to have her estate probated was Eliza J. Enos. Most of Enos's estate was her interest in the "Quincy House," a hotel that she owned but probably did not manage. When she died in 1859, the hotel was valued at $16,000.[69] Eliza J. Enos perhaps learned from the example of her mother-in-law, Salome B. Enos. Pascal and Salome Enos came to Springfield in 1823, after President James Monroe commissioned Pascal Enos to open a federal land office there. Pascal Enos died in 1832, and Salome Enos was left to manage the family estate, which then held "small commercial value in dollars." For the next forty-five years Salome Enos "husbanded her resources, cared for and protected that property with frugal industry for years and brought her children one of the largest estates in the city."[70]

Several women in Sangamon County wrote wills to protect the interest of their heirs. These women of means often held land and bequeathed the property so that their children would receive the land, either in trust or outright, when they reached maturity. Only twenty-seven Sangamon County women had wills when they died during the four decades from 1821 to 1860, but this sampling of propertied women further illustrates the active role that women played in the Sangamon County economy.

As early as 1828, and with increasing frequency through the next three decades, women in Sangamon County wrote wills to maintain control over the division of their property. During the 1850s alone twelve women wrote wills, and executors filed sixteen wills in probate court, a reflection of the increasing number of Sangamon County women who owned and bequeathed property. Typically, these women wrote their wills so that executors could pay all outstanding debts, then bequeathed their property to heirs as they saw fit. In almost every instance the author assigned her assets to her children, either directly or by trust. Daughters and impoverished sons often received special notice in women's wills, and Sangamon County women often conditioned their bequests by requiring that the property remain in the name of a daughter, separate from a son-in-law's estate.

These early wills trace the passing by frontier women of small fortunes in personal property and dower real estate on to their children, not unlike intestate division of property. Fanny Hamby's 1832 will was limited to paying her debts, and her executor was her creditor, who converted her personal estate into exactly the amount she owed him.[71] Sarah Braken's 1828 will divided her personal estate, which was valued at $17.56, among her children. Braken also left her dower property to her children, a gesture that ensured safe transfer of the land to the rightful heirs.[72]

Typical of wills written by women in Sangamon County was Mary Firey's in which she transferred land held in trust, on her behalf, to a new trust established for her children until their maturity, at which time they were bestowed with the full right of ownership.[73] Also representative was Margaret Renshaw's 1842 will in which she bequeathed a substantial farm to her children. Renshaw left a sixty-acre parcel to her son and a forty-acre parcel to her daughter for each to begin a farm. She gave each child half of the housewares and equal shares of farm stock.[74]

Several wills exhibited the propensity of women to favor female heirs, often transferring trust property from their own name to their daughter's or granddaughter's name. Women who transferred property exclusively to their daughter(s) sought to control their property so that their daughters had at least the same measure of support that their mother had garnered, without interference from husbands. Jane McCann put all her property in trust for her daughter and specifically excluded her son-in-law from access to the title to the land. Thus, no matter what became of her daughter's marriage, Jane McCann ensured some financial support for her daughter.[75] Christiana Griffith changed her will just before her death in 1852 and directed her executor to sell all fifteen town lots that she owned and to divide the proceeds equally among her three daughters. Her two sons received a watch and a set of books, respectively.[76] Maria Barbara Beck, who held a trust by inheritance, appointed her eldest daughter trustee of the property. Upon Beck's death in 1859 her daughter became trustee and held and managed the property, which included a small farm with necessary implements and stock, until her youngest sibling came of age, whereupon the estate was divided among all of Beck's heirs.[77]

The wealthiest Sangamon County women's estates included wills. Eliza Enos left her hotel, the Quincy House, to her two nephews, her sister's sons. The value of her interest was such that she had the executor sell some of her interest in the hotel periodically to pay for the boys' education.[78] When Sarah Cannon died in 1857, her estate included lots in Springfield and Decatur, Illinois, valued at approximately $2,300. Cannon arranged for the education of her daughters and had the property put in trust for them; she also required that the property go directly to her daughters and not to their husbands.[79] Women in Sangamon County understood the realities of their disability before the common law and actively sought to make their daughters' lives better by ensuring them some form of separate property on which to hinge a secure future.

The number of wills written by women increased toward the end of the 1850s, and property bequeathed became less agricultural in nature. City lots and housing became regular features in wills as Sangamon County's population grew and as Springfield grew as a city. Women held property in diverse ways. The shift away from rural real estate and agricultural property occurred as such property, along with personal property, generally became smaller parts of the overall value of women's estates in Sangamon County. More women held town homes and had monetary assets. At least two Sangamon County women counted out-of-state slaves among their assets. Beverly Powell's will stated the conditions of manumission for her slave James in Virginia.[80]

JUDGE THOMAS DRUMMOND AND THE "SHIELD AGAINST IMPROVIDENCE"

In *Lane v. Dolick et al.*, a federal case tried in Illinois in 1854, Margaret Lane tried to remove the defendants from two town lots they owned in Belleville, Illinois. During her marriage Margaret and her husband, James, conveyed the lots—property Margaret Lane brought into the marriage—to a man named Dolick and others. Margaret Lane wanted to remove the defendants because of some confusion, on her part, regarding the nature of the conveyance. The deed language was clear; however, the certificate was inconsistent with the type of transaction. The statutes required a very specific acknowledgment when a married woman conveyed her own real property, but in this case the court official wrote the certificate incorrectly. When a married woman conveyed property, a court official had to interview her away from the presence of her husband, and the judge in Margaret Lane's case saw inconsistencies in this aspect of the conveyance. In his opinion in *Lane v. Dolick et al.* Judge Thomas Drummond made a prophetic statement about the statutory protections of married women: "It seems to me, if the guards which have so long been thrown around the estates of married women as a shield against the improvidence, folly, or imprudence of the husband, are to be removed, it must be by the Legislature, and not by the courts."[81]

Drummond implied that Lane, and the court official who recorded her relinquishment of dower, did not fully recognize the effect of the transaction that she was undertaking at the behest of her husband. The court clerk could not have explained the conveyance to Margaret Lane—as he was required to do—if he did not understand that the property was hers to begin with. Drummond asserted that the court could not ignore that infringement, no matter how small, because the law was established to protect married women and their property in situations in which uncertainty prevailed. The court decided the case for Margaret Lane, and she regained ownership of the property in question.[82] While Drummond could not change the legal protections of married women in the courts, he foresaw legislative changes. Seven years after he wrote his opinion, the Illinois legislature enacted its first law specifically defining the rights of married women to own property.[83]

Married women's property rights in Illinois during the antebellum period were well established in a group of laws that were hidden among several different chapters of Illinois statutes. While dower represented an old remedy for women facing the harshness of the common law, it also limited the dividend of a lifetime of work to one-third of the value of a man's (and without absolute title in real estate). Nevertheless, women in Sangamon County pushed for their thirds in increasing numbers, and widowed land managers populated the county's countryside. Changing attitudes toward women and their role in the family and society made this phenomenon less of an aberration as the years went by.

As their estates reflect, Sangamon County women actively managed the land they held, whether they owned it or simply held a life estate. Many women increased the value of their property and worked hard to maintain the family farm. A widow's children benefited doubly from her productivity: in support during her lifetime and in valuable property after her death. By 1861 women throughout Sangamon County owned land outright or managed land on behalf of their husband's heirs. In either case a widow had the opportunity to obtain financial security for herself and her family.

Married women's property rights in Illinois changed most dramatically in 1861, when the state legislature approved a law allowing separate equitable estates for married women. For the first time a married woman could own real estate separately from her husband. Her property was not subject to her husband's debts, and he could not convey her property without her joining him in the conveyance. The new law allowed a woman to keep her inheritance or other property that she brought into the marriage. For an enterprising woman the law meant that property she obtained by her own means remained hers unless she chose otherwise.[84] The new law was the culmination of a continuum of extralegal changes in attitude away from the ancient idea of marital unity. That married women were allowed to own property was not a major change in the day-to-day life of women in Sangamon County. They had seen some measure of property rights through dower and trusts, and widows were often managers of their families' fortunes. Throughout the antebellum period women had profited from the land they managed but did not own; thus the 1861 reform was a natural advance in the property rights of women.

Illinois followed several other states in enacting separate estates for married women. More than a decade earlier New York established similar rights for women. Illinois, however, enabled women to profit from and own land acquired during marriage, unlike earlier reforms in other states.[85] Dower was still a part of late nineteenth-century Illinois chancery dockets, but with less and less frequency as women gained more from owning their own land. As they realized the profit from property ownership, and these profits were protected from the dealings of their husbands, women were better able to prepare for life as widows and to ensure inheritance for their children.

For many years Sangamon County women were part of the growing market economy despite their marginal legal status. Married women held land in trust and maintained property to pass on to their children. Widows actively sought their thirds and increasingly exercised their financial independence during widowhood. They represented a significant proportion of farmers in an agricultural community, and even when they did not own the land they farmed, they proved to be successful caretakers of their farms so that the next generation could grow.

Notes

1. Caroline H. Dall, *The College, the Market, and the Court; or, Woman's Relation to Education, Labor, and Law* (1867; rpt., New York: Arno, 1972), 347–54.

2. Motion to Dismiss, 24 March 1857, *Davenport v. Davenport et al.*, in *The Law Practice of Abraham Lincoln: Complete Documentary Edition*, ed. Martha L. Benner and Cullom Davis et al. (DVD; Urbana: University of Illinois Press, 2000), hereafter cited as *LPAL*.

3. John Davenport died May 31, 1852. Petition for Dower, 15 November 1855, *Davenport v. Davenport et al., LPAL.* Lucy Davenport was probably thirty-one when she wrote the motion (U.S. Census Office, Seventh Census of the United States [1850], Woodford County, Illinois, ms.).

4. Reva B. Siegel, "Home as Work: The First Woman's Rights Claims Concerning Wives' Household Labor, 1850–1880," *Yale Law Journal* 103 (March 1994): 1086–94; Dall, *College, the Market, and the Court,* 353–54. In *"A Secret to Be Burried": The Diary and Life of Emily Hawley Gillespie, 1858–1888* (Iowa City: University of Iowa Press, 1989), Judy Nolte Lensink records the life of a midwestern farm woman who was keenly aware of her contribution to the family profits and by the 1870s and 1880s was using her earnings to make purchases for both personal and family benefit.

5. "An Act in Relation to the Earnings of Married Women," 24 March 1869, *Public Laws of the State of Illinois* (1869), 255.

6. James Kent, *Commentaries on American Law* (1827; rpt., Buffalo: William S. Hein, 1984); St. George Tucker, *Blackstone's Commentaries, with Notes of Reference to the Constitution and Laws of the Federal Government of the United States and of the Commonwealth of Virginia*, 5 vols. (1803; rpt., New York: Augustus M. Kelley, 1969). These two commentaries were part of the basic education for antebellum lawyers. While they both espoused the paternal protections of coverture, they made different arguments in defending marital unity. See Norma Basch, *In the Eyes of the Law: Women, Marriage, and Property in Nineteenth-Century New York* (Ithaca, N.Y.: Cornell University Press, 1982), 60–64.

7. Tucker, *Blackstone's Commentaries*, 2:441.

8. James Kent, *Commentaries on American Law*, 2d ed. (1832), 2:106, quoted in Lawrence M. Friedman, *A History of American Law*, 2d ed. (New York: Simon and Schuster, 1985), 208.

9. Tucker, *Blackstone's Commentaries*, 2:441.

10. Kent, *Commentaries on American Law*, 2:109–21.

11. Dower was first codified in Illinois statutes in 1819, "An Act for the Speedy Assignment of Dower," 12 February 1819, *Laws of Illinois* (1819), 12–13; "An Act for the Speedy Assignment of Dower, and Partition of Real Estate," 6 February 1827, *Revised Code of Laws of Illinois* (1827), 183–87; "Dower," 3 March 1845, *Revised Statutes of the State of Illinois* (1845), 198–203.

12. Kermit L. Hall, *The Magic Mirror: Law in American History* (New York: Oxford University Press, 1989), 158–60.

13. John Mack Faragher, *Sugar Creek: Life on the Illinois Prairie* (New Haven, Conn.: Yale University Press, 1986), 138.

14. "Act for the Speedy Assignment of Dower," 12–13.

15. "Dower," 198–203.

16. Ibid., 200.

17. Salmon, for instance, found negligent enforcement of private examinations by officials in New York and Pennsylvania, while Massachusetts did not maintain any provisions for private examinations. See Marylynn Salmon, *Women and the Law of Property in Early America* (Chapel Hill: University of North Carolina Press, 1986), 6–7, 186–87.

18. Ibid., 199; Hall, *Magic Mirror*, 158–59.

19. "Property of Married Women," *(Springfield) Illinois State Register*, 5 April 1850. This act was similar to the New York law of 1848, which was the first of its kind.

20. "An Act to Protect Married Women in their Separate Property," 21 February 1861, *Public Laws of the State of Illinois* (1861), 140. In the narrow sense this reform did not aid women who could have benefited from receiving land from their indebted husbands in a trust. In a broader sense women gained because these acts began to recognize women as individuals with legal standing when it came to family property.

21. Hall, *Magic Mirror*, 159; Salmon, *Women and the Law of Property*, 96–97.

22. Elizabeth Bowles Warbasse, *The Changing Legal Rights of Married Women, 1800–1861* (New York: Garland, 1987), 300–7.

23. Ibid., 158–60; Friedman, *History of American Law*, 208–11.

24. Friedman, *History of American Law*, 210–11.

25. "Act to Protect Married Women," 140.

26. Petition for Dower, 15 November 1855, *Davenport v. Davenport et al.*, LPAL. Lucy

Davenport's petition claimed the land was acquired during coverture, which would have been August 23, 1843 (the date of John and Lucy Davenport's wedding) through May 31, 1852, when John Davenport died. John Davenport left three children: Lucy, born in 1846; Joseph, born in 1850; and Maria, who was probably an infant when her father died.

27. Minutes of Testimony, November 1855, *Davenport v. Davenport et al., LPAL.*

28. Deed of Trust, 24 May 1854, *Davenport v. Davenport et al., LPAL.*

29. Affidavit for Continuance, 8 October 1857, *Davenport v. Davenport et al., LPAL.*

30. Decree, 30 March 1857, *Davenport v. Davenport et al., LPAL;* Decree, 5 October 1858, *Davenport v. Davenport et al., LPAL.*

31. William H. Herndon, "An Unpublished Letter from Lincoln's Law Partner," in *Abraham Lincoln: Tributes from his Associates, Reminiscences of Soldiers, Statesmen, and Citizens* (New York: Thomas Y. Crowell, 1895), 20–21. Herndon was writing about women's voting rights but began the passage by reflecting generally on women's rights.

32. Dall, *College, the Market, and the Court,* 350–51.

33. Abraham Lincoln to Joseph Gillespie, 29 March 1850, *Lincoln conducted legal research for Stout, LPAL.*

34. L. Burlingame to Abraham Lincoln, 24 September 1859, *Burlingame asked Lincoln to represent Moor, LPAL.*

35. Abraham Lincoln to Joseph Means, 11 May 1858, *Lincoln provided legal advice to Means, LPAL.*

36. Surveyor's Appointment, March 1851, *Neale v. Britton, LPAL.*

37. Power of Attorney Appointment, 8 December 1855, *Mahoney v. Welles et al., LPAL;* Mary Welles to Abraham Lincoln, March 1855, *Welles et al. v. Hofferkemp et al., LPAL;* Mary Welles to Thompson, Green, and Co., 9 April 1855, *Welles et al. v. Hofferkemp et al., LPAL.*

38. Abraham Lincoln to John D. Johnston, 4 November 1851, in Roy P. Basler, ed., *The Collected Works of Abraham Lincoln,* 8 vols. (New Brunswick, N.J.: Rutgers University Press, 1953), 2:111–13.

39. William H. Davenport took over his father's property, valued at $2,000 in 1850, and eventually held six hundred acres of farmland in Woodford County. See Census Office, Seventh Census (1850), Woodford County; *Past and Present of Woodford County* (Chicago: LeBaron, 1878), 597–98.

According to probate papers, Lucy Davenport did receive $277.75 from the estate, along with basic personal property (bedding, kitchenware, milk cow, etc.) allowed by statute valued at $277.86½. Administrators sold John Davenport's personal property at auction for $1,032.74 to pay debts. See Lucy Davenport estate file, #138, Woodford County Circuit Court, Eureka, Illinois.

40. Of 107 dower cases from Sangamon County's first court session in 1821 through 1860, 62 (58 percent) had a decree allowing assignment of dower. Widows brought suit in 75 of the cases, and in 34 instances the widow was successful in obtaining a decree. See Sangamon County Circuit Court records, Illinois Regional Archives Depository, University of Illinois at Springfield, hereafter cited as ISRAD.

41. Faragher, *Sugar Creek,* 107.

42. Paulina Fobes estate file, #1097, Sangamon County Court, ISRAD.

43. Petition to Sell Real Estate, March term 1856, *Kirsch & Moffett v. Kirsch et al., LPAL;* Administrator's Report, 10 May 1856, *Kirsch & Moffett v. Kirsch et al., LPAL.*

44. Decree, 27 August 1859, *Kirsch v. Kirsch et al., LPAL.*

45. Decree and Master in Chancery's Report, 27 August 1863, *Herndon v. Kirsch et al.*, *LPAL*; Guardian's Report, 6 May 1864, *Herndon v. Kirsch et al.*, *LPAL*.

46. "Dower," 202.

47. Exhibit of Estate, 2 November 1839, *West v. Stevens et al.*, *LPAL*; Petition for Dower, 21 November 1839, *West v. Stevens et al.*, *LPAL*; Decree, November term 1839, *West v. Stevens et al.*, *LPAL*.

48. Agreed Statement of Facts, n.d., *McNutt et ux. v. Reynolds*, *LPAL*; Declaration, 8 May 1846, *McNutt et ux. v. Reynolds*, *LPAL*; Order, 20 October 1846, *McNutt et ux. v. Reynolds*, *LPAL*.

49. Quit Claim Deed, 29 August 1851, *Porter v. Ridgely*, *LPAL*; Quit Claim Deed, 2 September 1851, *Porter v. Fulkinson*, *LPAL*; Quit Claim Deed, 27 April 1854, *Porter v. Sangamon County*, *LPAL*; Quit Claim Deed, 27 April 1854, *Porter v. Porter*, *LPAL*; Quit Claim Deed, 23 February 1852, *Porter v. Hoffman et al.*, *LPAL*. The court assigned dower to Porter in *Porter v. Hoffman et al.* and *Porter v. Clinton*, *LPAL*.

50. Answer, 2 September 1851, *Porter v. Sangamon County*, *LPAL*; Quit Claim Deed, 27 April 1854, *Porter v. Sangamon County*, *LPAL*.

51. Decree, 2 March 1852, *Porter v. Hoffman et al.*, *LPAL*; Decree, 24 March 1852, *Porter v. Hoffman et al.*, *LPAL*; Quit Claim Deed, 23 February 1852, *Porter v. Hoffman et al.*, *LPAL*.

52. The court dismissed *Porter v. Sweet, Porter v. Campbell, Porter v. Hough, Porter v. Johnson, Porter v. Johnson, Porter v. Francis, Porter v. Stone, Porter v. Alkire, Porter v. Lindsay, Porter v. Tipton,* and *Porter v. Rose.* Porter reached settlements in *Porter v. Campbell, Porter v. Lyon, Porter v. Wright,* and *Porter v. Carpenter & Wood.* See Sangamon County Circuit Court, ISRAD. Porter also obtained settlements from James Sutton on March 4, 1852, for $100, Deed Record JJ, 116; James Troy on June 23, 1854, for $25, Deed Record PP, 233; and Aaron Biedler on November 3, 1855, for $30, Deed Record TT, 629, Sangamon County Court, ISRAD.

53. Andrew Porter alleged the insolvency of William Porter's estate in his answer. Answer, 6 April 1852, *Porter v. Porter*, *LPAL*; Bill of Appraisement, 9 May 1856, William Porter estate file #925, Sangamon County Court, ISRAD.

54. Richard H. Chused, "Married Women's Property Law, 1800–1850," *Georgetown Law Journal* 71 (1983): 1392–95.

55. Chused points out that the first reforms appeared in territorial Arkansas in 1835. Mississippi also reformed its laws regarding married women's property in 1839, and several states followed its example. See Chused, "Married Women's Property Law," 1398–400. Reformers regarded Illinois as liberal in certain aspects of family law. Dall notes that as early as 1829, married Illinois women could convey their property held in trust to anyone they chose, with or without their husband's approval. Illinois women also had the right of first refusal in administering their husband's estates and in serving as their children's guardian. See Dall, *College, the Market, and the Court,* 349–51.

56. Catherine Mischler estate file, #78, Sangamon County Court, ISRAD.

57. Nancy Sayles estate file, #278, Sangamon County Court, ISRAD.

58. Jane Davis estate file, #418, Sangamon County Court, ISRAD.

59. Margaret Renshaw, Will, Sangamon County Probate Record I&J, 422–27, ISRAD.

60. Elizabeth Morgan estate file, #1040, Sangamon County Court, ISRAD.

61. Elizabeth Mathews estate file, #884, Sangamon County Court, ISRAD.

62. Fobes estate file.

63. Elizabeth Langley estate file, #748, Sangamon County Court, ISRAD.

64. Faragher, *Sugar Creek,* 107.

65. Census Office, Seventh Census (1850), Sangamon County, Illinois, ms.

66. Faragher, *Sugar Creek,* 107.

67. Eliza Rape estate file, #1143, Sangamon County Court, ISRAD.

68. Elizabeth Trainer estate file, #908, Sangamon County Court, ISRAD.

69. Eliza J. Enos estate file, #1424, Sangamon County Court, ISRAD.

70. Joseph Wallace, *Past and Present of the City of Springfield and Sangamon County, Illinois,* 2 vols. (Chicago: S. J. Clarke Publishing, 1904), 2:997–98.

71. Fanny Hamby estate file, #110, Sangamon County Court, ISRAD.

72. Sarah Braken estate file, #63, Sangamon County Court, ISRAD.

73. Mary Firey estate file, #378, Sangamon County Court, ISRAD.

74. Margaret Renshaw estate file, #504, Sangamon County Court, ISRAD.

75. Jane McCann estate file, #804, Sangamon County Court, ISRAD.

76. Christiana Griffith estate file, #1023, Sangamon County Court, ISRAD.

77. Maria Barbara Beck estate file, #1460, Sangamon County Court, ISRAD.

78. Enos estate file.

79. Sarah Cannon estate file, #1341, Sangamon County Court, ISRAD.

80. Beverly Powell estate file, #660, Sangamon County Court, ISRAD.

81. *Lane v. Dolick et al.* in *McLean's Reports,* U.S. District Court of Illinois, October term 1854, 206.

82. *Lane v. Dolick et al.,* 200–209.

83. "Act to Protect Married Women," 140.

84. Ibid.

85. Warbasse, *Changing Legal Rights of Married Women,* 300–301.

PART 3

"Case" Studies

6

The Law in an Illinois Corner: The Impact of the Law on an Antebellum Family

STACY PRATT McDERMOTT

During the early nineteenth century immigrants from New England, the middle Atlantic states, and the South settled Illinois, and they brought their legal assumptions with them. Included among this common law baggage were specific patterns of settling inheritance and property disputes. Lawyers and lawmakers brought the common law to the frontier and used it, tested it, and eventually transformed it to suit the unique conditions of the prairie settlements it governed. While the state legislature outlined the structure of the law and the Illinois Supreme Court adjudicated the use of common law as precedent, the people governed by these rules were often miles and miles removed from the process of lawmaking. However, the law reached out from the state capital to even the most remote locales and directly affected the lives of individuals.

Nancy Robinson Dorman was one such individual. Her life and the story of her and her husband's bitter fifteen-year legal battle with her stepfather over the property of her deceased father illustrate the ways in which the law affected the lives of women. Nancy Dorman's struggle to assert her rightful claim to her father's estate became the basis for the convoluted and complex legal case of *Dorman et ux. v. Lane,* which went to the Illinois Supreme Court three times.[1] An examination of the case illustrates the process of estate administration and illuminates the vulnerable position that women and minors held in matters of the law and property. The case reveals the ways in which the structure of antebellum Illinois law viewed women and children as marginal, but it also reveals the intent of Illinois legislators, judges, and juries to protect women and children from the harsh realities of a male-dominated economic and social reality. The case offers an example of the legal position of women and children within the structure of antebellum Illinois law while documenting how one woman finally received judicial answers to her complicated legal and familial questions.

Although Nancy Dorman and her husband faced a complicated legal battle, like many other antebellum Illinois families they placed their faith in the law; through their persistence in that effort, they tested the limits of that law. Family-related issues represented an expanding component of circuit court dockets in Illinois. As the social, economic, and political landscape of the West altered and transformed familial relationships, Illinoisans sought answers to their questions of inheritance and property disputes from Illinois's fledgling legal system. They expected satisfaction in answers that the lawyers, judges, and juries provided, and they entrusted the law with the critical matters of their lives. In the *Dorman* case the opinion of the highest court in the state validated their personal faith in the law and represented the faith that many antebellum Americans placed in the laws that governed them. The *Dorman* case was a victory for the Dorman family and for other families faced with similar difficulties.

The documents and proceedings of *Dorman et ux. v. Lane* tell two complementary tales, one personal and one archetypical. The story of Nancy Robinson Dorman's pursuit of her legal claim to her father's estate is the story of the effect of the law on one antebellum Illinois woman. Surrounding the story of Nancy Dorman's personal legal experience lies the larger story of how the law affected women in antebellum Illinois and throughout the region. That story exposes with illustrative detail the legal situation of women and shows how they fared in matters of property before the bar in the years leading up to the Civil War. However, the case is not simply an example of a woman's challenge of a father's authority. The case also depicts the resolve of a young couple to challenge the authority of a prominent, politically connected man in order to gain ownership of a tract of land that had been a legacy from her father. The case illustrates the importance that antebellum families placed on the ownership of land and details their willingness to put themselves at risk in order to obtain it.[2]

This story began in the summer of 1815, when Christopher Robinson married Mary Lafferty in the heavily wooded and rolling hills of Gallatin County, Illinois. In 1819 the couple had a baby daughter, Nancy.[3] Life along the Ohio River in the southeastern corner of the newest state in the Union was good for the young family. Shawneetown, the center of the thriving river community in which the Robinsons lived, attracted a distinguished list of lawyers, politicians, and businessmen. The county offered many opportunities for industrious young men like Christopher Robinson, who amassed a considerable amount of property. Although no record regarding his occupation survives, Christopher Robinson appears to have steadily purchased land and heavily invested in Bank of Illinois stock.[4]

Gallatin County was home to a growing community of frontier families whose lives reflected the rise and fall of the waters of the Ohio River. The security of the county was set against the backdrop of those floodwaters, the wolves that inhabited the forests that blanketed the entire area, and the proximity of whites and Shawnee, who did not always share the frontier cooperatively.[5] Christopher Robinson made a good start for his family, but life on the Illinois frontier was unsettled and potentially dangerous. In late 1819 he died of unknown causes, leaving his young wife and baby daughter to fend off those dangers by themselves.

Christopher Robinson died intestate with considerable personal property and at least 480 acres of land in Shawneetown that his widow and daughter inherited according to the provisions of Illinois law. Widows received one-third of an estate's real and personal property as dower, and the surviving children shared the remainder equally.[6] As the sole child, Nancy Robinson was entitled to the remaining two-thirds of her father's estate and would receive the other third when her mother died.[7] Christopher Robinson also left behind considerable debts, including a note for $1,008.87 due to the Bank of Illinois, which became the principal liability of his estate.[8]

Mary Robinson served as administratrix and John Brown served as administrator of Christopher Robinson's estate.[9] By April 1823 the estate had settled nearly $1,000 of its debts to various creditors, including at least one outstanding promissory note for land that Christopher Robinson bought before he died. The two administrators were unsuccessful in collecting debts that others owed to the estate. When they were unable to satisfy the $1,008.87 debt, the Bank of Illinois agreed to renew the note, allowing Mary Robinson the extra time she needed to satisfy the debt. Later, after collecting more of the debts owed to the estate, a total of $1,574.69 in cash remained.[10]

The personal and real property that made up Mary Robinson's dower is unknown, but it probably was not sufficient to support her and her baby daughter indefinitely. In August 1821 she married John Lane.[11] Marriage was the most realistic economic and social option for widows. During this period on the Illinois frontier the death of a husband left the typical widow without any means of economic survival whatsoever, and these women had few choices. From the perspective of most widows, especially those with children, a man was necessary for economic survival. As a result, most widows chose to move in with parents or siblings or to remarry.[12]

According to early nineteenth-century standards, Christopher Robinson had prospered. However, even if he had lived long enough to amass a fortune large enough to support his widow and his daughter, it was extremely uncommon for widows, especially those as young as Mary Robinson, to remain unmarried. Twenty-seven-year-old John Lane was an affluent and prominent member of the community, an active member of the local Democratic Party, and one of the county commissioners who had granted Christopher Robinson an appointment as a road supervisor shortly before his death. Mary Robinson had probably known Lane through her husband's business dealings with him. As his wife, Mary Robinson would benefit from Lane's economic and social status and secure her daughter's future, and she probably accepted his proposal of marriage without much hesitation. To Mary Robinson, John Lane may have represented the economic protection she needed for her and her child against the severe conditions of the Illinois frontier. John Lane may have also offered Mary the emotional support and the companionship she lost when her husband died.[13]

As Mary Robinson Lane's husband, John Lane became a party to the promissory note that his wife, as administrator of her deceased husband's estate, owed the Bank of Illinois. He also gained legal control of the property of Christopher Robinson's estate. Mary Lane died in 1822, less than a year after marrying John Lane, leaving Nancy Robinson in the custody and care of her stepfather. Typically, a court-appointed guardian would take legal control of an orphaned child and perform custodial duties. In Nancy Robinson's case the court appointed no guardian, and John Lane, whose reputation in the county was that of a successful, respectable citizen, became her de facto guardian. Because Nancy Robinson was younger than fourteen, she was unable to choose her guardian, and apparently and perhaps unsurprisingly, no one challenged John Lane's assumption of the role of her guardian.[14] Although there is no legal record of his guardianship, his role in that capacity was probably that of a typical stepparent: he assumed responsibility for her care and support.

After Mary Robinson Lane's death, John Brown became the sole administrator of Christopher Robinson's estate. In 1826 he collected several debts still owed the estate and sold a quarter of a section of land and one lot in Shawneetown for $177. That additional income, combined with the prior balance of $1,574.69, equaled just over $2,500. John Brown also cashed nearly $1,500 in Bank of Illinois stock and dividends. By the end of the year the estate was nearly settled; the administrators had paid virtually all the debts, with the exception of the renewed note due to the Bank of Illinois.[15]

In 1826 John Lane satisfied the bank note out of his own assets, probably to gain complete legal control of his stepdaughter's inheritance. In November of the same year John Brown completed the settlement of Christopher

Robinson's estate, which the Gallatin County probate justice of the peace examined and signed into the record. John Lane then filed a suit in the Gallatin County Probate Court to obtain reimbursement from Christopher Robinson's estate, and the court ruled in his favor. The estate allegedly had no assets other than the real property that then belonged to Christopher Robinson's minor orphan daughter, Nancy Robinson, and was under the control of John Lane, who was acting as her guardian.

Perhaps uncertain of the authority of the probate court to sell the property to pay the debt, Lane, with the assistance of John Brown, petitioned the Illinois General Assembly to pass "An act authorizing the sale of lands belonging to the estate of Christopher Robinson, deceased," which it did on January 5, 1827.[16] In the years following the passage of this act John Brown, as the estate's surviving administrator, sold 480 acres of land in three parcels. George Addison Lane and Isaac Alexander Lane, two of John Lane's minor sons, purchased 160 acres for $300 and in November 1827 sold the land to their father for $307.[17] In May 1833 Samuel Seaton purchased 160 acres for $550 and John A. McClernand purchased the other 160 acres for $200.[18] Five years later McClernand conveyed to the State of Illinois a right-of-way through the acreage he had purchased from Robinson's estate to allow the Alton and Shawneetown Railroad to lay a single line of track through the property.[19] Whether John Lane and John A. McClernand manipulated the sale of land from Nancy's Robinson's inheritance in anticipation of the coming of the railroad is not clear. What is certain, however, is that through these careful transactions John Lane effectively stole his stepdaughter's inheritance. The estate received a total of $1,057 from these sales, a price that Nancy Robinson would later contend was well below the land's market value.

As a minor, Nancy Robinson had no legal standing.[20] She did not legally own the property of her inheritance, and she had no legal recourse against the manipulative actions of a stepfather who did not have her best interests in mind. All minor heirs in the antebellum period were at the mercy of those people who cared for them or, in some cases, those people who did not. The law's perception of children in antebellum America was changing, and in Illinois the courts used and expanded the English common law doctrine of *parens patriae*, which helped to protect a minor's property from misuse.[21] Illinois law provided protection for minors against the misdeeds of a guardian. In section 6 of "An Act Concerning Minors, Orphans, and Guardians," enacted in 1827, the law required that a court-appointed guardian "render a fair and just account of his said guardianship to the court of probate."[22]

Illinois law also gave courts of probate the power to remove guardians for "good and sufficient reasons" and appoint others.[23] The law for minors was firmly in place legislatively, but the question of Nancy Robinson's guardianship appears never to have been an issue. No documents that detail the exact legal situation of John Lane's guardianship of his stepdaughter survive, and the reasons why the probate court never interfered with John Lane's default status as her legal guardian are unknown. In the absence of a guardian, either familial or court appointed, who carefully protected children and the property they were to inherit, a minor heir and her inheritance were at risk.

When Nancy Robinson's mother died, John Lane became her only guardian. Illinois law possessed no authority to monitor or investigate John Lane's fitness for that role without a formal legal challenge. Nancy Robinson's situation was precarious, and her predicament was not uncommon.[24] In the cases of *Cowls v. Cowls* (1846) and *Young v. Lorain et al.* (1850) the Illinois Supreme Court would uphold the removal of guardians by ruling that the court of chancery had the power to remove them in all cases.[25] In those cases outside advocates of the minors in question recognized the legal insecurity of the minors' interests and acted on their behalf. Unfortunately, Nancy Robinson had no such advocates.

In 1837, ten years after her stepfather gained control of a portion of her inheritance, eighteen-year-old Nancy Robinson married William M. Dorman (1812–64), a young farmer, in Gallatin County. Dorman was not a wealthy man, and the property that his new wife had lost to her stepfather's family certainly would have been appealing. Nancy Robinson Dorman may have remained bitter about what she felt to be her stepfather's mismanagement of her father's estate. Perhaps she resented her stepfather's care over the years.[26] Whatever the motivating factor, on June 23, 1837, the Dormans filed an ejectment suit in Gallatin County Circuit Court against John Lane and his heirs to recover the property he had sold, including the 160 acres that the estate had sold to Lane's sons.[27] By that time both of Lane's sons had died, and although details regarding their deaths are unknown, records show that John Lane was in possession of the property in question at the time the Dormans brought the suit. At any rate, filing suit against such a powerful individual probably represented an enormous risk for the young, struggling farm couple. William Dorman, a staunch Democrat, jeopardized his personal standing among Democratic leaders of the county, who wielded significant political, economic, and social power in the region. William and Nancy Dorman's lawsuit was also likely to anger her politically connected stepfather. Given the risks of filing such a lawsuit, the land in question must have been important to the Dormans; regardless of the risks, William Dorman initiated the suit on behalf of his wife.

Nancy Dorman again had no legal standing, this time as the result of her marital status rather than her age.[28] Coverture, which institutionalized women's marginal status, denied her and all married women the right to own property or file a suit in a court of law in their own names.[29] William Blackstone's oft-quoted description details the harsh reality of coverture: "The very being or legal existence of the woman is suspended during the marriage, or at least is . . . consolidated into that of the husband: under whose wing, protection, and cover, she performs every thing."[30] For Nancy Dorman to gain possession of the real property of her inheritance, her husband had to file the suit on her behalf. If their suit was successful, Nancy Dorman would still not legally own the property. Although she would obviously benefit financially from her husband's ownership of the property, William Dorman would be the direct beneficiary of any judgment they obtained because marital unity declared that the couple was a single legal entity.[31]

In the November 1837 term of the Gallatin County Circuit Court, at which Judge Walter B. Scates presided, the jury found that the 1827 legislative act that had allowed John Brown, the estate's administrator, to sell Christopher Robinson's property was unconstitutional because it had invaded the province of the judicial branch.[32] The court then invalidated the estate sale and found for the plaintiffs. John Lane immediately appealed the decision to the Illinois Supreme Court. One of the attorneys that he retained for the appeal was a political ally, John A. McClernand, who had previously purchased 160 acres from Robinson's estate and used it for the Alton and Shawneetown Railroad right-of-way. In the assignment of errors McClernand argued that the circuit court's ruling for the Dormans in the ejectment suit was unconstitutional because it had rejected the authority of the legislative act that had allowed John Lane to sell land to pay the debts from Christopher Robinson's estate.[33]

The Illinois Supreme Court thought otherwise. In the December 1841 term the state's highest court affirmed the lower court's judgment for the Dormans.[34] In the opinion Associate Justice Theophilus W. Smith carefully examined common law precedent and stated clearly the statutory intent of legislative acts to relieve creditors. During the antebellum period it was common for the Illinois General Assembly to pass acts to relieve creditors with claims against indebted estates.[35] The acts generally called for the sale of property, the proceeds of which were divided among the creditors. Smith wrote that those acts to relieve creditors "were for the benefit of all the creditors of the estates without distinction."[36]

The Illinois Supreme Court said the state legislature had passed an unconstitutional act and argued that when legislators passed "An act authorizing the sale of lands belonging to the estate of Christopher Robinson, de-

The Illinois State Capitol in Springfield, where the Illinois Supreme Court heard the appeals of William and Nancy Dorman in 1841, 1844, and 1851. Courtesy of the Illinois State Historical Library, Springfield.

ceased," they directed "the sale for the benefit of two persons exclusively," thereby violating the fundamental basis for such acts.[37] The Illinois General Assembly had discriminated in favor of two creditors over the interests of others. Smith concluded his opinion by declaring the court's "conviction that the act is in direct conflict with the provisions of the constitution cited, and it is consequently inoperative and void."[38]

John Lane was probably fairly certain his appeal in the ejectment suit would fail, because immediately after his attorneys filed the appeal in the Illinois Supreme Court, Lane petitioned the Gallatin County Probate Court to grant him the authority to act *de bonis non administratis* (to complete the administration of Christopher Robinson's estate).[39] In December 1837 the court granted Lane the ability to administer the unsettled part of Christopher Robinson's estate. The jury in the ejectment suit had declared the original sale of the 480 acres void; therefore, the land reverted to the estate as unsettled. Lane argued that the $1,008.87 debt, which he had incurred when he paid the Bank of Illinois note for the estate in 1826, was also unsettled. In the September 1841 term Lane, as the new administrator of Christopher Robinson's estate, filed a petition to sell real estate in the Gallatin County Circuit Court to pay the unsettled debts of the estate.

The legal battle between John Lane and William and Nancy Dorman must have generated considerable interest in the community, because the case featured an impressive cast of legal practitioners. In addition to McClernand, Lane hired Henry Eddy, a distinguished member of the Shawneetown bar, who would die before the conclusion of the case.[40] Samuel D. Marshall (1812–54) and Edward Jones represented the Dormans. In the fall of 1841 Marshall, a confident twenty-nine-year-old Yale graduate, was a well-respected member of the southern Illinois bar and a prominent Illinois Whig. As editor of a Whig newspaper, Marshall's standing in the community was impressive. Although Jones was well known in Gallatin County as an eccentric, loud-talking man, he enjoyed an excellent reputation as a skilled Whig lawyer.[41] The case likely represented a politically charged battleground for Gallatin County political factions, a virtual war between strong-willed Whig and Democratic Party operatives. Although no records survive that would conclusively document the charge, Marshall may have taken on the Dormans' case as a political assault on John Lane, a former sheriff and prominent Gallatin County Democrat.[42]

As the sitting judge of the Third Judicial Circuit, Illinois Supreme Court Justice Walter B. Scates presided over the case of *Lane v. Dorman et ux.*[43] In September 1842 the court granted the petition to sell real estate, allowing Lane to resell the property in question. Adding another prominent individual to the case's list of participants, Marshall immediately contacted Abraham Lincoln in Springfield to handle the Dormans' appeal to the Illinois Supreme Court. Lincoln and Marshall were friends and fellow Whigs, and Marshall probably asked for Lincoln's support because of the two attorneys' mutual political interests but also because Lincoln was developing a statewide reputation as a capable appellate attorney.

In a letter to Marshall dated November 11, 1842, Lincoln wrote that he had "looked into the Dorman and Lane case till I believe I understand the facts of it; and I also believe we can reverse it. In the last I may be mistaken, but I think the case at least worth the experiment." He agreed to take the case on a contingency fee basis, writing: "I will do my best for the 'biggest kind of a fee' as you say, if we succeed, and nothing if we fail."[44] Lincoln was perhaps simply doing a favor for a friend, but given his political intentions, Lincoln may have taken the appeal to maintain ties to Marshall as a strong political ally in southern Illinois. By taking the case, Lincoln was assisting a fellow Whig as well as working for a potentially large fee.[45]

William Dorman filed his $1,500 appeal bond on December 3, 1842.[46] With the contingency fee agreement in place, Lincoln filed the assignment of errors in the case five days later. Lyman Trumbull, a prominent attorney and Illinois secretary of state—later a state supreme court justice and U.S. senator—entered the joinder in error for John Lane.[47] Trumbull was also a Democrat.

In the assignment of errors Lincoln outlined six specific points of fact that he believed the lower court had failed to consider in its judgment for Lane. First, Lane had received $300 worth of bank dividends related to his $1,008.87 payment to the Bank of Illinois, and the court should have viewed Lane's receipt of those dividends as an offsetting payment against the estate's debt to Lane. Second, the court rejected evidence of Lane's receipt of mesne profits, which in this case was the value of Lane's use of the land from Christopher Robinson's estate while he had held possession of it.[48] Third, Robinson's estate did possess sufficient personal effects to pay the estate's debts. Fourth, Lane should have applied to the debt the profits from the estate's sale of land. Fifth, Lane's possession of the land should also have applied to the debt. Sixth and finally, the lower court should not have allowed the sale of the land in the first place.[49]

In February 1843 Lincoln presented these arguments before the Illinois Supreme Court at Springfield and honed his final point by adding that any sale of the property in question was barred and destroyed when the administrator failed to make such application before the time set in the statutes— one year—had elapsed. Trumbull, appearing for Lane, argued that Lincoln was now introducing errors that he had not included in the original filing. According to Trumbull's argument, the court should not look at those errors, however flagrant they may have appeared. Trumbull also rejected the evidence that Lincoln proffered: Lane's receipt of money before his petition to sell the land to cover the estate's debt to him. Early in March the court continued the case to the next term. Then, during the December 1843 term the court continued the case for another year.

During the December 1844 term the Illinois Supreme Court ordered the attorneys for Lane and the Dormans to reargue the case.[50] Finally, late in January 1845 the Illinois Supreme Court reversed and remanded the lower court's verdict for Lane. In his opinion for the court Justice James Shields wrote that Lane had allowed fifteen years to pass before applying for the sale of real estate to pay the estate's debt to him and that "it would be extremely hazardous for this court to sanction such gross negligence, and particularly in a case where the same person was both administrator and creditor." Shields went on to add that John Lane "permitted the order to lie dormant for the space of fifteen years, to continue a lien upon the real estate, and after such an extraordinary lapse of time, he applies to the circuit court, and without offering any excuse for this unreasonable delay."[51]

On this point Shields cited the sixth section of an amendment to an act relative to the settlement of estates. The amendment, which the Illinois General Assembly approved in February 1831, stated that "no suit shall be brought against any executor or administrator for or on account of any claim or demand against the intestator or intestate, unless such suit shall be brought within one year next after such executor or administrator shall have settled his accounts with the court of probate."[52] He also noted that in the lower court, the Dormans had provided proof of Lane's receipt of $300 in bank dividends. The court further found that Lane had benefited personally, and not as administrator, from mesne profits and that the lower court had erred by refusing to allow testimony and evidence regarding those profits. The lower court had not evaluated evidence of potential set-offs of the debt to Lane in the form of both the dividends and mesne profits.

Through this case the Illinois Supreme Court established a new rule in the law of estate administration: after one year had passed since the settlement of an estate, the estate's administrator could not sell the estate's real property to pay debts. Rather than simply determining that fifteen years was excessive in this case, the court ruled specifically on the point of time and eliminated the possibility of future appeals questioning the appropriate time allowable between the settlement of an estate and the sale of property to pay debts.[53]

The supreme court's decision had two direct effects in the case of *Dorman et ux. v. Lane.* It permitted Lane to amend his petition in the circuit court to sell real estate and seek an exception to the one-year rule, and it forced the circuit court to consider the evidence regarding mesne profits. In a separate opinion of the court Scates, who had been the presiding judge in the lower-court decision, agreed with the reversal of the circuit court's decision, although not for the reasons stated in Shields's opinion. In effect, Scates was agreeing with the reversal of a verdict over which he had presided.[54] In a separate opinion Scates argued that the probate court was actually in a better position to rule on the circumstances of Christopher Robinson's estate settlement and administration. He questioned the jurisdiction of the circuit court to rule on the matter.

In June 1845, a few months after the supreme court's decision, Lincoln wrote to Marshall: "I learn this morning at the clerk's office that Lane has not, as yet, taken out the order remanding it [the *Dorman* case]; and I think it possible he may have abandoned it."[55] Lane, however, had done no such thing. The high court's decision had not discouraged him. He was still determined to deny his stepdaughter her inheritance.

On December 30, 1845, Lincoln wrote Marshall that Lane had filed a new petition in the Gallatin County Circuit Court "to avoid paying the cost of taking the case between Dorman and him back from the Supreme Court." Lincoln also wrote that he "together with Judge Logan, will try to frame a plea within law or in abatement, out of the fact of the pendency of the old case, that shall blow them up with their new case." He also noted that Lane was nearly out of time. Illinois law required that a remanded supreme court case be refiled in the circuit court within one year. Lincoln asked Marshall to keep quiet about the time limitation "lest they hear of it, and take the claim."[56] At that point Marshall took over as the Dormans' attorney in the new action before the circuit court.

Lane had asked the Gallatin County Circuit Court to reinstate the original action against the Dormans and retry his case for a petition to sell the 480 acres previously sold to settle John Lane's claim against Christopher Robinson's estate. On October 30, 1846, Marshall filed William Dorman's affidavit requesting a change of venue from Gallatin County. In the affidavit Dorman declared that "he verily fears that he will not receive a fair trial of the said cause in said court on account that the honorable judge of said court is prejudiced."[57]

Samuel Marshall perhaps also felt that John Lane's status in Gallatin County was such that potential jurors and court officials would be biased against the Dormans. The court agreed with Dorman's request for a change of venue and moved the trial to nearby White County. Because Scates was sitting as the circuit court judge there as well, the court probably granted the request for reasons other than a prejudiced judge. Whatever the reason, on March 13, 1847, Lane's attorneys filed an amended petition in the White County Circuit Court to sell real estate. Attorneys for the Dormans filed their demurrer to the amended petition. Yet after one continuance the court overruled the demurrer and found that the amended petition was sufficient in law and would stand as filed.[58]

After at least nine witnesses testified and the court had granted a handful of continuances, Scates ruled during the March 1849 term. On March 3 the court denied the Dormans' claim and allowed Lane to sell the property once again. A dejected Marshall wrote Lincoln on April 20, 1849, detailing the loss. Marshall wrote that he felt "more interest in this case than all the business put together to which I ever attended."[59] While Marshall had originally taken the case for political reasons, he had developed a personal attachment to the Dormans' cause. What had started as a political assault against John Lane and a circle of powerful Gallatin County Democrats had become a personal struggle to help the Dormans regain the land to which they were entitled. Perhaps Marshall had assumed a paternal responsibility to secure Nancy Dorman's inheritance. He had, in effect, become the advocate that she had lacked as a child. After consulting with other attorneys, including Lincoln, as to the validity of another appeal, Marshall decided to appeal the decision from the White County Circuit Court to the Illinois Supreme Court. Dorman filed an appeal bond in May, and the case began its third journey to the highest court in the state.

On August 8, 1849, John Lane died, and the Dormans suffered yet another delay in their long legal battle. Appellee attorneys asked the court to substitute the name of John C. Yost on the docket. Yost, Lane's son-in-law and the administrator of his estate, asked the court for a continuance, which it granted. In November 1850 Scates, no longer a justice of the Illinois Supreme Court, represented Yost and asked that his client be made party to the appeal. Scates's involvement in the case as a litigator at this point may well have confirmed the Dormans' complaint that the judge had been prejudiced against them.

After another continuance Lincoln filed the assignment of errors in December 1851, arguing that the White County Circuit Court had "ordered the sale of the lands, where as it should not have." Again, Lincoln argued on six points. First, the lower court should have barred Lane from selling the land because the appropriate time for a sale had passed. Second, the order did not "ascertain the amount of debt for which the land is ordered to be sold." Third, the lower court did not determine whether selling only part of the two tracts in question might be sufficient. Fourth, Lane's attorneys presented "nothing of the proceedings of the administrator de bonis non." Fifth, the court failed to consider the value of the personal property of Christopher Robinson's estate in settling the debt to Lane. Sixth, the court made a $1,008.87 allowance to the administrators (John Brown and John Lane) in the estate settlement "without any person being appointed by the Probate court to contest their claim."[60]

Lincoln's sixth point referred to the failure of the court to appoint a guardian *ad litem* to protect Nancy Robinson's interests as Christopher Robinson's minor heir. John Lane had been Nancy Robinson's guardian by default, but he did not have legal standing in that role. As noted earlier, Illinois law required the appointment of a guardian for the legal benefit of minor heirs who had interest in the lands being sold. Nancy Robinson had no such protection.

By 1852 the Illinois Supreme Court consisted of only three justices—Chief Justice Samuel H. Treat, Justice John D. Caton, and Justice Lyman Trumbull, who had previously served as Lane's attorney in the lower court.[61] On January 31, 1852, the supreme court reversed the decree of the White County Circuit Court that allowed John Lane to sell the land. In a simply argued, very brief opinion in which he cited no authorities, Treat found that the estate's debt to the Bank of Illinois was fully satisfied through the 1827 sale of land and that "it was not revised by the subsequent recovery of the lands by the heir." He added that only the purchasers of the original land sold had any cause to complain and that none had ever made any attempt to recover the

The reconstructed courtroom in which Lincoln represented the Dormans before the Illinois Supreme Court. Court was held in this room from 1839 to 1876. Courtesy of the Lincoln Legal Papers, Springfield, Illinois.

purchase price. Ironically, of course, John Lane's sons had been two of the original purchasers.

The language and tone of Justice Treat's opinion suggest the court was irritated by John Lane's repeated attempts to maintain possession of his step-daughter's inheritance. Treat wrote that "there is an insuperable objection to this petition." In closing, Treat adamantly noted that "the petition does not disclose the least necessity for the application; and the court consequently erred in overruling the demurrer, and in granting a license to sell the real estate. The judgment is reversed."[62]

Thirty-two years after Christopher Robinson's death and fifteen years after the Dormans initiated their legal battle with John Lane, Nancy Robinson Dorman's struggle to gain possession of her father's estate was finally over. Nancy Dorman died in 1851 or 1852, nearly ten years before the passage in 1861 of Illinois's Married Women's Property Act, which granted married women the legal standing necessary to own land in their own names.[63] On May 8, 1853, William Dorman finalized the end to his and his wife's long and bitter legal struggle by settling their attorney's fees. Lincoln received $100 for his legal services in the case and signed a quitclaim deed voiding the bond that the Dormans had signed back in 1845. Later that month Samuel Marshall also accepted $100 for representing the Dormans. Both the Dormans and their attorneys had invested a great deal of time, passion, and energy in the effort, and after three grueling circuit court trials and three trips to the Illinois Supreme Court, the Dormans had full right to and possession of Nancy Dorman's inheritance. The value of the land at the time is unknown, but it was worth at least $1,200, and probably more than twice that amount, and well worth the $200 in legal fees.[64] According to surviving records, the Dorman family maintained that hard-earned property. William Dorman farmed the land, raised five sons, and prospered. By 1860 he had accumulated real estate holdings totaling $6,000 and personal property worth $800.[65]

William Dorman died in the spring of 1864. His widow and second wife, Sophia Dorman, filed a petition for partition to divide the real property of her husband's estate, including the land for which William and Nancy Dorman had fought so hard. The petition asked the court to divide the property among the widow, Sophia Dorman; William and Nancy Dorman's sons; and William and Sophia Dorman's four children. The commissioners appointed in the partition case found no equitable way to divide the property among the heirs and sold the land to settle the estate. Upon the settlement of William Dorman's estate later that year, William and Nancy Dorman's children received the final benefits of the inheritance that their grandfather had left nearly forty-five years earlier.[66]

It may appear ironic that after the Dormans' long personal and legal battle to retain their property, Christopher Robinson's grandchildren did not inherit the land. The economic realities of the frontier directly affected the lives of the Dorman family, as had the law. Nancy and William Dorman were undaunted. They accepted their struggles like most antebellum Illinoisans and took pleasure in the resulting triumphs wedged between the hardships. For them, ownership of the land, even for a time, was worth the struggle. After all, owning their own land was why most settlers went west into Illinois and beyond in the first place.

Throughout their lives Nancy Robinson Dorman and William Dorman, who was a staunch Democrat, felt sincere appreciation for the men who had fought their legal fight and brought Illinois law to life in their little corner of the state. In 1846 the couple named their fourth son Samuel in honor of Samuel Marshall, despite their beloved attorney's active participation in Illinois Whig politics. William Dorman also remained a loyal friend and supporter of Abraham Lincoln and campaigned for Lincoln during the senatorial and presidential races. Years after the case Frank Eddy, the son of attorney Henry Eddy, remembered that his friend William Dorman had said many times that "Lincoln and Marshall recovered my wife's land and made me what I am and would not charge me a cent and I will vote and fight for them to show my gratitude." The younger Eddy also remembered that had Nancy Dorman lived to have another son, the couple would have named him after Abraham Lincoln.[67] The Dormans' appreciation reveals the importance they placed on the property in question and the meaning they attached to their struggle for Nancy Dorman's inheritance. The Dormans put their trust in the hands of two respectable and capable attorneys, Lincoln and Marshall, who understood their struggle and successfully navigated the legal system to obtain justice for their clients. Their faith in the legal system was not uncommon in antebellum Illinois. More and more families were turning to the courts to solve the challenging issues in their increasingly complicated family relationships.

The Dormans were in many ways a typical antebellum family. Property, inheritance, and estate administration were concerns for families across the state and throughout the country, and family dynamics played a significant role in how those issues played out in each family that faced them. The Illinois Supreme Court's ultimate opinion in the Dormans' legal struggle reflects the court's responsiveness to antebellum petitioners in family matters. As family-related legal issues became a growing part of the court dockets in jurisdictions throughout the United States, families like the Dormans increasingly used the courts to settle important issues in their ever-changing family circumstances. The law was not removed from the corners of the state and the remote localities of the nation; rather, the law permeated society at all levels in such a way as to embrace it, inform it, and shape it.

Notes

1. *Et ux.* was a common abbreviation of *et uxor,* "and wife." The foundation of the contextual research for this case is the work of William D. Beard in a case presentation published by the Lincoln Legal Papers. Susan Krause also contributed to that effort. This essay borrows heavily from their research, and I am grateful for their earlier contributions. Although no scholarship regarding the frontier Illinois family exists and few studies have integrated the history of the law, this study of one Illinois family's legal experiences is grounded by many historical studies of the colonial and antebellum American family, including Norma Basch, *In the Eyes of the Law: Women, Marriage, and Property in Nineteenth-Century New York* (Ithaca, N.Y.: Cornell University Press, 1982); Stephanie Coontz, *The Social Origins of Private Life: A History of American Families, 1600–1900* (London: Verso, 1988); Carl N. Degler, *At Odds: Women and the Family in America from the Revolution to the Present* (New York: Oxford University Press, 1980); Michael Grossberg, *Governing the Hearth: Law and the Family in Nineteenth-Century America* (Chapel Hill: University of North Carolina Press, 1985); Steven Mintz, *A Prison of Expectations: The Family in Victorian Culture* (New York: New York University Press, 1985); and Helena M. Wall, *Fierce Communion: Family and Community in Early America* (Cambridge, Mass.: Harvard University Press, 1990). These contributions to the history of the American family form a foundation for understanding the general circumstances of American families and provide much of the context for an understanding of this complicated case study in Illinois family law.

2. James E. Davis, *Frontier Illinois* (Bloomington: Indiana University Press, 1998), 218.

3. Nancy Robinson's birth date is unknown. She may well have been born in 1820 after her father's death.

4. Copy of Statement of Estate Settlement, 30 November 1826, *Dorman et ux. v. Lane,* in *The Law Practice of Abraham Lincoln: Complete Documentary Edition,* ed. Martha L. Benner and Cullom Davis et al. (DVD; Urbana: University of Illinois Press, 2000), hereafter cited as *LPAL.*

5. For detailed geographical and historical descriptions of Gallatin County, see *History of Gallatin, Saline, Hamilton, Franklin and Williamson Counties, Illinois* (Chicago: Goodspeed, 1887), 13–28.

6. Dower represented a life estate for a widow. She had full right to one-third of the real and personal property of her husband's estate for use during her lifetime. See "An Act for the Speedy Assignment of Dower, and Partition of Real Estate," 6 February 1827, *Revised Code of Laws of Illinois* (1827), 183–87; "An Act to Regulate Administrations and the Descent of Intestate Estates, and for Other Purposes," 23 March 1819, *Laws of the State of Illinois* (1819), 230–31. Dower assignment of one-third of the deceased husband's estate was typical, and most men died intestate (see Jane H. Pease and William H. Pease, *Ladies, Women, and Wenches: Choice and Constraint in Antebellum Charleston and Boston* [Chapel Hill: University of North Carolina Press, 1990], 105). The one-third rule had also been the standard in the colonial and early national periods (see Mary Beth Norton, *Founding Mothers and Fathers: Gendered Power and the Forming of American Society* [New

York: Alfred A. Knopf, 1996], 111). For a description of the legal provisions for widows in the United States, see Marylynn Salmon, *Women and the Law of Property in Early America* (Chapel Hill: University of North Carolina Press, 1986), 141–84.

7. Throughout the eighteenth and nineteenth centuries, land could pass to daughters either through intestacy distributions or through wills (Norton, *Founding Mothers and Fathers,* 114).

8. For a general overview of women and inheritance in America, see Carole Shammas, Marylynn Salmon, and Michel Dahlin, "Inheritance Law and the Rights of Women and Children in the Nineteenth Century," in *Inheritance in America from Colonial Times to the Present* (New Brunswick, N.J.: Rutgers University Press, 1987), 83–101.

9. Illinois estate law provided the decedent's spouse with the right to administer the estate. If the spouse relinquished this right, the law allowed a family member the next opportunity before creditors of the estate could apply. John Brown was a farmer in Gallatin County, Illinois (Gallatin County Court Will Record, I:67).

10. Copy of Statement of Estate Settlement, 30 November 1826, *Dorman et ux. v. Lane, LPAL.*

11. John Lane (1794–1849) was born in Kentucky and was one of the earliest settlers of Gallatin County. He was a shopkeeper, sheriff, county commissioner, militia captain, director of the State Bank of Illinois, and unsuccessful candidate for both houses of the Illinois General Assembly. See *History of Gallatin . . . Counties,* 43, 61, 122.

12. For a detailed history of women's experiences in this period farther to the east, see Nancy F. Cott, *The Bonds of Womanhood: "Women's Sphere" in New England, 1780–1835* (New Haven, Conn.: Yale University Press, 1977).

13. Anya Jabour describes the ideal of companionate marriage in *Marriage in the Early Republic: Elizabeth and William Wirt and the Companionate Ideal* (Baltimore: Johns Hopkins University Press, 1998).

14. For the law on guardians see "An Act Concerning Minors, Orphans and Guardians," 2 February 1827, *Revised Code of Laws of Illinois* (1827), 301.

15. Copy of Statement of Estate Settlement, 30 November 1826, *Dorman et ux. v. Lane, LPAL.*

16. By statute the probate courts in Illinois had the authority to sell real estate to pay the debts of an estate. The law protected dower rights against such sales. See "An Act Authorizing the Sale of Lands Belonging to the Estate of Christopher Robinson, Deceased," 5 January 1827, *Laws of the State of Illinois* (1827), 5.

17. Gallatin County Circuit Court Deed Record D, 5 May 1833, 4–5; Gallatin County Circuit Court Deed Record D, 31 May 1833, 6–8.

18. Gallatin County Circuit Court Deed Record H, 5 May 1838, 314–16.

19. No deed record of the Lanes' purchase survives, but the amount represents the total realized from the sale of the land by Brown ($1,057) minus the two separate sales of $550 and $200 for which deed records are available. For John Lane's purchase of the land from his sons, see Gallatin County Circuit Court Deed Record A, 30 November 1827, 327–28.

20. Sec. 2 of "An Act to Amend an Act, Entitled 'An Act Concerning Practice in Courts of Law,'" 9 February 1831, *Laws of the State of Illinois* (1831), 113–14, allowed minors to sue by a next friend, an adult who assumed responsibility for the court costs in the case. However, without knowledge of such a legal provision and without an advocate, a child as young as Nancy Robinson had no legal standing.

21. Grossberg, *Governing the Hearth,* 142.

22. "Act Concerning Minors," 301–2.

23. Ibid., 302.

24. Wall, *Fierce Communion*, 149.

25. *Cowls v. Cowls*, 8 Ill. (3 Gilman) 435 (1846); *Young v. Lorain et al.*, 11 Ill. 624 (1850).

26. By the beginning of the nineteenth century social and economic forces were challenging the ideal of a father's sovereign rule, and Nancy Dorman's willingness to challenge her stepfather's management of her inheritance represents that shift. See Steven Mintz and Susan Kellogg, *Domestic Revolutions: A Social History of American Family Life* (New York: Free Press, 1988), 55.

27. Ejectment was a common legal action used to regain possession of real property and damages for unlawful detention.

28. Norma Basch discusses the legal ramifications of marital unity in "Invisible Women: The Legal Fiction of Marital Unity in Nineteenth-Century America," *Feminist Studies* 5 (Summer 1979), reprinted in *History of Women in the United States*, ed. Nancy F. Cott, vol. 3: *Domestic Relations and Law* (Munich: K. G. Suar, 1992), 132–52. Three other major contributions to the understanding of the history of women and their roles in society inform this study: Cott, *Bonds of Womanhood;* Linda Kerber, "Separate Spheres, Female Worlds, Woman's Place: The Rhetoric of Women's History," *Journal of American History* 75 (June 1988): 9–39; and Laura McCall and Donald Yacovone, eds., *A Shared Experience: Men, Women, and the History of Gender* (New York: New York University Press, 1998).

29. Norma Basch, "The Emerging Legal History of Women in the United States: Property, Divorce, and the Constitution," *Signs: Journal of Women in Culture and Society* 12 (Autumn 1986): 100.

30. St. George Tucker, *Blackstone's Commentaries, with Notes of Reference to the Constitution and Laws of the Federal Government of the United States and of the Commonwealth of Virginia*, 5 vols. (1803; rpt., New York: Augustus M. Kelley, 1969), 2:442.

31. Pease and Pease, *Ladies, Women, and Wenches*, 90–91.

32. *Lane et al. v. Doe ex dem. Dorman et ux.*, 4 Ill. 237 (1841).

33. Assignment of Errors, 1 January 1840, *Lane et al. v. Doe ex dem. Dorman et ux.*, Illinois Supreme Court (I-SC) case file 967, Illinois State Archives.

34. The Illinois Supreme Court justices who heard the appeal were Chief Justice William Wilson and associate justices Thomas C. Browne, Samuel D. Lockwood, Theophilus W. Smith, Sidney Breese, Walter B. Scates, Samuel H. Treat, and Stephen A. Douglas.

35. The Illinois General Assembly passed dozens of these private acts between 1818 and the enactment of the 1842 Federal Bankruptcy Act.

36. *Lane et al. v. Doe ex dem. Dorman et ux.*, 4 Ill. 244 (1841).

37. Ibid.

38. Ibid., 245.

39. *De bonis non administratis* means "of the goods not administered." When an administrator was appointed to succeed another who had left the estate partially unsettled, he was said to be granted administration *de bonis non;* that is, of the goods not already administered. See *Black's Law Dictionary*, 5th ed. (St. Paul, Minn.: West, 1979), 363.

40. John Alexander McClernand (1812–1900) was admitted to the bar in 1832 and became a successful and prominent attorney in Illinois. Editor of the *Gallatin (Ill.) Democrat* and *(Shawneetown) Illinois Advertiser*, he was a staunch Jacksonian Democrat and antiabolitionist who went on to become a general in the Union Army. See "John A. Mc-

Clernand," Biography, *LPAL;* John M. Palmer, *The Bench and Bar of Illinois* (Chicago: Lewis, 1899), 194–95.

Eddy was a Whig, but his popularity among Shawneetown Democrats suggests that party politics played a less important role in his standing in the community. He was a popular newspaper editor and well-known attorney. Shawneetown, which was a Democratic stronghold, elected Eddy, despite his Whig connections, to serve as its representative to the state's first constitutional convention. Lane must have hired Eddy for his talents as a lawyer and not for his political affiliation. See Palmer, *Bench and Bar,* 853–54.

41. Palmer, *Bench and Bar,* 852.

42. John Lane was a lifelong Democrat and for a time identified politically with the radical Locofoco Democrats. In 1840 he served as a delegate at the group's Illinois convention (*Sangamo [Springfield, Ill.] Journal,* 28 February 1840).

43. Walter Bennett Scates (1808–87) became judge of the Third Judicial Circuit in Illinois in 1836. He served as an Illinois Supreme Court justice from 1841 until 1847. He was reelected to the bench in 1853 and became chief justice of the court two years later. Between his tenures on the court he maintained a successful law practice. He later served in the Civil War under Gen. John A. McClernand. See "Walter B. Scates," Biography, *LPAL.*

44. Abraham Lincoln to Samuel Marshall, 11 November 1842, *Dorman et ux. v. Lane, LPAL.* In February 1845 the Dormans signed a bond for deed in which they agreed to convey eighty acres of land to their attorneys—Lincoln, Marshall, and Jones—if the lawyers successfully represented them.

45. David Herbert Donald, *Lincoln* (New York: Simon and Schuster, 1995), 110.

46. Appeal bond, 19 November 1842, *Dorman et ux. v. Lane, LPAL.*

47. Lyman Trumbull (1813–96) was admitted to the Illinois bar in 1837, enjoyed a successful legal practice, and served as an Illinois Supreme Court justice from 1848 to 1853. After his service on the court he went on to a successful political career as a member of Congress, both as a representative and as a senator. He spent most of his political life as a Democrat but joined the Republican Party after its formation in 1856. See "Lyman Trumbull," Biography, *LPAL.*

48. Mesne profits are the value of the use or occupation of land, usually measured in rents and profits, during the time someone possessed the land, such as the period that John Lane held Nancy Robinson Dorman's inheritance. See *Black's Law Dictionary,* 1090.

49. Assignment of Errors, 8 December 1842, *Dorman et ux. v. Lane, LPAL.*

50. The supreme court in 1842 consisted of the following justices: Chief Justice William Wilson, Justices Samuel D. Lockwood, Thomas C. Browne, Walter B. Scates, Samuel Treat, John D. Caton, Richard M. Young, James Shields, and Jesse B. Thomas.

51. *Dorman et ux. v. Lane,* 6 Ill. 147 (1844). James Shields (1810–79) was an Irish immigrant who was admitted to the bar in 1836 and served on the Illinois Supreme Court from 1843 to 1845. See "James Shields," Biography, *LPAL.*

52. "An Act to Amend an Act, Entitled 'An Act Relative to Wills and Testaments, Executors and Administrators, and the Settlement of Estates,'" 14 February 1831, *Laws of the State of Illinois* (1831), 191–92.

53. *Dorman et ux. v. Lane,* 143.

54. During the antebellum period Illinois Supreme Court justices were at various times assigned to serve as judges in their local circuit courts. Although it was not uncommon for justices to recuse themselves in matters representing potential conflicts of interest, the

ethical and professional standards in antebellum American legal practice were very different from those of the modern day.

55. Abraham Lincoln to Samuel Marshall, 20 June 1845, *Dorman et ux. v. Lane, LPAL.*

56. Abraham Lincoln to Samuel Marshall, 30 December 1845, *Dorman et ux. v. Yost, LPAL.* Stephen T. Logan (1800–80) was Lincoln's law partner from 1841 to 1844. By 1845 Logan was a judge and no longer Lincoln's partner, but Lincoln consulted the judge and referred the case to him before Lincoln left for Washington to assume his new duties as a representative in Congress. See "Stephen T. Logan," Biography, *LPAL.*

57. Affidavit for change of venue, 30 October 1846, *Dorman et ux. v. Yost, LPAL.*

58. Decree, 11 September 1847, *Dorman et ux. v. Yost, LPAL.*

59. Samuel Marshall to Abraham Lincoln, 20 April 1849, *Dorman et ux. v. Yost, LPAL.*

60. Assignment of Errors, December term 1851, *Dorman et ux. v. Yost, LPAL.*

61. The makeup of the Illinois Supreme Court changed twice during the years spanning the *Dorman* case. Nine justices heard the first and second appeals, but after the constitutional convention of 1848 only three justices sat on the state's highest court. Samuel H. Treat (1811–87) served as an Illinois circuit court judge before becoming an Illinois Supreme Court justice in 1841. He became a U.S. District Court judge in 1855, a position he held until his death. John D. Caton (1812–95) was a practicing attorney in Illinois before his appointment to the Illinois Supreme Court in 1842. He served on the state's highest court until his retirement in 1864 and as its chief justice for the last nine years of his tenure. See "Samuel H. Treat," Biography, *LPAL;* "John D. Caton," Biography, *LPAL.*

62. *Dorman et ux. v. Yost,* 13 Ill. 127 (1851).

63. "An Act to Protect Married Women in their Separate Property," 21 February 1861, *Public Laws of the State of Illinois* (1861), 143.

64. The original purchasers paid $1,057 for the land when John Lane sold it. Part of the property was sold for $1,200 in 1869 to pay the debts of William Dorman's estate. See Gallatin County Circuit Court Order Book 1, 12 October 1869, 61–63.

65. U.S. Census Office, Eighth Census of the United States (1860), Gallatin County, Illinois, ms.

66. Order Book, 12 October 1869, Gallatin County Circuit Court records, Gallatin County Courthouse, Shawneetown, Ill.

67. Frank Marshall Eddy to William H. Herndon, 21 March 1888, *Dorman et ux. v. Lane, LPAL.*

7

"Infamous Outrage and Prompt Retribution": The Case of People v. Delny

SUSAN KRAUSE

Courts in antebellum Illinois seldom dealt with the criminal charge of rape, and the charge of statutory rape was even more uncommon. When they appeared at all on the record, the disposition of rape cases was generally perfunctory. The grand jury often did not find enough evidence to indict; when it did, the state's attorney often did not prosecute. In those few instances of prosecution the chastity of the woman became an issue. However, the victimization of children aroused both public sentiment and the courts, as several newspaper accounts make clear. The nearly complete documentation of Abraham Lincoln's twenty-five-year law practice before his presidency presents a body of evidence with which to explore just such an occurrence of statutory rape in the cultural context of this antebellum midwestern region. *People v. Delny* is the only case of "the infamous outrage" of statutory rape among Abraham Lincoln's cases. Did the combination of age and gender make girls doubly vulnerable in the eyes of antebellum courts and therefore in need of special protection? Charges of raping a girl brought courts and juries into action, both to defend female virtue and to uphold childhood innocence. Did courts mete out rapid justice to defend the ideal of the republican family under siege by divorce, desertion, and male licentiousness? Perhaps, but it also seems that Thomas Delny, an Irish immigrant laborer, represented the social reformers' archetype of a scourge upon society.

This study contributes to a growing historical literature on rape by examining sexual assault in the context of an important midwestern state. Many of the early historical and contemporary studies reflect modern feminist views and analyses of rape, the family, and sexuality. More recent scholarship focuses on the historical issues of sex, love, and violence across racial boundaries and on regional American variations in criminal prosecutions of rape.

The conclusions of this case study contribute to recent historical literature on rape and the legal system in the United States.[1]

Although this case study focuses on an instance of statutory rape, it also sheds light on the prosecution of rape charges brought by adult women during the same period. The patterns of rape prosecution in Abraham Lincoln's Illinois confirm the conclusions of several studies of sex and the law, which have other regional and temporal bounds. Illinois courts' action and inaction reveal different attitudes regarding adult and child victims of rape. Women were discouraged from reporting rapes because courts historically did not prosecute the rapists, and women were unwilling to subject themselves to public scrutiny and humiliation as victims. But in the rape of a child consent was not an issue, and such rapes galvanized the courts. Peter W. Bardaglio's and Victoria E. Bynum's examinations of rape in the racially charged nineteenth-century South find that male attitudes about coercion, consent, and respectability proved an obstacle to prosecution.[2] Similarly, Laura F. Edwards examined southern society's divisions of rich and poor women and found that courts protected poor women from rape only in theory. Unlike elite women, poor women had to prove themselves worthy before a court accepted their charges; this case-by-case denial of charges by the courts gave the "appearance that decisions were based solely on the merits of individual women's complaints."[3] Barbara S. Lindemann and Cornelia Hughes Dayton examined seventeenth-century legal prosecutions of rape in Massachusetts and Connecticut, respectively, and found higher conviction rates for the rape of a child than for the rape of a single woman; they also found differences in rates of conviction based on social standing of both victim and perpetrator.[4] These issues of the court's uneven treatment of adult and child rape victims, and other, broader issues of society's reactions to immigration and temperance, provide the context for examining the case of *People v. Delny.*

In May 1853, while the Tazewell County Circuit Court was hearing cases in Pekin, Illinois, Paul N. Rupert accused Thomas Delny of attempting to rape or raping Jane Ann Rupert, Rupert's seven-year-old niece. The sheriff promptly arrested Delny and brought him before a local magistrate.[5] Justice of the Peace T. J. Pinkham and neighboring Justice of the Peace James Harriott examined the witnesses and evidence against Delny and set his recognizance bond at $2,000. Delny failed to provide good and sufficient sureties for his bond, and the sheriff jailed him until trial.[6] The court also required the prosecutor's witnesses—Paul N. Rupert, Joseph S. Maus, Lewis Carpenter, Robert C. White, Ira Rathbone, Mary White, and Sarah Rathbone—to post $100 bonds to ensure that they would appear to give evidence before the grand jury and before a trial jury if necessary.[7]

The Tazewell County Courthouse in Pekin, Illinois, where a jury found Thomas Delny guilty of the rape of Jane Ann Rupert. Courtesy of the Illinois State Historical Library, Springfield.

Because the May 1853 term of the Tazewell County Circuit Court had already met for eight days, the court had handled all the criminal cases and dismissed the grand jury. State's Attorney David B. Campbell was no longer in town, possibly because he had gone to the next county on the Eighth Judicial Circuit. Judge David Davis called for a special grand jury and appointed Abraham Lincoln as state's attorney pro tem to prosecute Delny.[8] Lincoln had twelve cases on the docket that term in Tazewell County, but none was a criminal case. After hearing the evidence and the witnesses for the prosecution, the grand jury found a true bill of indictment against Delny in the rape of Jane Ann Rupert. Grand jury foreman David Mark signed the bill and passed it along to the circuit court. The list of witnesses before the grand jury included young Jane Ann. In addition to Paul N. Rupert, Joseph S. Maus, and Catharine Rupert, who had testified before the justices of the peace, the grand jury heard evidence from Dr. L. A. McCook and Joseph C. Hinsey. The indictment charged that Thomas Delny, "a male above the age of fourteen years . . . violently, and against her will, feloniously did ravish and carnally know [her]; contrary to the form of the statute in such case . . . and against the Peace and dignity of the . . . People of the State of Illinois." It further declared that Jane Ann Rupert was a female child "under the age of ten years, to wit of the age of seven years."[9]

The early criminal codes of Illinois were adopted from the common law of England when Illinois became a state in 1818.[10] The laws passed by the first general assembly defined rape and statutory rape and prescribed the penalty: "That any person or persons who shall have carnal knowledge of a woman forcibly and against her will, or who shall aid or abet, counsel, hire, or cause or procure any person or persons to commit the said offence, being of the age of fourteen years, shall unlawfully know and abuse any woman child under the age of ten years with or without her consent, shall, on conviction suffer death."[11] In 1830 the General Assembly amended the penalty for a rape conviction, setting it to a prison term from one year to life.[12]

In his famous *Commentaries* William Blackstone discussed the eighteenth-century English laws of rape. Specifically with respect to "an infant under twelve years of age," he noted that she could be a competent witness if she understood the concept of the oath. If she did not understand oaths, she could still be heard to give information, although that testimony alone would not be enough to convict. Noting the secretive nature of the crime and the absence of other proof, other witnesses could provide corroboration as to the time, place, and circumstances that would give credence to the child's testimony. Additionally, the law allowed into evidence whatever the child might have told her mother or relatives about the crime, but conviction should not be grounded only on the unsupported accusation of "an infant under years of discretion." Blackstone continued that although seemingly competent witnesses might prove not to be credible, the value of trial by jury was that the jurors were "triers of the credit of the witnesses, as well as of the truth of the fact."[13]

Blackstone also noted that in civil law, a prostitute or common harlot could not charge injury for seduction, because she had no chastity. However, in the circumstance of rape such an unchaste woman might have "forsaken that awful course of life" and so might bring charges in a court of justice. He cautioned, though, that the jury had to weigh the credibility of her evidence carefully and that of other corroborating witnesses. Specifically, the jury must judge if the "party ravished" and the witnesses were of good fame who, if after learning of the offense, searched for the offender. The jurors should also determine whether the victim concealed the injury when she had the opportunity to make it known; did she cry out to be heard? He cautioned that while rape was a most detestable crime, punishable by death, it was an accusation easily made but hard to prove. It was even harder for an innocent suspect to refute.[14]

Thomas Delny came to trial for the rape of Jane Ann Rupert before the Tazewell County Circuit Court on May 10, 1853. Judge Davis presided, and the court furnished Delny, who apparently had no lawyer, with a copy of the indictment and a list of the witnesses against him.[15] Delny pleaded not guilty. The prosecution called the same witnesses that had appeared before the grand jury. The defendant subpoenaed six witnesses, including the same Dr. Mc-Cook called by the prosecution, Constant Filbert, Dutch Billy the Cooper, someone named Simonds, Henry Bloom, and M. Hoyl.[16] Neither the courts nor the newspapers recorded the testimony of witnesses, so the testimony that the jury heard that day remains unknown. After hearing the evidence, the jury found Delny guilty and sentenced him to the penitentiary for eighteen years. Davis's docket entry gives further details of the sentence. It was to include one year in solitary confinement and the remaining seventeen years at hard labor.[17] The cost to the State of Illinois for the trial of Thomas Delny was $11.60, including $5 for prosecuting attorney Abraham Lincoln.[18] Within two days of his arrest Delny had been tried and found guilty. Three days later he began his sentence at the Illinois State Penitentiary in Alton.[19]

While the court documents provide a neat and orderly account of the offense and trial, local newspapers suggest a more turbulent series of events. The *Springfield Daily Register* carried a small article mentioning the trial and Lincoln's involvement. AN AWFUL CRIME AND SPEEDY PUNISHMENT headlined the terse facts without ever naming Delny or Jane Ann Rupert. The newspaper reported that "a mob came very near getting possession of the base wretch and hanging him."[20] Four days later and just across the river from Pekin where Delny had been tried, the *Peoria Weekly Democratic Press* published a more vivid account of the mood of the community, under the headline INFAMOUS OUTRAGE AND PROMPT RETRIBUTION. The newspaper reported that upon learning that Delny had "committed a horrible outrage upon the person of a little girl, seven years of age, daughter of a widow" the "citizens became justly incensed, seized the scoundrel, who denied the charge." They "took him to the river, tied a rope about his neck, with a huge weight to the end of it, and threatened to throw him into the stream, if he did not confess his guilt." The newspaper also reported that Delny confessed on the condition that he have a fair trial and that on the same evening a grand jury rendered a true bill of indictment.[21]

An examination of the community context of *People v. Delny* illuminates some of the other reasons that emotions ran high. Unfortunately, few witnesses before either the justices of the peace or the grand jury left traces in the public record. Only Jane Ann Rupert, her uncle Paul N. Rupert, and Catharine Rupert, probably Jane Ann's aunt, are listed in the census.[22] None of the defendant's witnesses appear in the record; several were listed on the subpoena by only one name or by their occupation.[23] Eight of the twelve trial jurors named appear in the 1850 federal census for Tazewell County. Seven of the eight were farmers, and all were born outside Illinois—in New England, Pennsylvania, Virginia, or Ohio. Five jurors also had daughters younger than ten, a personal attribute that may have influenced their ability to judge the evidence fairly in a trial involving statutory rape.[24] These jurors reflected the character of Pekin, Illinois, in 1853. The city had received its charter in 1849, with a population of about fifteen hundred, who were described as a mixture of "original frontiersmen, Indians, veterans of two wars, river men, farmers, and . . . the first few hard-working German immigrants." The city also had a few Irish residents. Pekin had its share of violence, until a new element began to appear with the construction of churches and the organization of the Sons of Temperance. In 1850 the population surged to 1,840, fueled by German immigration.[25]

Thomas Delny, according to the Convict Register for the Illinois State Penitentiary, was born in Ireland, had lived in Illinois for only two years, and was a miner. His parents lived in Canada, and he was not a member of any church or temperance society. He was forty and had dark brown hair and gray eyes, with a light complexion and powder marks and scars on his cheek, forehead, and nose. He could read and write and often drank to excess.[26] The descriptions of Delny and his jurors reveal a great deal about the conflicts in American society in the 1850s. Agrarian America was reeling from an influx of Irish immigrants hired to construct the proliferating network of railroads and of German immigrants who were fueling new industry and capitalism. With these transitory immigrant laborers came disruption, violence, and local resentment.

It is not surprising that the penitentiary description of Thomas Delny notes his excessive drinking. Irish intemperance shocked many Americans, who made no allowance for the laborious and frugal existence they lived. Irish laborers' association with the Catholic church, traditionally distrusted and feared in the United States, compounded the offense.[27] Five million immigrants came to the United States between 1845 and 1854, when the entire population of the country was only twenty million people. Of the five million immigrants, two million were Irish and 1.5 million were German. Economic dislocation and opportunity fueled this massive migration. Discontent with European conditions and a heightened awareness of opportunities in the United States, coupled with dramatic decreases in the cost of passage brought on by sheer volume and competition, made migration financially possible for the poorer classes. But the Irish immigrants, fleeing the social and economic ravages of the potato famine, were too impoverished to become independent farmers and virtually monopolized the unskilled labor force in American cities. They also responded to the lure of labor agencies seeking workers in the canal and railroad construction booms. German immigration peaked between 1846 and 1855 in response to crop failures in Europe. Artisans and tradesmen joined the pauper immigrants after the worsening agricultural and economic conditions and the revolutions of 1848 and 1849. The Germans concentrated in the upper Mississippi and Ohio valleys, although they were more evenly distributed throughout the countryside than the Irish. Mass immigration intensified the social difficulties of pauperism, disease, and criminality. Native-born Americans interpreted poverty and difficulties in adjusting to a new way of life as inborn depravity.[28]

The simultaneous rise in the rates of immigration and violence was not limited to any one area. Fifty years earlier Chester County, Pennsylvania, had experienced an increase in the rate of assaults after the arrival of Ulster Scots, Irish, and nonpietist Germans swelled the population. The jurors in the case of *People v. Delny,* who migrated from settled areas like Pennsylvania to Illinois, brought with them the belief that the Scots-Irish were more likely to engage in violent behavior than the pacifist Germans. Additionally, laborers represented a disproportionate percentage of the suspects in cases of personal violence. In their examination of violent crimes in Pennsylvania before the nineteenth century, G. S. Rowe and Jack D. Marietta cite a number of Chester County court cases in which children had been sexually assaulted and describe how "even children were not safe from neighbors and workmen who entered their homes easily and often."[29]

Thomas Delny's occupation as a miner put him in a small minority within the community of Pekin. Although seventeenth-century explorers found coal in Illinois, by 1840 only 152 men scattered across nineteen counties mined coal in the state.[30] In Peoria, across the Illinois River from Pekin, only eight men were employed in mining.[31] In Pekin these early mines were simple operations of a few men that removed outcroppings of coal from the hillsides.[32] That Thomas Delny was Irish and a laborer who often drank to excess put him in a class widely perceived as disruptive, if not dangerous.

Pekin was along one of the small railroads that eventually would connect to the ambitious, newly chartered Illinois Central Railroad that ran north and south through the state. Contractors building the Illinois Central hired more than ten thousand men to build the railroad, which, when finished, was the longest in the United States. Most of the first laborers for the Illinois Central were Irish. They proved to be both hard workers and hard drinkers, and the rough-mannered foreigners soon became unpopular within the local communities along the railroad.[33] A series of violent riots between laborers and railroad contractors in 1853 in LaSalle and Decatur, Illinois, confirmed many people's worst fears about these new outsiders.[34] Thomas Delny had been in Illinois since 1851, a few years before the primary influx of immigrants, but the people of Pekin no doubt associated him with all other Irish immigrants after the events of 1853. Newspapers chronicled murders, rapes, and violence stemming from immigrant drunkenness. Reformers sought to quell disorder by outlawing the sale of liquor, and the most ambitious reformers engaged in their own mob actions.[35]

In such a climate it is little wonder that the allegation that an Irish miner had raped a child aroused a lynch mob in Pekin. Ian R. Tyrrell suggests that "temperance reformers championed their cause not to eliminate liquor alone but to eradicate the central social problems of Jacksonian society: crime, immorality, poverty, and insanity."[36] Intemperance seemed to promote these growing social problems. The New England economic boom of the 1840s and 1850s drew unprecedented numbers of unskilled, transient workers, and their attendant social problems, to small communities undergoing economic development. The temperance movement sought to control and reform the laboring poor.[37] This boom reached the Midwest in the 1850s. Until then, prohibition efforts were aimed at creating a "more coherent social order out of chaotic frontier conditions." Until transportation advances changed the regional economy, midwesterners distilled corn liquor for local and regional consumption. The opening of eastern markets for corn products and the influx of New England immigrants changed the character of the fledgling temperance movement in the Midwest. As in New England, the emphasis began to shift to promote self-help among people of modest means and to create an industrialized society of disciplined workers.[38]

The Pekin lynch mob that threatened Delny is also rooted in a historical context of vigilante action. W. Fitzhugh Brundage cites the obscure origins of lynchings in seventeenth-century Ireland and eighteenth-century America. Mob violence was an established custom by the end of the colonial period and "a truly national phenomenon" by the antebellum period. Mobs in the North "threatened—and in several instances murdered—abolitionists, Mormons, Catholics, immigrants and blacks." As lynching spread across the country by the mid-1850s, mobs increasingly "ignored existing legal institutions and meted out extralegal punishment."[39]

Concomitant with the immigration and temperance upheaval in the midnineteenth century were changes within the American family. Michael Grossberg describes the new republican family in his study of the emergence of American family law in the nineteenth century. He found that "alterations in the households of the era occurred symbiotically with those social, economic, and political developments that marked the path toward a predominantly bourgeois, capitalist society." The new private institution of the family elevated the status of mothers and children as their roles placed "an emphasis on domestic intimacy." The new Enlightenment ideas about child development and the environment contributed to an increased affection in the raising of children. As childhood extended, society viewed children as more "vulnerable, malleable charges with a special innocence and with particular needs, talents, and characters."[40] Indeed, Abraham Lincoln's contemporaries portray him as too kind and gentle with his own children, taking great pleasure in their freedom from the tyranny of parental restraint. He was just as indulgent with children not his own, and he had a special relationship with the neighborhood children, which he seldom accorded most adults.[41]

Much as the temperance movement reacted to the ill effects of liquor abuse on society, self-appointed monitors organized to protect and defend the new idealized family model. By 1853 the reaction to Jane Ann Rupert's rape may have been fueled by the influence of the vocal protectors of the family who warned that "divorce and desertion, [and] male licentiousness . . . threatened the very fabric of the republic."[42] The rape of a child produces a strong reaction at any time, but in this context the response was vigilantism.

Although Peter Bardaglio's recent study of sexual violence against children focused on the late nineteenth-century South, the southern patriarch's duty to defend his offspring from external dangers applied during this earlier period as well: "Rape challenged the power of the male household head to protect the women, children and other dependents in this family, and damaged his standing in the community. By violently gaining access to the sexuality of a girl or woman, the rapist not only achieved control over the female, but also undercut the public authority of her father or husband."[43] The community of Pekin assumed the paternal role to the fatherless child Jane Ann Rupert when it pursued and prosecuted Thomas Delny for her rape.

Perhaps because of who he was and what he represented to the people of Pekin, Delny engendered a more dramatic response than did several others accused of statutory rape in central Illinois during this period. Sexual impropriety runs through a variety of cases in which Abraham Lincoln and his partners participated. Such charges as adultery, fornication, and prostitution within the context of divorce or slander, as well as the economic ramifications of bastardy and seduction, peppered antebellum court dockets. The ideal of female purity was upheld by paternalistic laws that punished those that strayed from the ideal and those that slandered those ideals.[44] However, the reality in central Illinois between 1836 and 1860 was that the state's attorney failed to prosecute most rape cases. Men charged with rape typically attempted to prove that the victim was habitually guilty of "lewd" sexual behavior. In his twenty-five-year career as a lawyer, Abraham Lincoln was involved in only seven cases involving charges of rape or assault with intent to rape. The state's attorney did not prosecute in four cases, and the court dismissed two cases in which Lincoln represented the defendant. *People v. Delny*, the only case involving a child victim, was the only one that went to trial. Of the seven, it was also the only case in which Lincoln served as the prosecuting attorney.[45]

There is only one reported appeal of a rape conviction to the Illinois Supreme Court between 1836 and 1861, the years of Lincoln's legal practice. The highest state court reversed and remanded the Bureau County case of *Barney v. People* at its April 1859 term in Ottawa, based on two errors. First, the jury panel had been sworn in once at the beginning of the term rather than for each case. The "solemnity of calling the juror before the prisoner, in the presence of the court . . . gives the prisoner a comfortable assurance that he is to have a fair and impartial trial." Second, the high court concluded that the lower court had erred in refusing a jury instruction that pertained to the victim's actions: "The husband of the prosecutrix was, at the time the rape as alleged by her to have been committed, an able-bodied man, and was at the said time within a few rods of the said place where the rape is alleged by her to have been committed, that he might easily have heard her had she made any outcry; that the prosecutrix made no outcry; that she and her husband remained for an hour or an hour and a half with the defendant, in a friendly manner, then these circumstances raise a strong presumption that no rape was committed." The court found that it was possible that a rape had occurred under such conditions, if true, but that "those circumstances must, in all unbiased minds, raise a strong presumption against such a consummation."[46]

That few prosecutions for the crime of rape went forward in Illinois during this period was not unusual. In a census of the actions and special proceedings in the Circuit Court for Chippewa County, Wisconsin, for crimes against sexual morality, only one case of rape, and no cases of assault with intent to rape, appeared between 1855 and 1864.[47] In 119 years (1682–1801) in Chester County, Pennsylvania, only fifty-seven cases of rape and thirty-nine cases of attempted rape appeared in the record.[48] Similarly, rape was also an infrequent charge in the Sangamon County Circuit Court in Lincoln's home county. Rape or assault with intent to rape appeared only seventeen times between 1836 and 1860, or only once every seventeen months, in a county that had a concentrated population. In fact, this court heard no such cases between 1836 and 1841, and nine of the seventeen rape or assault cases occurred in 1860. Of these seventeen cases, grand juries dismissed three as lacking sufficient evidence for indictment, the state's attorney ultimately did not prosecute four more, and the court struck from the docket or dismissed eight.

The court set aside the guilty verdict in one case and rendered a guilty verdict in only one case. Two cases involved children: *People v. Clarkson,* which the grand jury dismissed as "no true bill," and *People v. Ernst,* which resulted in a guilty verdict and a prison sentence.[49]

The context and outcome of *People v. Clarkson,* which occurred seven years after the *Delny* case and sixty miles away, provide an interesting contrast. James J. Clarkson was an alderman and a member of the Springfield City Council when E. H. Woods accused Clarkson of the attempted rape of Woods's ten-year-old daughter. The two highly partisan Springfield newspapers—the Democratic *Illinois State Register* and the Whig *Illinois State Journal*—gave running accounts of the public proceedings and the examination of Alderman Clarkson by a justice of the peace over a two-week period. The newspaper described the girl, "who told a straight-forward story," as "quite good looking and about the usual size of girls of her age."[50] The *Illinois State Register* declared: "We do not feel disposed to make a long notice of the matter, for it savors too much of filthiness to be dished up for the entertainment of *our* readers; but we consider it proper to state that Clarkson's counsel took the position on Saturday morning, in their arguments before the examining court, that the charge had been made for the purpose of breaking him down in this community, and that the father of the girl was acting partly from outside influence, and partly from revengeful motives—counsel making the distinct charge that Woods had attempted to take improper liberties with Clarkson's wife."[51]

Unlike Thomas Delny in Pekin, James J. Clarkson was a prominent member of the Springfield community. In addition to serving as an alderman, he was the manager of the *Illinois State Democrat,* a Springfield newspaper that claimed to represent democracy and to combat the political "heresies" of Stephen A. Douglas.[52] Clarkson was bound over after his public examination, to appear at the next term of court.[53] After posting his bond of $1,000, Clarkson resigned from the city council, stating, "I shall endeavor to meet and successfully combat the charges against me; and I hope that you may enjoy no less happiness than usual, from the recollection that during my absence—my sickness—you ruined my character and blasted my name, without giving me the opportunity of defending myself from the most damnable conspiracy ever concocted."[54]

The *Illinois State Journal* published Nancy M. Clarkson's denial that Woods had ever acted inappropriately toward her and later noted the rumor that James J. Clarkson had left town.[55] The harm to the child was seemingly subverted to the politically motivated charges and countercharges. Indeed, it is unclear from the newspaper accounts whether the rape had occurred in the previous two months or two days, as the newspaper asserted first one and then the other. The extant court records for *People v. Clarkson* are few. During the April 1860 term of the Sangamon County Circuit Court, the grand jury declined to indict Clarkson, and the court discharged the bail bond and dismissed the case.[56] The *Illinois State Journal* noted soon afterward that both the principal witness for the prosecution in *People v. Clarkson* and the girl's father had left town. It also reported the editor's contention that Clarkson would not have been indicted even if the girl had appeared before the grand jury. Public sentiment was that the girl's father had been "decidedly mysterious" during the entire investigation. The editor agreed with those who said that the girl's father had falsely accused Clarkson.[57] During that same term the court granted Nancy Clarkson, represented by Abraham Lincoln, a divorce from James J. Clarkson on the grounds of adultery with lewd women and desertion from the state after an indictment in the rape of a young girl.[58]

Where was the public outrage against Clarkson? While the newspaper noted that a large audience assembled to witness the examination of Clarkson "charged with an outrage of a brutal character upon a little girl," there is no hint of a vigilante response. Indeed, in a strange juxtaposition a newspaper article immediately preceding a report of the Clarkson proceedings recounts that some women in an adjoining county had burned the clothing and even cut down and burned the latticework porch of a woman whose misdeed had been to lead "from the paths of virtue (actually seduced!) the republican sheriff of Logan county, together with other innocent and unoffending citizens! Wives taking vengeance upon a worthless woman, who had seduced their poor defenseless husbands! What next?"[59] Outrage for criminal wrongs seems to have been very selective. Not only the social and political standing but the ethnicity, occupation, and even the gender of the accused contributed to the intensity of the public response. In the case of *People v. Clarkson* it seems that Woods used the potential for public reaction to the alleged rape of his child to attempt to undermine a political adversary. While the grand jury did not find enough evidence to indict Clarkson in the rape of the child, the court nonetheless demonstrated its protective paternalism toward Mrs. Clarkson in granting her a divorce from an adulterous husband of questionable moral character.

In the only other criminal prosecution for the rape of a child in the Sangamon County Circuit Court during the period 1836–61, the grand jury indicted Jacob Ernst on four separate counts. Again, the local newspaper carried the story and expressed outrage, although no overt community reaction developed. In summarizing the various activities of the court in session, the newspaper, mistakenly referring to Ernst as "Ernst Hoffman," reported that "a monster in [human] shape . . . was placed [on trial] for having made improper advances to his step-daughter, a girl 13 years old. The [crime] was pretty clearly established to the satisfaction of almost everybody in court, but the circumstances developed during the trial are of [such] revolting character that we are compelled [to avoid] publishing them in detail." No doubt the recent death of the mother of the "unhappy young [girl]" contributed to community reaction to the crime. Unlike Thomas Delny, Ernst was represented by an attorney who introduced some witnesses to establish his client's general good character. The Sangamon County Circuit Court tried Ernst at its June 1861 term; after deliberating for only an hour, the jury found him guilty of raping his twelve-year-old stepdaughter, Katherine Hoffman.[60] The court sentenced Ernst to five years in the penitentiary, and the judge overruled a motion by Ernst's attorneys for a new trial and arrest of judgment.[61] The court convicted Ernst of one charge of assault to commit rape, but it struck a second charge of assault to commit rape and two charges of rape against him in the August 1861 term.

The few charges of rape, and assault to commit rape, appearing on the Sangamon County Circuit Court docket (seventeen in twenty-five years) suggest that either few men committed rape or that prosecutors and victims found that charges of rape were difficult and painful to prove. While chastity or reputation did not have a role in the rape of a child, it is probable that it was a key element in cases where adult women were victims. In the small sample of rape cases from Abraham Lincoln's own law practice, only one of the seven known rape cases—*People v. Delny*—resulted in a conviction. In only one other case does the extant record provide evidence of the defense. In *People v. Roberts* the state's attorney refused to prosecute Roberts in the rape of Elizabeth Harland after Lincoln pleaded his client not guilty and attempted to prove that Harland was habitually guilty of lewd conduct.[62]

The only insight into Abraham Lincoln's personal response to the crime of rape is a reminiscence of Civil War prosecutions in which he sat as the ultimate judge. According to the judge advocate general, Lincoln "sought excuses to spare soldiers condemned to death by court martial" but he was prompt to punish those who had committed outrages upon women.[63] In considering six rape convictions, Lincoln granted only one pardon. In this instance, a congressman personally sought the pardon, and the request was based on later evidence by comrades that the alleged rape had occurred in a "household which was more barroom-brothel than a normal home" and that the woman and her grown daughter were lewd.[64] In the cases of two other convicted rapists Lincoln reduced the sentences: one from life imprisonment to two years because of the young age of the assailant, and the other to six months from the sentence of hard labor until the end of the enlistment. In the remaining three cases Lincoln let stand the sentences of execution, imprisonment for three years, and imprisonment for fifteen years.[65]

According to antebellum Illinois law, the court could sentence individuals convicted of rape to life imprisonment in the state penitentiary. The legislature made no substantive changes in Illinois rape law until 1887 when the age of male responsibility for statutory rape was raised to sixteen and the age of the female victim from ten to fourteen.[66] Thomas Delny was to serve his sentence of eighteen years at hard labor for the rape of Jane Ann Rupert at the Illinois State Prison in Alton, in southwestern Illinois along the Mississippi River. The State of Illinois leased the penitentiary to a private individual who operated the prison on the profits of convict labor. A criminal sentenced to hard labor could be leased to work during the day in the nearby town of Alton. In 1855 the state penitentiary housed 332 prisoners in 152 cells and had been cited ten years earlier by prison reformers for extensive overcrowding and deplorable living conditions. By 1857 not only was the prison administration under attack for the conditions but the Alton community was exhibiting hostility toward the prison's effect on property values. Additionally, labor groups complained of unfair competition from convict labor. These objections, and the condition of the buildings, soon led to a plan for the construction of another prison in Joliet in northern Illinois and the clos-

Alton, Illinois, ca. 1861. At the lower right is the state penitentiary, where Thomas Delny was imprisoned from 1853 to 1859. Courtesy of the *Telegraph,* Alton, Illinois.

ing of the Alton penitentiary. The new prison was to be built with convict labor, and by 1859 all prisoners were to be removed from Alton.[67]

The closing of the state penitentiary at Alton had unforeseen consequences for Thomas Delny. Sebastian Wise and Peter Wise owned and operated a large steam-driven flour mill on the Mississippi River bank adjacent to the penitentiary in Alton. During 1856 and 1857 they had rebuilt the mill and warehouses, at a time when a large portion of the convicts were slated for removal to Joliet. The Alton community leaders welcomed the removal of the penitentiary not only because it opened up the best tracts of land in the city for development but also because the absence of prisoners produced a new demand for "the labor of at least four hundred able bodied mechanics."[68] Sebastian and Peter Wise probably leased laborers from the penitentiary to staff their nearby milling operation.

On February 11, 1859, Sebastian Wise of Alton wrote to Gov. William H. Bissell, reminding him of an earlier conversation and making application for a pardon for Thomas Delny. "Will your Excellency, then, extend to Delney the clemency, of which I think him well worthy & deserving?" Governor Bissell endorsed the request and thereby pardoned Delny.[69] On Febru-

The Wise brothers' mill in Alton, Illinois, ca. 1896, where Thomas Delny apparently worked while serving his eighteen-year sentence for rape. D. R. Sparks purchased the mill in 1880 and changed its name. Courtesy of Donald J. Huber, Alton, Illinois.

ary 22, 1859, Delny was discharged from the Alton prison after serving less than six years of an eighteen-year sentence for the rape of seven-year-old Jane Ann Rupert.[70]

Executive pardon was the only means by which Delny could be released from prison in fewer than eighteen years.[71] In the antebellum era the pardon process was typically initiated by a petition signed by respected citizens from a prisoner's home area. A pardon was not usually recognition of a prisoner's rehabilitation; rather, it was an expression of sympathy from the community. It was also frequently a practical matter of freeing a prisoner so that he, rather than the community, could provide for the support of the family he left behind. Sebastian Wise's petition for a pardon for Thomas Delny was not accompanied by the signatures of any citizens of either Alton or Pekin.

Between 1847 and 1858 approximately 3,826 inmates had been housed at Alton, the state's only prison. An overwhelming number of inmates were convicted for the crime of larceny. Only forty-two were incarcerated for the crime of rape or attempting to commit rape, representing merely 1 percent of the prison population. Of the forty-two men incarcerated for rape, eleven (26 percent) were Irish, at a time when Irish immigrants represented an average of 2.85 percent of the total Illinois population. Thomas Delny was one of only five inmates whose sentence exceeded ten years. The governor pardoned thirteen of the forty-two inmates, who served an average of 38 percent of their sentence for rape; three of the thirteen were Irish.[72] While Thomas Delny's release did not occur as a result of the usual circumstances of community support for pardons, he likely benefited from the changing circumstances at the prison. On the eve of the prison closure in 1859 Sebastian Wise, a wealthy miller, requested clemency for a laborer who had probably been leased to him over the years.[73]

What happened to Thomas Delny and Jane Ann Rupert after 1853 is not known. Other questions remain unanswered as well, but this case study suggests some conclusions. Why did only the rape of a child, and not rape in other cases, rouse public sentiment and legal action? Why, once confronted by legal action, did the courts deal with the issue of rape so unevenly? Public sentiment and court action in Delny's conviction suggest that who Delny was and what he represented were as significant as the crime he committed. The Irish immigrant laborer received swift and severe punishment and barely avoided the consequences of a lynch mob. In contrast, the Springfield alderman, Clarkson, escaped with damage only to his reputation, position, and marriage. The "monster" stepfather, Ernst, received a degree of punishment somewhere in between. Despite the republican family's valuing of women and children, the courts in antebellum central Illinois seemed to possess little tender consideration for adult victims of rape but reacted in a paternal fashion to protect victims who were minors.

Blackstone's delicate commentaries on the criminal charge of rape provide other clues to the courts' response. Lawrence M. Friedman's analysis of women victims makes the point that while men beat, harassed, and raped women, men also carried out justice "using men's standards and men's consciousness." The legal statutes covered male biases and assumptions regarding who was a respectable woman and what constituted consent. Friedman also notes the difficulty in getting reliable statistics on the numbers of rapes and concludes that it was "always among the least-reported, least-prosecuted, and least-punished of the major crimes." The law did not favor women victims and discouraged them from reporting rape. Thus they rarely subjected themselves to the public shame, trauma, and stigma in a court of law.[74] These obstacles probably explain the few rape charges brought before the Sangamon County Circuit Court during this twenty-five-year period. They may also help to explain the reaction to the rape of Jane Ann Rupert. The rape of an unquestionably innocent girl crystallized the application of the law laid bare of other biases and assumptions.

The case of *People v. Delny* is illustrative of the few charges of rape to be prosecuted in the courts of antebellum Illinois. The apparently limited legal protection provided to women who brought such charges, and subjected themselves to public examination and countercharges of lewd behavior, almost certainly resulted in the underreporting of the crime. However, the sexual assault of a child galvanized the community and the court into action to defend both female virtue and childhood innocence by the application of law based on unquestioned purity. "An awful crime and speedy punishment" succinctly summarized the mood of the community and the court's role in calming the community's fears. While older attitudes of patriarchal male dominance and the subordination of women may have persisted in the limited prosecution of rapes of adult women, these gave way to paternalistic justice when applied to a child. This case also demonstrates the community's reaction to a number of disquieting social undercurrents as well. Thomas Delny embodied the stereotype of the drunken Irish immigrant at the heart of the labor violence of 1853 and may have been both a guilty rapist and a victim of the climate of the 1850s. Paradoxically, he may also have benefited from another circumstance equally beyond his control: the closing of the state penitentiary at Alton and a pardon from the governor based on the value of his labor to a local manufacturer. Abraham Lincoln, indulgent father and later compassionate president, had little compassion for those guilty of crimes against women. Perhaps this attribute helps to explain why *People v. Delny* is the only case in which Lincoln served as state's attorney.

Notes

1. For one of the earliest feminist investigations see Susan Brownmiller, *Against Our Will: Men, Women, and Rape* (New York: Simon and Schuster, 1975). For discussions of the legal and social issues of family, violence against women, and women's history, see Nancy F. Cott, *The Bonds of Womanhood: "Women's Sphere" in New England, 1780–1835* (New Haven, Conn.: Yale University Press, 1997); Elizabeth Pleck, *Domestic Tyranny: The Making of Social Policy against Family Violence from Colonial Times to the Present* (New York: Oxford University Press, 1987); Jill K. Conway, *The Female Experience in Eighteenth- and Nineteenth-Century America: A Guide to the History of American Women* (New York: Garland, 1982); Rosemarie Tong, *Women, Sex, and the Law* (Towowa, N.J.: R. Rowland and Allanheld, 1984); Joseph F. Kett, *Rites of Passage: Adolescence in America, 1790 to the Present* (New York: Basic Books, 1977); Kathy Peiss and Christina Simmons, eds., *Passion and Power: Sexuality in History* (Philadelphia: Temple University Press, 1989). For a discussion of sex, love, and race see Martha Hodes, ed., *Sex, Love, Race: Crossing Boundaries in North American History* (New York: New York University Press, 1999). For regional and international studies see Garthine Walker, "Rereading Rape and Sexual Violence in Early Modern England," *Gender and History* 10 (April 1998): 1–25; Mary E. Odem, "Cultural Representations and Social Contexts of Rape in the Early Twentieth Century," in *Lethal Imagination: Violence and Brutality in American History,* ed. Michael A. Bellesiles (New York: New York University Press, 1999), 353–70; Carolyn A. Conley, "No Pedestals: Women and Violence in Late Nineteenth-Century Ireland," *Journal of Social History* 28 (Summer 1995): 801–18; and Manon vander Heijden, "Women as Victims of Sexual and Domestic Violence in Seventeenth-Century Holland: Criminal Cases of Rape, Incest, and Maltreatment in Rotterdam and Delft," *Journal of Social History* 33 (Spring 2000): 623–44.

2. Peter W. Bardaglio, *Reconstructing the Household: Families, Sex, and the Law in the Nineteenth-Century South* (Chapel Hill: University of North Carolina Press, 1995); Victoria E. Bynum, *Unruly Women: The Politics of Social and Sexual Control in the Old South* (Chapel Hill: University of North Carolina Press, 1992). See also Jennifer Wriggins, "Rape, Racism, and the Law," in *The Legal Response to Violence Against Women,* ed. Karen J. Maschke (New York: Garland, 1997), 1–39; Mary Frances Berry, "Judging Morality: Sexual Behavior and Legal Consequences in the Late Nineteenth-Century South," *Journal of American History* 78 (December 1991): 835–56.

3. Laura F. Edwards, *Gendered Strife and Confusion: The Political Culture of Reconstruction* (Urbana: University of Illinois Press, 1997), 8–9.

4. Barbara S. Lindemann, "'To Ravish and Carnally Know': Rape in Eighteenth-Century Massachusetts," *Signs: Journal of Women in Culture and Society* 10 (Autumn 1984): 63–82; Cornelia Hughes Dayton, *Women before the Bar: Gender, Law, and Society in Connecticut, 1639–1789* (Chapel Hill: University of North Carolina Press, 1995).

5. U.S. Census Office, Seventh Census of the United States (1850), Tazewell County, Illinois, ms. The 1850 census reported that Paul A. (N.) Rupert and Noah I. Rupert were forty and thirty-eight years old, respectively. Both were born in Virginia and their households were listed next to each other in the record. It seems likely that they were brothers. Noah I. Rupert died sometime between the 1850 census and the 1853 rape.

6. Mittimus, 8 May 1853, *People v. Delny,* in *The Law Practice of Abraham Lincoln: Complete Documentary Edition,* ed. Martha L. Benner and Cullom Davis et al. (DVD; Urbana: University of Illinois Press, 2000), hereafter cited as *LPAL.*

7. Recognizance of Witnesses, 9 May 1853, *People v. Delny, LPAL.*

8. Judge's Docket, May term 1853, *People v. Delny, LPAL.*

9. Indictment for Rape, 9 May 1853, *People v. Delny, LPAL.*

10. Leslie A. Cranston, *Early Criminal Codes of Illinois and Their Relations to the Common Law of England* (DuQuoin, Ill.: Cranston, n.d.), 5, 15.

11. "An Act Respecting Crimes and Punishments: Rape," 23 March 1819, *Laws of the State of Illinois* (1819), 219.

12. "An Act to amend an Act entitled, 'An Act Relative to Criminal Jurisprudence,' approved 6 January 1827, and to Provide for the Regulation and Government of the Penitentiary," 15 February 1821, *Laws of the State of Illinois* (1830), 110.

13. St. George Tucker, *Blackstone's Commentaries, with Notes of Reference to the Constitution and Laws of the Federal Government of the United States and of the Commonwealth of Virginia,* 5 vols. (1803; rpt., New York: Augustus M. Kelley, 1969), 4:213–14.

14. Ibid., 4:212–14.

15. The judge's docket does not provide the name of an attorney for the defendant. See Judge's Docket, May term 1853, *People v. Delny, LPAL.*

16. Order, 10 May 1853, *People v. Delny, LPAL;* Subpoenas, 9–10 May 1853, *People v. Delny, LPAL.*

17. Jury Verdict, n.d., *People v. Delny, LPAL;* Judge's Docket, May term 1853, *People v. Delny, LPAL.*

18. Fee Book [April term 1851–October term 1855], p. 166, *People v. Delny, LPAL.*

19. Illinois State Penitentiary, Convict Register No. 3 (15 May 1847 to 31 December 1854), Nos. 649–1644, p. 319, Illinois State Archives, Springfield.

20. *Springfield (Ill.) Daily Register,* 14 May 1853.

21. *Peoria (Ill.) Weekly Democratic Press,* 18 May 1853.

22. Census Office, Seventh Census (1850), Tazewell County.

23. Subpoena, 10 May 1853, *People v. Delny, LPAL.*

24. Census Office, Seventh Census (1850), Tazewell County. Those found in the 1850 census are Henry Gillum, John S. Young, Enoch Morse, James Fuller, Daniel Hodgson, John Waldon, David Shay, and William Glasgow.

25. *The Pekin Centenary, 1849–1949: A Souvenir Book Commemorating 100 years of Community in the City of Pekin, Illinois* (Pekin, Ill.: Pekin Association of Commerce, 1949), 9–11, quotation on 9.

26. Illinois State Penitentiary, Convict Register No. 3, 319.

27. Marcus Lee Hansen, *The Atlantic Migration, 1607–1860: A History of the Continuing Settlement of the United States* (Cambridge, Mass.: Harvard University Press, 1940), 303.

28. Maldwyn Atlen Jones, *American Immigration* (Chicago: University of Chicago Press, 1960), 92–93, 95–105, 111–12, 118, 130–32; Mark Wyman, *Immigrants in the Valley: Irish, Germans, and Americans in the Upper Mississippi Country, 1830–1860* (Chicago: Nelson-Hall, 1984), 53–57. See also W. J. Rorabaugh, *The Alcoholic Republic: An American Tradition* (New York: Oxford University Press, 1979).

29. G. S. Rowe and Jack D. Marietta, "Personal Violence in a 'Peaceable Kingdom,'" in *Over the Threshold: Intimate Violence in Early America,* ed. Christine Daniels and Michael V. Kennedy (New York: Routledge, 1999), 24–31, quotation on 31.

30. David Ross, "History of Coal Mining in Illinois: An Address Delivered before the State Mining Institute in Annual Session at DuQuoin, Illinois, May 26, 1916," (Hartford, Conn.: Aetna Life Insurance, 1916), 3–4.

31. S. O. Andros, "Coal Mining in Illinois," *Illinois Coal Mining Investigations* 13 (1915): 33.

32. *Sesquicentennial History Book, 1824–1974, Commemorating 150 years of Growth and Development in the Celestial City* (Pekin, Ill.: Pekin Chamber of Commerce, 1974), 59.

33. Paul W. Gates, *The Illinois Central Railroad and Its Colonization Work* (1934; rpt., New York: Johnson Reprint, 1968), 96.

34. David Lee Lightner, "Labor on the Illinois Central Railroad, 1852–1900" (Ph.D. diss., Cornell University, 1969), 41–45, 50.

35. Wyman, *Immigrants in the Valley,* 173, 181; Arthur Charles Cole, *The Era of the Civil War, 1848–1870,* vol. 3 of *The Centennial History of Illinois* (Springfield: Illinois Centennial Commission, 1919), 205–6, 211.

36. Ian R. Tyrrell, *Sobering Up: From Temperance to Prohibition in Antebellum American, 1800–1860* (Westport, Conn.: Greenwood, 1979), 4.

37. Ibid., 5, 9–10.

38. Ibid., 244.

39. W. Fitzhugh Brundage, *Lynching in the New South: Georgia and Virginia, 1880–1930* (Urbana: University of Illinois Press, 1993), 3–5, quotation on 4. While the tradition of mob violence is most often associated with racial conflicts in the South before the Civil War, whites who deviated from the community standards of behavior were the victims of mobs, not blacks. Blacks accused of raping white women in the antebellum South were executed by the state, and owners were compensated for their loss.

40. Michael Grossberg, *Governing the Hearth: Law and the Family in Nineteenth-Century America* (Chapel Hill: University of North Carolina Press, 1985), 4, 6, 8, 10.

41. Michael Burlingame, *The Inner World of Abraham Lincoln* (Urbana: University of Illinois Press, 1994), 57–59.

42. Grossberg, *Governing the Hearth,* 10.

43. Peter W. Bardaglio, "Children, Sexual Violence, and the Law in the New South," in *Childhood in Southern History,* ed. Ted Ownby (University: University Press of Mississippi, forthcoming).

44. One hundred twenty-six legal cases in the more than five thousand legal cases cited in *LPAL* contain the subject heading of "sexual relations." Usually, but not always, these cases involve illicit sexual relations.

45. In the Sangamon County Circuit Court, *People v. Anderson, People v. Tunison,* and *People v. Black;* in the Tazewell County Circuit Court, *People v. Beal* and *People v. Beal;* in the De Witt County Circuit Court, *People v. Roberts,* all in *LPAL.*

46. *Barney v. People,* 22 Ill. 160–61 (1859). Although the Reconstruction-era South admittedly had a unique character, Bardaglio offers some comparison of numbers of appellate cases for males convicted of rape or attempted rape. He found approximately 345 such appeals in the published records of the state courts of the South between 1865 and 1899. Mary E. Odem, found 112 statutory rape cases in Alameda County, California, between 1910 and 1920. See Bardaglio, "Children, Sexual Violence, and the Law"; Mary E. Odem, *Delinquent Daughters: Protecting and Policing Adolescent Female Sexuality in the United States, 1885–1920* (Chapel Hill: University of North Carolina Press, 1995), 76.

47. Francis W. Laurent, *The Business of a Trial Court: One Hundred Years of Cases* (Madison: University of Wisconsin Press, 1959), 122. Eighteen cases of rape and eleven cases of assault with intent to rape are reported for the complete period of Laurent's study (1855–1954).

48. Rowe and Marietta, "Personal Violence in a 'Peaceable Kingdom,'" 25.

49. Judge's Dockets, 1836–61, Sangamon County Circuit Court, Lincoln Legal Papers, Springfield, Ill.

50. *(Springfield) Illinois State Register,* 2–8 February 1860, 13 February 1860 (quotation).

51. *Illinois State Register,* 13 February 1860.

52. Franklin William Scott, *Newspapers and Periodicals of Illinois, 1814–1879* (Chicago: R. R. Donnelley and Sons, 1910), 72, 324. Clarkson also edited and published the *Trestle Board,* a Masonic newspaper. The *Illinois State Register* noted that Clarkson was editor of "the Danite organ," a reference to a secret society of Mormons (8, 13 February 1860).

53. *Illinois State Register,* 8, 13 February 1860.

54. *(Springfield) Illinois State Journal,* 22 February 1860.

55. *Illinois State Journal,* 17 February 1860.

56. Judge's Docket, April term 1860, *People v. Clarkson, LPAL.*

57. *Illinois State Journal,* 4 May 1860.

58. Divorce Decree, April term 1860, *Clarkson v. Clarkson, LPAL.*

59. *Illinois State Register,* 11 February 1860.

60. *Illinois State Register,* 28–29 June 1861; *Illinois State Journal,* 29 June 1861, correctly reported Jacob Ernst's name. The *Register* continued to refer to him as Hoffman, apparently in some confusion with his stepdaughter's name.

61. Judge's Docket, June special term 1861, *People v. Ernst,* Sangamon County Circuit Court, Illinois Regional Archives Depository, University of Illinois at Springfield.

62. Affidavit for Continuance, 15 May 1855, *People v. Roberts, LPAL.*

63. Burlingame, *Inner World of Abraham Lincoln,* 136.

64. Thomas P. Lowry, *Don't Shoot That Boy: Abraham Lincoln and Military Justice* (Mason City, Iowa: Savas, 1999), 248.

65. Ibid., 245–48. Lowry identified six cases of rape that Lincoln reviewed.

66. Hurbert S. Feild and Leigh B. Bienen, *Jurors and Rape: A Study in Psychology and Law* (Lexington, Ky.: Lexington Books, 1980), 264. In 1905 the legislature again raised the age of responsibility for the male, to seventeen, and that of the female victim to sixteen, added language to specify "not his wife," and added a proviso that allowed marriage to the victim before trial to preclude conviction. In 1955 the legislature reduced the age of responsibility for males to fourteen, and in 1967 it increased the minimum penalty to four years in prison.

67. William Robert Greene, "Early Development of the Illinois State Penitentiary System," *Journal of the Illinois State Historical Society* 70 (August 1977): 187–91.

68. McEvoy and Bowron, *Alton General City Directory, and Business Mirror, for 1858* (Alton, Ill.: Courier Steam Printing, 1858), 6–8, 9 (quotation), 129. In addition to the flour mill, the Wise brothers owned the steamer *Columbus.* The two men also donated the land for the Saints Peter and Paul Catholic Church, built in Alton in 1855. See Charlotte Stetson, *Alton, Illinois: A Pictorial History* (St. Louis, Mo.: G. Bradley, 1987), 40, 45.

69. Sebastian Wise to William H. Bissell, 11 February 1859, *People v. Delny, LPAL.*

70. Illinois State Penitentiary, Convict Register No. 3, 319.

71. In 1811, while Illinois was still a territory, the governor obtained the power to grant reprieves and pardons. After Illinois was admitted as a state in 1818, and in subsequent state constitutions, the governor retained that power. See John H. Wigmore, *The Illinois Crime Survey* (Chicago: Blakely, 1929), 429.

Abraham Lincoln petitioned for the pardon of at least twenty men in Illinois between 1842 and 1860. Successive governors granted each a pardon. Lincoln had defended ten of these men in their criminal trials. See Harry E. Pratt, "Lincoln's Petitions for Pardon," *Illinois Bar Journal* 30 (February 1942): 235.

72. Illinois State Penitentiary, Convict Register No. 3 (May 1847–July 1855) and Registrar of Prisoners (May 1847–August 1858), Illinois State Archives; Wyman, *Immigrants in the Valley,* 44; John Clayton, *The Illinois Fact Book and Historical Almanac, 1673–1968* (Carbondale: Southern Illinois University Press, 1970), 38.

73. U.S. Census Office, Eighth Census of the United States (1860), Madison County, Illinois, ms., 153.

74. Lawrence M. Friedman, *Crime and Punishment in American History* (New York: Basic Books, 1993), 215–17, quotation on 217.

8

Her Day in Court: The Legal Odyssey of Clarissa Wren

DANIEL W. STOWELL

Antebellum Illinois law made liberal provisions for women to obtain divorces and sometimes alimony from husbands who had mistreated them. In the moral climate of antebellum America the law condemned women and men who committed adultery, although criminal prosecutions for adultery were generally on the wane. Adultery was one of the most widely accepted grounds for divorce in the United States. It was also one of the most successful. When men or women sued for divorce on the ground of adultery, they were more likely to obtain a divorce than on any other basis except desertion.[1]

When Aquilla Wren divorced his wife, Clarissa Wren, for her acts of adultery and her hostility to him, she persistently pursued an alimony payment from him despite significant cultural and legal obstacles. Even though Aquilla Wren died during the course of the proceedings, Clarissa Wren demanded her day in court and took her case all the way to the Illinois Supreme Court. There, a rising young lawyer named Abraham Lincoln argued her cause. The majority of justices in the state's highest court, wearing their paternalistic face, insisted that, though a jury had found Clarissa Wren guilty of adultery and of other offenses against her husband, she should have an opportunity to present her case for alimony or dower. Such a decision would hardly be expected from a patriarchal court intent on upholding male dominance of women.

Aquilla Wren (1797–1844) and Clarissa Jones (b. 1811) married in Jackson County, Ohio, in January 1826. In 1829 the Wrens, like many other Americans, journeyed westward for a new start. They settled in Springfield, Illinois, where Aquilla Wren opened a store. A year later Aquilla and Clarissa Wren moved seventy miles north to the small village of Peoria, where he opened another dry goods store, purchased land, and became one of the town's leading merchants. The state legislature had organized Peoria County in 1825 with Peoria as the county seat. By the early 1830s Peoria had only twenty-one log cabins and seven frame houses. The town did not incorporate until 1835. However, Peoria grew into an important port on the Illinois River during the next decade. In the mid-1840s more than forty riverboats made hundreds of arrivals annually in Peoria. By 1844 the town had 1,619 inhabitants.[2]

Aquilla Wren's fortunes grew with Peoria. In March 1832 he was elected as a county commissioner. In 1833 he sold several town lots to Isaac Underhill, a new settler who became a real estate dealer himself. By 1834 Wren owned and operated a steamboat ferry across the river to Tazewell County.[3]

In February 1835 the Illinois legislature passed a bill to incorporate the State Bank of Illinois and appointed twenty-four men, including Aquilla Wren, as commissioners of the State Bank. Two years later, in the midst of Democratic assaults on the State Bank of Illinois as unconstitutional, the young Whig state representative Abraham Lincoln defended the State Bank before the Illinois House of Representatives. Insisting that the commissioners could not be bribed, Lincoln read the name of each commissioner, including that of Aquilla Wren. "These are twenty-four of the most respectable men in the State," Lincoln insisted. "Probably no twenty-four men could be selected in the State, with whom the people are better acquainted, or in whose honor and integrity, they would more readily place confidence."[4]

In 1836 Aquilla Wren again served as a county commissioner. By the early 1840s Wren owned a store, a sawmill, and a ferry crossing the Illinois River at Peoria. In 1841 Wren was elected a trustee and city assessor for Peoria. He was also actively engaged in lending money.[5] Although Wren's business and reputation grew in the 1830s and early 1840s, his marriage faltered. The Wrens had no children, or at least none who survived into the 1840s. The couple was not alone, however; by the early 1840s Aquilla Wren's brother, Clarissa Wren's father, and some of her cousins lived nearby in Peoria County.

In 1843 Aquilla Wren engaged a talented team of lawyers, including Norman H. Purple, George T. Metcalfe, and Onslow Peters, to represent him in his divorce case against his wife.[6] Early in September 1843 Wren filed his bill for divorce with the clerk of the Peoria County Circuit Court, charging his wife with numerous counts of adultery. While the Wrens lived in Springfield in 1830, he insisted, she committed adultery with Willard Center, Lockwood Center, William Stanley, and Abraham Minier. Wren also declared that his wife "has been in habits of improper intimacy" and had committed adultery with Jacob Darst, a clerk in Aquilla Wren's store.[7] Specifically, Aquilla Wren charged that in the summer of 1838 or 1839, his wife had sent away her servant girl and spent the night alone with Darst; that in 1838 she had complained to several neighbors that her husband "would ruin Darst by taking him down the river" and that it was a pity as "he (Darst) was such a pretty nice young man"; that in the summer of 1838 Clarissa Wren and Jacob Darst were in her bedroom alone for some time; that they were again alone at Darst's brother's house "for some time" in the fall of 1842; and that his wife and Darst were frequently alone at the home of her father, Henry Jones, for a period of six weeks in the fall of 1842. Aquilla Wren also alleged that in the summer of 1841 Clarissa Wren "peeped through a key hole to see a young man undress and go to bed." On another occasion, Aquilla Wren claimed, she allegedly asked a neighbor where Johanns Adams "got his *skin* now his wife was dead."[8]

In addition to various acts of adultery and immorality, Aquilla Wren charged that his wife publicly expressed her desire to "ruin" him, refused to cook for him, and "concealed or destroyed various valuable deeds and other papers." He claimed that she told several people that she "could stand over him and see him draw his last breath with pleasure, and that she hoped the brother of said complainant, then sick, would die." Aquilla Wren's bill concluded that his wife's conduct had been "lewd, lascivious, immodest, unkind and cruel, that she has in various ways endeavored to injure and vex complainant in his domestic relations, in his feelings, in his business, property and reputation." In sum, she was "no longer worthy [of] the name of a wife in the confidence and affection of a husband."[9]

On September 4, 1843, the circuit clerk issued a summons directing the sheriff of Peoria County to bring Clarissa Wren before the court on the third Monday of October 1843. Clarissa Wren hired the Springfield law firm of Stephen Trigg Logan and Abraham Lincoln, as well as the local legal partnership of Elihu N. Powell and William F. Bryan, to represent her.[10] On the third day of the October session Clarissa Wren filed her answer to her husband's allegations. She denied that she had committed adultery with anyone in Springfield. While they lived there, "a malicious and unprincipled woman" had attempted to "propagate such a report." She also denied having any "improper intimacy" with Jacob Darst or any other person in Peoria County. Clarissa Wren further contradicted Aquilla Wren's charges by declaring that she never sent her servant girl away in order to be alone with Jacob Darst. At the girl's "earnest request" Clarissa Wren had allowed her to leave for one night. However, since Darst was Clarissa Wren's cousin and another hired man was present, she saw "no impropriety in it." She did not recall the comments about Darst that her neighbors attributed to her, but if she had said them, she could not "conceive it to be either ground of divorce or of scandalous imputation against her." She had stayed at her father's house in October 1842 for a few days, not to see Darst but because she was compelled to do so "by the barbarous and cruel conduct and morose temper" of Aquilla Wren. Darst was a boarder at her father's house, but "she could see no reason why this should prevent her seeking her natural asylum from the cruel and inhuman treatment of her husband."[11]

According to Clarissa Wren, her husband sent her a letter while she was at her father's house, entreating her to return to him. She enclosed a copy of the letter, dated October 30, 1842, as evidence to support her case:

> Dear Clarissa
>   I send you this letter by Sylvester. I was utterly astounded yesterday when I found you were gone perhaps forever I beseech you to come back before it is too late. . . . I still believe you have some *love* for me yet. I never knew more for you until now. O! if you had only told me your intention. . . . Let me now appeal to all your better feelings. I shall wait with open arms to receive you. For God sake don't let me appeal in vain I write this with tears in my eyes and a heart so full it is allmost ready to burst if you know my anguish of my soul you would come to me with the wings of the Eagle. Yes I no my Clarissa has not so far forgotten me as to be *Deaf* to my entreaties
>   Your loving husband
>   A Wren

Clarissa Wren found it "most strange and unaccountable that he should have evinced such anxiety to be reconciled to and receive back a woman who had been guilty of that adulterous[,] lewd[,] lascivious[,] and immodest course of life" that he now charged against her. She returned to her husband in the fall of 1842, and they lived together until August 1843, when she was again "compelled by the threats and violence" to leave him and return to her father's house. She accused him of striking her and of throwing a bucket of cold water on her while she was in bed one morning. After the latter incident she refused to cook for him any longer; before, she had "always endeavored faithfully to discharge her domestic duties." She denied all other charges that Aquilla Wren made against her, including trying to injure him, "tho she has had much provocation to do so."[12]

After Clarissa Wren filed her answer, both sides began to develop lists of witnesses and take depositions from witnesses that lived too far away to attend court. Aquilla Wren requested depositions from sixteen witnesses in Rock Island County, Sangamon County, and Tazewell County in Illinois and from Athens County in Ohio. He subpoenaed at least twenty-seven more witnesses from Peoria County. Clarissa Wren requested a deposition from one witness in Bureau County, Illinois, and subpoenaed at least fifty witnesses before and during the trial. In November and December 1843 Clarissa and

Aquilla Wren obtained the depositions of eight people in four different counties. Although women made up roughly one-quarter of the witnesses requested by each party and one-quarter of those who eventually testified, the form of their testimony reveals a significant gender pattern. Of the ten women who offered testimony in the case, only three appeared in court. The other seven women testified by deposition.[13]

Clarissa Wren deposed Margaret Hasler, a newly married German teenager who lived in Bureau County, north of Peoria. In the summer of 1843 Hasler had lived with the Wrens for two and a half weeks. During this time, she said, Aquilla Wren was "very cross towards his wife." In contrast, Clarissa Wren "was very kind to him all the time that I lived there." When asked how many times she heard Aquilla Wren swear at Clarissa Wren, she said she did not know how many times, but she did not remember ever hearing Clarissa Wren swear at Aquilla Wren or call him "hard names." Much of the deposition and cross-examination dealt with whether Hasler and Clarissa Wren or Aquilla Wren prepared breakfast for him and his laborers on the day that she left the Wrens' service.[14]

From Rock Island County, on the Iowa border, Aquilla Wren obtained the testimony of Lockwood J. Center, one of the men with whom Wren accused his wife of committing adultery. Center lived in the Wrens' neighborhood in Springfield from October 1829 to April 1830. He testified that Clarissa Wren's conduct "did not become a married or single Lady" and he "new her to be unfaithful and untrue to her companion." When asked whether she had "carnal connection with any other person than her husband," Center answered, "She had." When asked whether she committed adultery with any person during the time that he knew her, he answered, "She did."[15]

From Tazewell County, across the Illinois River from Peoria, Aquilla Wren obtained the depositions of Eunice A. Armstrong, Eliza A. McCoy, and Levina Colbert. Eunice Armstrong was the stepmother of the Wrens' hired man, Sylvester Armstrong. She and her husband rented their home from Aquilla Wren. She testified that Clarissa Wren made threats to ruin Aquilla Wren, wished him dead, and frequently called him "the Old Devil." She also declared that Clarissa Wren complained that her husband abused her, but Eunice Armstrong thought Aquilla Wren "treated his wife kindly so far as I saw." Aquilla Wren complained to her that "he had suffered more than a thousand deaths at this woman's hands." After Clarissa Wren refused to cook for him, Aquilla Wren ate his meals with the Armstrongs. A few days later Clarissa Wren encountered his dog when she came to the Armstrongs' house. She said to the dog, "Go away you scoundrel you have taken up your board here and I will have nothing to do with you." Under cross-examination Armstrong declared that as far as she knew, Clarissa Wren "always had everything in good order" in her home.[16]

Levina Colbert had known the Wrens for seven years and had lived with them for a few weeks after she first met them. She had "never seen any harm in Mr. Wren or either of them." Eliza A. McCoy had known the Wrens for more than a year. She had "never known any thing but kindness on the part of Mr. Wren." When asked whether the duties performed by Clarissa Wren while keeping house for her husband were very laborious, McCoy replied, "I never thought them laborious she did her own work like other woman. I never saw Mrs Wren milking but two or three times and then she was milking alone."[17]

In Sangamon County, Aquilla Wren obtained testimony from Willard R. Center, Elizabeth Stanley, and Leonora Neal. Willard R. Center knew the Wrens when they lived in Sangamon County in 1829 and 1830. When asked whether Clarissa Wren was guilty of any "immodest, unchaste, or lewd conduct," Center refused to answer the question "in that shape." When asked whether she had "carnal connexion with any person except her husband," Center answered, "I know that she had it" within the five or six months of his acquaintance with the Wrens. When asked "with whom had she such carnal connexion," Center replied, "I decline answering." His answer is unsurprising, given that he was one of the four men with whom Aquilla Wren accused his wife of having sexual relations while they lived in Springfield.[18]

Elizabeth Stanley had lived in the same house with the Wrens in Springfield in 1829 and 1830. She testified that Lockwood Center and Willard R. Center had each visited Clarissa Wren alone in her room when Aquilla Wren was out of town. At one point Clarissa Wren told Stanley that she "considered her self in a famieliway" (pregnant). Stanley also recalled a conversation in which Clarissa Wren told her that "she did not love her husband but loved the young man [Lockwood Center] better and if he would run off with her she would go with him." Clarissa Wren also confided to Stanley that when the Wrens had lived in Ohio, she had agreed to elope with a man named Joseph Will. Leonora Neal was the daughter of Elizabeth Stanley, and she substantiated her mother's allegations regarding Clarissa Wren and Lockwood Center. Clarissa Wren also told Neal that "she considered herself in a family way by Willard Center" and that they had agreed to run off together.[19]

By the spring of 1844 Aquilla Wren was "boarding" at the Planter's House, a hotel at the corner of Adams and Hamilton Streets, across from the county courthouse.[20] The March 1844 term of the Peoria County Circuit Court began on Monday, March 4, in the courthouse in Peoria. John Dean Caton, an associate justice of the Illinois Supreme Court and the judge for the Ninth

Judicial Circuit, presided at the trial.[21] On the third day of the term the court opened the depositions in the case of *Wren v. Wren*. On March 8 Clarissa Wren, through her attorneys, filed a petition with the court for alimony *pendente lite*, or a temporary allowance for support and for preparing her case.[22] On the following day she withdrew her petition for temporary alimony, and the court granted her motion to file an amended answer. In her amended answer, filed on March 9, Clarissa Wren charged that her husband "has disregarded his marriage vows by repeatedly committing adultery with divers persons unknown" to her. Specifically, she charged that during the winter of 1839–40 and in the winter of 1841, while "absent down the Mississippi," Aquilla Wren "grossly and shamefully committed *adultery* with divers *Black & Mulatto* women to your respondent unknown." She discovered his "adulterous conduct" only after she had filed her original answer in October 1843.[23]

Fearing that her denials would be insufficient, Clarissa Wren's attorneys filed this amended answer to divert attention from her adulterous and scandalous behavior. By accusing Aquilla Wren of committing adultery with African-American women, they attempted to tap northern racial animosity. They hoped that the all-male jury would be more enraged by a man who violated moral standards *and* racial taboos than by a woman who was alleged to have breached the standards of female moral behavior. Clarissa Wren's attempt to interject race into the case suggests that racial hostility might overcome the double standard of moral behavior for men and women, or so she and her attorneys believed.[24]

On Tuesday, March 12, Clarissa Wren filed a motion for a continuance, but Caton denied the motion. Two of her lawyers, Elihu Powell and William Bryan, then tried to have the court dismiss the depositions of Willard R. Center, Elizabeth Stanley, and Leonora Neal. Aquilla Wren and his attorney Norman H. Purple filed affidavits opposing the dismissal of the depositions, and Caton apparently refused to dismiss the depositions. On Wednesday, March 13, Aquilla Wren filed his replication to Clarissa Wren's amended answer. In this document Aquilla Wren declared that his wife's amended answer was "untrue and false, in the whole and in every part and portion thereof."[25]

The filing of Aquilla Wren's replication ended the pleading process, and the parties "joined the issue," or submitted it to the court for its decision. On Thursday, March 14, Caton ordered the sheriff to impanel a jury of "twelve good and lawful men" to try the case. After several jurors were excused or challenged, only nine jurors remained. Caton ordered the sheriff to "return without delay" three more jurors. The judge swore the jurors "well and truly to try the issue joined and a true verdict give according to evidence."[26] The jury then began to hear the testimony of thirty-six witnesses—fourteen for

Aquilla Wren and twenty-two for Clarissa Wren. When the day ended before the jury had heard all the evidence, Caton ordered the sheriff to sequester the jury until 8 A.M. on Friday.[27]

On Friday and Saturday, March 15 and 16, the jury heard the remainder of the evidence. Purple, Aquilla Wren's attorney, provided the court with five instructions to issue to the jury. According to these instructions, the jury was to determine whether Clarissa Wren had committed adultery, whether she was guilty of any of the other charges, whether Aquilla Wren had condoned or forgiven his wife for any acts of adultery, whether Aquilla Wren had committed adultery, and whether he was guilty of any of the other charges his wife had made against him. After hearing nearly three days of testimony, the jury left the courtroom to deliberate. When it returned, the jury reported to Caton that it found Clarissa Wren guilty of committing adultery with Lock-

The Peoria County Courthouse, ca. 1854 (it was built in 1835), where the county circuit court heard the Wren divorce case. Courtesy of the Illinois State Historical Library, Springfield.

wood Center and Willard Center in Springfield in 1830 and of "improper intimacy" with Jacob Darst "not amounting to adultery." It also found her guilty of "endeavoring to injure complainant in his business, property, and reputation" and of "using improper language" about Aquilla Wren. However, the jury determined that Aquilla Wren had condoned or pardoned Clarissa Wren's acts of adultery in Springfield, as evidenced by his letter to her in October 1842. The jury further found Aquilla Wren not guilty of adultery and the other charges against him.[28]

According to the 1827 Illinois statute on divorce, "If it shall appear to the satisfaction of the court that the injury complained of was . . . done with the assent of the complainants for the purpose of obtaining a divorce, or that the complainant was consenting thereto, or that both parties have been guilty of adultery, when adultery is the ground of complaint, then no divorce shall be decreed." Because the jury found that Aquilla Wren had forgiven Clarissa Wren's adulterous acts of 1829 and 1830, these actions alone were insufficient to decree a divorce. Furthermore, if the jury had found Aquilla Wren also guilty of adultery, the court would not have been able to grant a divorce, according to the statute. After the jury announced its verdict, Clarissa Wren filed a motion for a new trial.[29]

In the May 1844 term of the Peoria County Circuit Court, Clarissa Wren filed an affidavit insisting that the members of the jury in the March trial "were all, or nearly all, the well known personal friends" of Aquilla Wren. Furthermore, Smith Frye, the sheriff who selected the jury, was "pecuniarily interested in procuring a verdict" against her.[30] Frye had purchased from Aquilla Wren some land in which Clarissa Wren had dower rights, but those dower rights would end with a divorce. William S. Moss, one of the jurors, also had a "pecuniary interest" in a verdict against her.[31] Another juror, Samuel T. McKean, had "previously to his sitting on said jury, expressed an opinion against her." For these reasons Clarissa Wren wanted a new trial.[32]

To support her accusations Clarissa Wren presented four affidavits. George Ford testified that he had a conversation with McKean at Farrell's drug store in Peoria a few days before the trial. Ford said that he thought the charges against Clarissa Wren were false, and "McKean replied with some warmth, that he, McKean, believed the said charges to be true." Leonard Summers and Nathaniel S. Tucker also testified by affidavit that they heard McKean admit that he had discussed the charges with Aquilla Wren, and McKean expressed his belief that Clarissa Wren was guilty. Powell and Bryan, Clarissa Wren's attorneys, testified by affidavit that McKean had told them under examination "that he had formed and expressed no opinion as to the guilt or innocence of the defendant of the charges alleged against her."[33]

On June 4, 1844, attorneys for both sides presented arguments regarding a new trial. To counter Clarissa Wren's allegations of a prejudiced jury, Aquilla Wren presented four affidavits. Samuel T. McKean testified that although Aquilla Wren had talked to him about the charges, McKean had "formed no opinion in favor either of the plaintiff or the defendant or against either." Another juror, Samuel Dunn, had also been present at Farrell's drug store and participated in the conversation among McKean, Ford, and Summers. Dunn was "confident" that McKean expressed no opinion about whether the charges against Clarissa Wren were true.

Juror William S. Moss testified that although he had purchased land from Aquilla Wren, the idea that he had a "pecuniary interest" in the verdict "never occured to his mind." Even though others later suggested that he did, Moss still believed that he "has not now any such interest." Sheriff Smith Frye testified that he selected the jurors for the entire session of the court without reference to this specific case and without thinking "who were friends or enemies of either party." Although he too had purchased property from Aquilla Wren, he did not believe that he had any "pecuniary interest" in the verdict. Clarissa Wren's attorneys objected to the filing of these affidavits, but the court overruled their objection. Aquilla Wren's attorneys also cross-examined George Ford and Leonard Summers before the court. Under cross-examination both witnesses moderated their version of the conversation in Farrell's drug store. After hearing arguments from the attorneys for each party and considering the issue, the court denied Clarissa Wren's motion for a new trial and took additional time to consider its ruling on the original bill for divorce.[34]

On June 15 Aquilla Wren's lawyers introduced depositions from Ralph L. Jones and Charles S. Awl stating that Clarissa Wren and Jacob Darst had both lived at her father's house since the trial in March.[35] On Monday, June 17, 1844, the Peoria County Circuit Court finally ruled on Aquilla Wren's bill for divorce. Caton ordered that "the bonds of matrimony between the said Aquila Wren and Clarissa Wren be from henceforth dissolved and that the marriage contract heretofore entered into between the said parties be and the same is hereby set aside[,] annulled and held wholly for nought." The court postponed its ruling on Clarissa Wren's application for alimony until the next term of court. The judge also ordered the master in chancery to determine and report on Aquilla Wren's assets, his yearly income, and the "amount necessary for the support and maintenance" of Clarissa Wren. According to the Illinois Supreme Court's 1835 decision in *Reavis v. Reavis*, alimony was to be "a yearly allowance commensurate to the support" of the wife and children "in proportion to the ability of the husband and her condition in life"; thus the court's request of the master in chancery to investigate Aquilla Wren's assets.[36]

Before the next meeting of the circuit court the dispute between Aquilla Wren and Clarissa Wren took an unexpected turn. On August 14, 1844, Aquilla Wren died of fever at the age of forty-seven.[37] Two weeks before his death Wren made his last will and testament. He directed that his "just debts" should be paid first. Then he gave $200 each to the daughters of his sister, Sarah Bobo of Athens County, Ohio. Wren bequeathed the remainder of his estate to his brother, Thomas Wren. Aquilla Wren also appointed William S. Moss, "my friend" *and* a juror in the recently ended divorce case against Clarissa Wren, as his executor. According to probate records, Aquilla Wren at his death owned $1,220 worth of personal property; 320 acres of land and seven town lots in Peoria, Illinois; and at least $3,000 in promissory notes, debts, and court judgments owed to him. He also owed several debts, but his estate probably amounted to several thousand dollars.[38]

On October 16, 1844, Abraham Lincoln, representing Clarissa Wren, filed the affidavit of Sheriff Smith Frye, which informed the court of Aquilla Wren's death. Lincoln also filed a motion to abate, or end, the case because of Aquilla Wren's death. Shortly afterward Lincoln recognized that asking for an abatement of the case without also asking for an appeal left Clarissa Wren with no legal options. Lincoln withdrew the motion to abate and filed a bill of exceptions to the court's actions. Clarissa Wren listed six specific exceptions to the court's actions: Smith Frye, the sheriff who selected the jury, had an interest in the outcome of the case; William S. Moss, one of the jurors, had an interest in the outcome of the case; Samuel T. McKean, another juror, had formed and expressed an opinion against Clarissa Wren before the trial; "a large majority" of the jurors were "strong personal friends" of Aquilla Wren's; the verdict was "against the law and evidence"; and the verdict did not "conform to the charges in the bill."[39]

Clarissa Wren's sixth exception was particularly strong, because Illinois law in 1844 provided seven grounds for divorce: adultery, bigamy, impotence, desertion, fraud, repeated cruelty, and habitual drunkenness. Although the jurors had decided that Clarissa Wren had committed adultery in 1830, they also declared that Aquilla Wren had forgiven his wife of her acts of adultery. Her "improper intimacy" with Jacob Darst did not meet the jury's definition of adultery, and her other "improper" behavior could only loosely be described as cruelty. However, in 1833 the legislature gave chancery courts "full power and authority to hear and determine all causes for a divorce, not provided for by any law of this state." No longer did a spouse have to suffer one of the enumerated injuries; if the court were "satisfied of the expediency" of decreeing a divorce, it could do so. The Peoria County Circuit Court had acted under this broad delegation of authority, and Clarissa Wren objected to its decision.[40]

After Caton signed and sealed the bill of exceptions, Lincoln again filed Clarissa Wren's motion to abate the case. The court abated the case "in so far as said suit is pending in this court." On Clarissa Wren's own motion, then, the court ended the consideration of alimony because of Aquilla Wren's death. As attorneys commonly did, Lincoln wrote out this complicated series of actions in the form of a decree before the clerk entered it into the court record.[41]

In the December 1844 term of the Illinois Supreme Court, Abraham Lincoln filed for Clarissa Wren a transcript of the case from the Peoria County Circuit Court and an assignment of errors. Lincoln specified that the Peoria County Circuit Court erred in denying Clarissa Wren's motion for a new trial, in denying her motion to set aside the verdict of the jury, and in "rendering a decree of divorce upon the verdict of the jury." Clarissa Wren requested that the supreme court place the case on the docket and publish a notice to identify any unknown appellees. The Peoria partnership of Powell and Bryan and the Springfield partnership of Logan and Lincoln represented her before the supreme court. Norman H. Purple, Onslow Peters, George T. Metcalfe, and Halsey O. Merriman represented the appellees.[42] As Aquilla Wren's executor, William S. Moss became one of the appellees in the case, but Clarissa Wren also named Thomas Wren, Smith Frye, and two of Aquilla Wren's nieces as appellees. Clarissa Wren could not remember the name of the other daughter of her sister-in-law, Sarah Bobo. Thomas Wren and Aquilla Wren's nieces were appellees because they were among the beneficiaries of Aquilla Wren's will. Frye was an appellee because both he and Moss had purchased land from Aquilla Wren on which Clarissa Wren had never relinquished her right of dower, as the law required.[43]

On Christmas Eve 1844 attorneys for Clarissa Wren and for William Moss presented arguments for and against her motion for a writ of *scire facias* to summon Moss, Frye, and Thomas Wren before the supreme court and for an order of publication to notify Sarah Bobo's daughters in Ohio of the appeal to the supreme court involving their interests. Elihu Powell, supporting the motion, argued that the divorce decree and the death of Aquilla Wren left Clarissa Wren unable to recover dower in the estate. However, if she could not reopen the case by making the executor and heirs parties to it, she would "lose all claim of maintenance out of his estate." Norman H. Purple and Onslow Peters, opposing the motion, insisted that the issue in the lower court was one of divorce and did not survive the death of Aquilla Wren. Abraham

Lincoln concluded the oral arguments and supported the motion by argu-ing that "a question of property, the right of dower or alimony is involved." Because the divorce decree barred Clarissa Wren from obtaining her dower and the abatement of the suit cut off her access to alimony, the action should continue "on account of the nature of the interests involved."[44] However, the court "not being sufficiently advised took time to consider." When they re-turned two days later, the justices granted Clarissa Wren's motion for a writ of *scire facias* and ruled that she could publish a public notice to compel the daughters of Sarah Bobo to appear before the court in March 1845.[45]

Lincoln's decision to invoke property as the issue was a brilliant maneu-ver to change the focus of the appeal. Rather than debate whether Clarissa Wren had committed any indiscretion to justify a divorce, Lincoln shifted the ground to a question of property. For nineteenth-century courts few, if any, subjects were as important as property. Lincoln insisted that if the supreme court refused to hear her appeal, it would violate her property rights. Although antebellum Illinois courts freely granted a divorce to a petitioner whose spouse had committed adultery, they were also scrupulous in their defense of prop-erty rights. Lincoln's oral argument persuaded the majority of the justices that the case was not merely about the dissolution of a marriage. Property rights of dower and alimony were inextricably linked to Aquilla Wren's petition for a divorce. Although he was dead and the issue of divorce per se was moot, the divorce decree had property implications for Aquilla Wren's nieces, his brother, his creditors, his debtors, and for Clarissa Wren.

When the Illinois Supreme Court began its 1845 session that December, Norman Purple had replaced Jesse B. Thomas, Jr. on the court. Powell and Lincoln, representing Clarissa Wren, presented a motion asking the court to compel the appellees to "join the issue." On December 18 Powell and Lin-coln presented oral arguments to the court in support of the motion, and Merriman and Jesse B. Thomas Jr. opposed it. Powell argued that according to the Illinois statute governing dower, a wife divorced for her own fault or misconduct lost her dower rights.[46] If an appellate court reversed the divorce decree, then she would again have a right to dower. Therefore, the husband's heirs and purchasers of land should be made parties to the case. Thomas argued that a writ of error applied only to those who had an interest in the subject matter of the case, not to those who had an interest only in the con-sequences of the case. The decree by the lower court was a divorce, "which is personal to the parties, and that decree has been affirmed by a higher power— by the death of one of the parties to the decree." Thomas further argued that if the supreme court reversed the judgment, the lower court could not retry the case. "Greater injustice would result to the heirs of Wren by a reversal,"

Thomas concluded, "than by a refusal of this court to open the case." The justices of the supreme court, "not being sufficiently advised took time to consider."[47]

On Monday, December 22, Justice Walter B. Scates, writing for the 7-1 majority, presented the opinion of the court. Justice Norman H. Purple recused himself from this case because he had been an attorney for Aquilla Wren in the case before the circuit court and earlier before the supreme court. Scates wrote that "the general rule at law is that the writ of error does not lie against any but him who is party or privy to the first judgment, his heirs, executors or administrators . . . yet there are exceptions." In the 1824 case of *Carr v. Callingham* the judges of the Kentucky Court of Appeals had "intimate[d] strongly that they would so frame a writ of error in a chancery cause, as to bring all that might be affected by the reversal before them." Although it was "a novel practice introduced by statute" to allow a writ of error in a chancery case when doing so would in effect retry the whole case, "it is a practice long indulged." Aquilla Wren's death rendered the question of divorce moot, but it also prevented further proceedings on the question of alimony.

However, if the decree granting the divorce was erroneous and Clarissa Wren could not appeal the decision because of a lack of appellees, it would "unjustly deprive" her "of all right to dower." Moss, as the executor of Aquilla Wren's will, did have an interest in the outcome of the case because of the court costs involved that might be charged to the estate. Furthermore, Thomas Wren and Sarah Bobo's daughters had an interest in the case because they might lose one-third of their inheritance if Clarissa Wren received her dower from Aquilla Wren's estate. If they were not parties to the case, they could lose such property "without a hearing." Likewise, Moss and Frye, who had purchased land from Aquilla Wren on which Clarissa Wren had not released her dower interest, could also lose a portion of their property if the court reversed the divorce decree. The majority of the court concluded, then, that "we should frame such a writ of error brought on a decree in chancery as will secure the interests of all who may be affected by it, while it affords a remedy to the plaintiff."[48]

Justice Richard M. Young dissented, insisting that the issue in the Peoria County Circuit Court was "a matter purely *personal*," that of the divorce of Aquilla Wren and Clarissa Wren. The "sole question" to be litigated in the supreme court was "the correctness or otherwise of the decree granting the divorce," even though the rights of others might be affected by the court's decision. Should the court permit Clarissa Wren to reverse a decree of divorce from her husband after his death? "I think not," Young concluded.[49]

On December 29 Thomas, Metcalfe, and Merriman, the attorneys for Moss, Frye, and Thomas Wren, filed a petition for rehearing. The attorneys asked for a rehearing because they had been "unable to furnish the court with any authorities or decisions and were compelled in consequence to submit the decision of the question upon argument only." They declared that the question at issue had "never before been raised in this court." Because it was "of considerable importance in principle, as well as to the parties to the suit," they wanted to provide the court with authorities to support their position.[50]

The court apparently denied the appellees' petition for a rehearing, and the parties finally joined the issue in the Illinois Supreme Court more than eighteen months after the Peoria County Circuit Court had decreed a divorce between Aquilla Wren and Clarissa Wren. On Saturday, January 3, 1846, William Bryan opened the oral arguments for Clarissa Wren on the issue of whether the circuit court had made errors. Norman H. Purple again recused himself. On January 10 Thomas filed a motion for a continuance in the case until the next term and supported his motion with an affidavit by Purple. Purple informed the court that although he had the "utmost confidence" in the abilities of former justice Thomas, who had argued the case in the current term, Purple believed that "it is important to the rights of the parties in interest in this case" that George T. Metcalfe present the oral argument for the appellees. Purple affirmed that Metcalfe "is very familiar with the whole case," but Metcalfe was sick and unable to attend court. Lincoln and Bryan opposed the motion for a continuance. After considering the issue for two days, the court granted the continuance to the next term.[51]

During 1846 Clarissa Wren's attempt to reverse the divorce decree against her took more unexpected turns. On October 8 Moss resigned his position as executor of Aquilla Wren's estate. On the same day Thomas Wren, Aquilla Wren's brother, became the administrator *de bonis non* of Aquilla Wren's estate by swearing an oath that he would "well and truly administer" the estate. Three weeks later, on October 29, Clarissa Wren married Amaziah Hart in Peoria in a ceremony performed by the minister John P. Tinkerton. When the Illinois Supreme Court convened in Springfield on December 16, Merriman informed the court of these changes in the status of the parties to the case. Because of the doctrine of coverture, in which the wife's legal personality was subsumed into that of her husband, Amaziah Hart became a party to his new wife's case. Thomas Wren and Moss were already parties to the case, but their relationships to the case had changed. Finally, Merriman, on behalf of Moss, Frye, and Thomas Wren, confessed the errors that Clarissa Wren had assigned. By consent of the parties the supreme court ordered the divorce decree "reversed[,] annulled[,] set aside[,] and wholly for nothing esteemed." Thomas Wren agreed to pay the costs of the case out of the assets of Aquilla Wren's estate.[52] Two and a half years, almost to the day, after the Peoria County Circuit Court granted Aquilla Wren's petition for a divorce from his wife, the Illinois Supreme Court reversed that decree. By judicial action Clarissa Wren, once the divorced adulteress, became the widow of Aquilla Wren, with her dower rights intact.

Lincoln or his partners were involved in seventeen similar cases between 1839 and 1861 in which husbands sued their wives and charged them with adultery. In twelve cases (71 percent) the court or jury found the defendant guilty and granted the divorce. In two of these cases the woman received alimony or a single payment in lieu of alimony. The court dismissed four other cases, which sometimes implied a reconciliation. The judgment in the last case is unknown, but in no case did the court find for the alleged adulteress.[53]

Clarissa Hart's second husband, Amaziah Hart, died on October 7, 1847, and as his widow, she administered the settlement of his estate. On April 13, 1848, the minister Samuel Ladd performed the marriage of Clarissa Hart to her third husband, farmer Sanford H. White, across the Illinois River in Tazewell County.[54] In 1850 she and her husband lived in Peoria County near her extended family. Her husband owned $1,800 in real property, but unlike nearly all married women in antebellum America, Clarissa Jones Wren Hart White owned $1,500 of real property in her own name.[55]

Clarissa Wren's odyssey through the Illinois courts in the 1840s reveals much about the role and experience of women within the court system. Clarissa Wren was clearly at a legal disadvantage when her husband, a prominent Peoria businessman, accused her of adultery and sued her for divorce. In the moral climate of the nineteenth century adultery remained a serious moral offense for both men and women, though clearly more so for women. Aquilla Wren also accused his wife of another serious infraction of married women's duties: failing to perform her "domestic duties." He employed a prominent set of lawyers and subpoenaed numerous witnesses. The jurors may also have been biased against her because they allegedly were all friends of her husband. She might also have noted that they were all men, but within this historical context the observation would have been of no use to her.

However, neither Illinois law nor the legal system left Clarissa Wren without opportunities for redress. She too employed leading attorneys and called even more witnesses than did her husband. Even when found guilty of adultery, "improper intimacy," and of trying to ruin her husband, she still appealed for alimony and had some chance for success. When Aquilla Wren died, she prosecuted a writ of error to the Illinois Supreme Court and won a hearing. By transforming the issue in the case into one of property, her attorney Abraham Lincoln invoked the powerful rights of dower and alimony. The supreme court accepted Lincoln's reasoning and allowed the writ of error with those who had an economic interest in the case as parties. Failing to prevent the appeal, the other parties capitulated and the supreme court reversed the divorce decree and restored Clarissa Wren's dower rights.

. . .

The stories of Nancy Robinson Dorman, Jane Ann Rupert, and Clarissa Wren illustrate how Illinois courts responded to the individual plights of women and children. A child when her stepfather seized and sold her inheritance, Nancy Robinson Dorman later challenged him in court and won, not once but three times, before the Illinois Supreme Court. Jane Ann Rupert, a young orphaned victim of sexual assault, found the court ready to listen to her story and to protect her from future harm by convicting and sentencing her attacker to prison. Like other women and children in antebellum Illinois, Clarissa Wren had access to the courts to challenge her husband's allegations and to press her claims for alimony or dower. Ultimately, she recovered her dower rights through a reversal of the divorce decree.

What do these stories disclose about the status of women and children before the courts of antebellum Illinois and about their experiences before those courts? First, women and children had access to courts to plead their cases. Second, women and children could expect a hearing before these courts with a reasonable chance of success. Third, these courts viewed women and children as objects of paternal care rather than patriarchal dominance. What, for example, might Nancy Robinson Dorman or Clarissa Wren have expected from a truly patriarchal court? John Lane had served as Nancy Robinson's guardian for much of her life and had paid some of her father's debts. He might well have expected to be able to profit from and even sell some of the land she inherited, given his new responsibilities in caring for her. Clarissa Wren, divorced because of her own adulterous, hostile, and "improper" actions, could hardly have anticipated a sympathetic hearing from a court committed to maintaining male dominance of women. The trial following the rape of Jane Ann Rupert is less surprising and suggests some of the limits of paternalism in antebellum Illinois; only when the victim was so young as to preclude any doubt about her moral character did juries consistently find attackers guilty of rape.

The other essays in this volume likewise show that women and children generally had access to the courts and, in some areas of the law, even special provisions, such as temporary guardians for children in inheritance cases and the ability to sue without court costs for women seeking divorce. Illinois law and Illinois circuit courts allowed women to end marriages that endangered them or left them economically vulnerable. Women were also quite successful in formally terminating marriages that deserting husbands had already dissolved in fact. Inheritance procedures allowed heirs to challenge unfavorable wills and to ensure equitable distribution of estates. A widow's right to dower, while rarely equal to the property or contributions that she brought to the marriage, was an object of particular concern for courts. Some women, like Margaret Porter of Sangamon County, derived considerable economic benefit from pointing out procedural irregularities that threatened her dower rights. Furthermore, while widows often did not own substantial real property, they did manage their deceased husband's property for the benefit of their children.

These essays also shed considerable light on Abraham Lincoln's legal and social environment. Through his law practice he became a vital part of hundreds of these individual and family tales of squabbling siblings, struggling widows, and failed marriages. While anecdotal evidence suggests that he did not enjoy these family-turned-legal conflicts, he did gain a firm grasp of the concerns and interests of a broad spectrum of people, from farm laborers to state officers. He also relished the opportunity to be a peacemaker and arbiter in disputes that might be settled amicably. His own paternalistic attitudes toward women and children resonated with those of many of his fellow lawyers and the judges in whose courts he practiced.

Finally, these forays into the family law of antebellum Illinois illuminate a society in transition, from small frontier hamlets nearly self-sufficient to growing towns and cities increasingly connected by railroads and webs of credit to the entire nation. Legal change mirrored social change; the expanding grounds for divorce, the increasing attention to the "best interests of the child," and the passage of a married woman's property act are among the most obvious of such changes. Increasingly through the antebellum era, paternalistic Illinois legislators, lawyers, and judges gave "tender consideration" to the interests of women and children.

Notes

1. See table 3.2 in Stacy Pratt McDermott's essay "Dissolving the Bonds of Matrimony" in this volume.
2. Newton Bateman, Paul Selby, and David McCulloch, eds., *Historical Encyclopedia of Illinois and History of Peoria County,* 2 vols. (Chicago and Peoria: Munsell Publishing, 1902), 2:239, 243.
3. S. De Witt Drown, *The Peoria Directory for 1844* (Peoria, Ill.: Author, 1844), 28, 43; *Peoria (Ill.) Register and Northwestern Gazette,* 28 April 1838, 9 April 1840.

4. *Sangamo (Springfield, Ill.) Journal*, 28 February 1835, 28 January 1837. For Lincoln's support of the State Bank, see Gabor S. Boritt, *Lincoln and the Economics of the American Dream* (1978; rpt., Urbana: University of Illinois Press, 1994), 13–24.

5. Aquilla Wren probate file #913, Peoria County Probate Case Files, Illinois Regional Archives Depository, Western Illinois University, Macomb, Ill.; Drown, *Peoria Directory for 1844*, 28, 53; *Peoria Register and Northwestern Gazette*, 3 December 1841.

6. Norman H. Purple (1803–63) moved to Peoria in 1837 to practice law. In August 1845 Gov. Thomas Ford appointed him as a justice of the Illinois Supreme Court to replace the resigning Jesse B. Thomas Jr. Purple held the position until the reorganization of the court in 1848. After resigning from the supreme court, Purple returned to Peoria to practice law. See Bateman, Selby, and McCulloch, *Historical Encyclopedia*, 2:538–39; *United States Biographical Dictionary: Illinois Dictionary* (Chicago: American Biographical Dictionary, 1876), 674–75.

George T. Metcalfe was a rising Whig attorney in Peoria. By 1844 he was Norman H. Purple's junior partner in the firm of Purple and Metcalfe.

Onslow Peters (1805–56) was admitted to the bar in Massachusetts but came to Peoria in 1837 to practice law. He later became the judge of the Sixteenth Judicial Circuit. See *The Biographical Encyclopaedia of Illinois of the Nineteenth Century* (Philadelphia: Galaxy, 1875), 360; John M. Palmer, ed., *The Bench and Bar of Illinois: Historical and Reminiscent*, 2 vols. (Chicago: Lewis, 1899), 2:306.

7. Jacob Darst (1815–after 1890) was born in Ohio. He came to Peoria in June 1835 and worked as a clerk for Aquilla Wren in his general merchandise store. In 1836 Darst went to Galena, where he worked in the lead mines. In 1838 he returned to Peoria and began speculating in land. He also piloted boats down the Mississippi River for Aquilla Wren. Darst operated a coal mine and continued to speculate in land. See *The History of Peoria County, Illinois* (Chicago: Johnson, 1880), 639; *Portrait and Biographical Album of Peoria County, Illinois* (Chicago: Biographical, 1890), 364–65.

8. Bill of Complaint, October 1843, *Wren v. Moss et al.*, in *The Law Practice of Abraham Lincoln: Complete Documentary Edition*, ed. Martha L. Benner and Cullom Davis et al. (DVD; Urbana: University of Illinois Press, 2000), hereafter cited as *LPAL*.

9. Ibid.

10. Stephen Trigg Logan (1800–80) was admitted to the bar in Kentucky and settled in Springfield, Illinois, in 1832. In April 1841 Abraham Lincoln became Logan's junior law partner. Their partnership continued until December 1844, when Logan entered a partnership with his son David Logan, and William H. Herndon became Lincoln's junior partner. See Allen Johnson, ed., *Dictionary of American Biography*, 11 vols. (New York: Charles Scribner's Sons, 1964), 6:365–66; Usher F. Linder, *Reminiscences of the Early Bench and Bar of Illinois* (Chicago: Chicago Legal News, 1879), 155–59; Palmer, *Bench and Bar of Illinois*, 1:166–69.

Elihu N. Powell (1811–71) was a prominent member of the bar in Peoria County. He joined in partnership with William F. Bryan in 1839. Powell became judge of the Sixteenth Judicial Circuit in November 1856. See *Peoria Register and Northwestern Gazette*, September 14, 1839; Palmer, *Bench and Bar of Illinois*, 1:306–7.

William F. Bryan was born in Pennsylvania in 1810 and in 1839 settled in Peoria, where he became Elihu N. Powell's law partner. See Palmer, *Bench and Bar of Illinois*, 1:311–15.

11. Summons, 4 September 1843, *Wren v. Moss et al.*, *LPAL*; Answer, 18 October 1843, *Wren v. Moss et al.*, *LPAL*.

12. Answer, 18 October 1843, *Wren v. Moss et al., LPAL.*

13. Notices to Take Depositions and Subpoenas, November 1843–March 1844, *Wren v. Moss et al., LPAL.*

The Wrens requested depositions from or subpoenaed eighty-four different individuals as witnesses; both parties subpoenaed nine of these people. Twenty-one (25 percent) of all those subpoenaed or deposed were women. There was no significant gender difference among the witnesses that each party requested to testify or among those witnesses that actually did testify. Of the forty-three witnesses that Aquilla Wren requested, ten (23 percent) were women. Of the fifty witnesses that Clarissa Wren requested, twelve (24 percent) were women. Only one woman (7 percent) was among those who actually testified in court for Aquilla Wren. Only two women (9 percent) appeared to testify for Clarissa Wren.

A more stark gender pattern did emerge among the deponents, however. Of the nine depositions filed in the case (Aquilla Wren obtained another deposition in March 1844), seven (78 percent) were by women. The two men who testified by deposition, Lockwood J. Center and Willard R. Center, had a specific reason for wanting to stay out of court: Aquilla Wren had accused his wife of committing adultery with each of them. Therefore, the jury ultimately received testimony from forty-four witnesses, of whom ten (23 percent) were women. Yet only three of those women appeared in court; the rest (70 percent) testified by deposition.

Other evidence supports the suggestion that a gender difference existed in the form of testimony. For example, Eliza A. McCoy from Tazewell County testified by deposition, but her husband, John A. McCoy, appeared in person to testify. Eunice A. Armstrong, also from Tazewell County, testified by deposition, but her stepson Sylvester Armstrong appeared in court.

14. Deposition, 19 December 1843, *Wren v. Moss et al., LPAL.*

15. Deposition, 18 November 1843, *Wren v. Moss et al., LPAL.* The clerk of the Rock Island County Circuit Court also asked Lockwood J. Center whether Clarissa Wren had admitted to him that she had committed adultery, "and if so with whom?" Center answered that he "did not recollect" hearing her say that she was guilty of committing adultery. The earlier questions did not require him to state with whom she had "carnal relations" or committed adultery. Because Center was alleged to have been one of the men with whom she had committed adultery, it is unsurprising that he "recollected" no admission on her part.

16. Deposition, 6 December 1843, *Wren v. Moss et al., LPAL.*

17. Ibid.

18. Deposition, 12 December 1843, *Wren v. Moss et al., LPAL.*

19. Ibid.

20. Drown, *Peoria Directory for 1844*, 110; Jerry Klein, *Peoria!* (Peoria, Ill.: Visual Communications, 1985), 176.

21. John Dean Caton (1812–95) moved to Chicago in 1833 and was admitted to the bar in 1835. In August 1842 Gov. Thomas Carlin appointed Caton to the Illinois Supreme Court. Seven months later Caton failed to win reelection, but Gov. Thomas Ford reappointed him to the court two months later. With the reorganization of the court in 1849 Caton remained on the bench and resigned in 1864. See Palmer, *Bench and Bar of Illinois*, 1:39–41.

22. Alimony *pendente lite* was a form of alimony specific to divorce cases. Most courts

routinely granted it, because married women, whether plaintiff or defendant, rarely had other means of support.

23. Decree, 6 March 1844, *Wren v. Moss et al., LPAL;* Decree, 7 March 1844, *Wren v. Moss et al., LPAL;* Circuit Court Transcript, 13 November 1844, *Wren v. Moss et al., LPAL.*

24. For the racial attitudes of antebellum northerners see Leon F. Litwack, *North of Slavery: The Negro in the Free States, 1790–1860* (Chicago: University of Chicago Press, 1961), 64–112; Charles N. Zucker, "The Free Negro Question: Race Relations in Antebellum Illinois, 1801–1860" (Ph.D. diss., Northwestern University, 1972); James Oliver Horton and Lois Horton, *In Hope of Liberty: Culture, Community, and Protest among Northern Free Blacks, 1700–1860* (New York: Oxford University Press, 1997). For attitudes toward "race-mixing" see Joanne Pope Melish, *Disowning Slavery: Gradual Emancipation and "Race" in New England, 1780–1860* (Ithaca, N.Y.: Cornell University Press, 1998), 122–26.

An 1829 Illinois law made interracial marriage a criminal offense: "No person of color, negro, or mulatto, of either sex, shall be joined in marriage with any white person, male or female, in this state, and all marriages or contracts entered into between such colored person and white person, shall be null and void in law; and any person so offending shall be liable to pay a fine, whipped in not exceeding thirty-nine lashes, and be imprisoned not less than one year; and every person so offending shall be held to answer in no other than a criminal prosecution, by information or indictment" ("An Act Respecting Free Negroes and Mulattoes, Servants, and Slaves," 17 January 1829, *Revised Code of Laws of Illinois* [1829], 111).

25. Decree, 9 March 1844, *Wren v. Moss et al., LPAL;* Decree, 12 March 1844, *Wren v. Moss et al., LPAL;* Motion, 13 March 1844, *Wren v. Moss et al., LPAL;* Affidavits, 13 March 1844, *Wren v. Moss et al., LPAL.*

26. Decree, 14 March 1844, *Wren v. Moss et al., LPAL.* The jurors were Samuel T. Mc-Kean, John Coyle, Thomas Frye, Samuel Dunn, Benjamin Miller, William S. Moss, John Harris, Bayles Campbell, James K. Gove, Gaius Jenkins, John McFarland, and George Hart.

The four jurors identifiable in the 1850 federal census—Coyle, Frye, Miller, and Gove—were all farmers. Their average age in 1844 was thirty-seven. An additional juror, Moss, identifiable in an 1844 Peoria city directory, was also a farmer and businessman and was forty-six years old. See U.S. Census Office, Seventh Census of the United States (1850), Peoria County, Illinois, ms.; Drown, *Peoria Directory for 1844,* 86.

27. Decree, 14 March 1844, *Wren v. Moss et al., LPAL.*

Witnesses for Aquilla Wren included R. L. Armstrong, Sylvester Armstrong, Anson Darst, Jacob Lineback, John Schock, James Green, Orson Rice, Charles S. Awl, George Divelbiss, James Murden, S. Stephen Guyer, Lydia Ann Darst, Hiram H. Degear, and Benjamin R. Beal. See Fee Bill, 23 May 1845, *Wren v. Moss et al., LPAL.*

28. Decree, 16 March 1844, *Wren v. Moss et al., LPAL.*

29. The term *condonation* in the canon law described the forgiveness by a person of his or her spouse for acts of adultery, with an implied condition that the injury would not be repeated. Cohabitation or "matrimonial intercourse" after learning of such infidelity was evidence of condonation, and condonation was a bar to a decree of divorce. The Illinois law of 1827 adopted this restriction on the granting of divorces. See John Bouvier, *A Law Dictionary Adapted to the Constitution and Laws of the United States of America,* 7th ed., 2 vols. (Philadelphia: Childs and Peterson, 1857), 1:264–65; "An Act Concerning Divorces," 31 January 1827, *Revised Code of Laws of Illinois* (1827), 181–83.

30. Affadavit, 27 May 1844, *Wren v. Moss et al., LPAL.* Smith Frye (1806–60) came to Peo-

ria in 1834 from Pennsylvania. He was a Democratic candidate for sheriff as early as 1840 and was elected sheriff of Peoria County in 1842. He served at least until 1845. He also speculated in land. In 1859 he was appointed as the U.S. marshal for the Northern District of Illinois. See *Peoria (Ill.) Democratic Press,* 5 March 1840; *Peoria Register and Northwestern Gazette,* 12 August 1842; *Peoria (Ill.) Daily Transcript,* 23 September 1859; Aaron Wilson Oakford, comp., "The Peoria Story: A Picture Story from Mid-America about the Lives and Family Ties of Folks in Peoria, Illinois" (1949–57), Virginius H. Chase Special Collections Center, Cullom-Davis Library, Bradley University, Peoria, Ill.

31. Affidavit, 27 May 1844, *Wren v. Moss et al., LPAL.* William S. Moss (1798–1883) was a prominent businessman and land speculator in Peoria and later in California. See Olive Davis, *From the Ohio to the San Joaquin: A Biography of William Moss, 1798–1883* (Stockton, Calif.: Heritage West Books, 1991), 64–109.

32. Affidavit, 27 May 1844, *Wren v. Moss et al., LPAL.*

33. Affidavits, 27 May 1844, *Wren v. Moss et al., LPAL;* Affidavit, 28 May 1844, *Wren v. Moss et al., LPAL.*

34. Circuit Court Transcript, 13 November 1844, *Wren v. Moss et al., LPAL;* Decree, 4 June 1844, *Wren v. Moss et al., LPAL.*

35. Affidavit, 15 June 1844, *Wren v. Moss et al., LPAL.*

36. Decree, 17 June 1844, *Wren v. Moss et al., LPAL; Reavis v. Reavis,* 2 Ill. 247 (1835). The master in chancery was an officer of the court who acted as an assistant to the judge. The master in chancery conducted investigations as in this case, took testimony, estimated damages, or sold property to execute judgments.

37. *Peoria Democratic Press,* 21 August 1844.

38. Will, Inventory of Notes Belonging to the Estate of Aquilla Wren, Inventory and Appraisement of the Personal Estate of Aquilla Wren, Inventory of the Real Estate of . . . Aquilla Wren, Aquilla Wren probate file.

39. Clarissa Wren's fourth exception had some validity because Aquilla Wren was a well-known businessman and civic leader. Juror John Coyle had served as a county commissioner with Wren in 1832. Juror Samuel T. McKean had served as a county commissioner with Wren in 1836. Aquilla Wren named juror William S. Moss as the executor of his will. See Drown, *Peoria Directory for 1844,* 28; Will, Aquilla Wren probate file. Lincoln's bill of exceptions appears in Circuit Court Transcript, 13 November 1844, *Wren v. Moss et al., LPAL.*

40. "An Act Respecting Divorce," 22 February 1819, *Laws of the State of Illinois* (1819), 35–37; "An Act Concerning Divorces," 31 January 1827, *Revised Code of Laws of Illinois* (1827), 181–83; "An Act Amending the Law Concerning Divorces," 4 December 1833, *Revised Laws of Illinois* (1833), 234–35.

41. Decrees, 16 October 1844, *Wren v. Moss et al., LPAL;* Bill of Exceptions, 16 October 1844, *Wren v. Moss et al., LPAL.*

42. Halsey O. Merriman (1815–54) was an attorney from Peoria County. From 1840 to 1844 he had been Norman H. Purple's partner. See *Peoria Register and Northwestern Gazette,* 9 April 1840; *Peoria Democratic Press,* 28 February 1844; *Peoria (Ill.) Weekly Republican,* 31 March 1854.

43. Order, 20 December 1844, *Wren v. Moss et al., LPAL;* Assignment of Errors, 20 December 1844, *Wren v. Moss et al., LPAL;* Motion, 20 December 1844, *Wren v. Moss et al., LPAL;* Affidavit, 20 December 1844, *Wren v. Moss et al., LPAL.*

44. *Wren v. Moss et al.,* 6 Ill. 560 (1844). For American attitudes toward property see

generally James W. Ely, Jr., *The Guardian of Every Other Right: A Constitutional History of Property Rights* (New York: Oxford University Press, 1992), 59–81; William B. Scott, *In Pursuit of Happiness: American Conceptions of Property from the Seventeenth to the Twentieth Century* (Bloomington: Indiana University Press, 1977).

45. Order, 24 December 1844, *Wren v. Moss et al., LPAL;* Order, 26 December 1844, *Wren v. Moss et al., LPAL.*

46. Jesse B. Thomas Jr. (1806–50) was admitted to the bar in Springfield in the late 1820s. In 1835 he was appointed as the attorney general for the State of Illinois. He became a justice of the Illinois Supreme Court in 1843 and served until he resigned in August 1845. He was reappointed to the court in January 1847 and served until the reorganization of the court in December 1848. He later moved to Chicago and practiced law there. See Palmer, *Bench and Bar of Illinois,* 1:44, 177; 2:1094; Frederic B. Crossley, *Courts and Lawyers of Illinois,* 3 vols. (Chicago: American Historical Society, 1916), 1:338.

According to an 1827 law, if a court decreed a divorce for the fault or misconduct of the wife, "she shall forfeit her dower." Furthermore, "if a wife voluntarily leave her husband and commit adultery, she shall be forever barred her dower, unless her husband be voluntarily reconciled to her, and suffer her to dwell with him" ("An Act for the Speedy Assignment of Dower, and Partition of Real Estate," 6 February 1827, *Revised Code of Laws of Illinois* [1827], 185).

47. Order, 18 December 1845, *Wren v. Moss et al., LPAL; Wren v. Moss et al.,* 7 Ill. 72 (1845).

48. *Wren v. Moss et al.,* 7 Ill. 72 (1845); *Carr v. Callingham,* 3 Litt. 377 (1824). Illinois justices William Wilson, Thomas C. Browne, Samuel D. Lockwood, Samuel H. Treat, John D. Caton, and Gustavus P. Koerner joined Walter B. Scates in the majority opinion. Richard M. Young dissented, and Norman H. Purple recused himself.

49. *Wren v. Moss et al.,* 7 Ill. 72 (1845).

50. Order, 29 December 1845, *Wren v. Moss et al., LPAL;* Petition for Rehearing, December term 1845, *Wren v. Moss et al., LPAL.*

51. Order, 10 January 1846, *Wren v. Moss et al., LPAL;* Affidavit, 10 January 1846, *Wren v. Moss et al., LPAL;* Order, 12 January 1846, *Wren v. Moss et al., LPAL.*

52. Peoria County Marriage Records, Peoria County Clerk's Office, Peoria, Ill.; *Marriage Licenses Issued in Peoria County, 1825–1860* (Peoria, Ill.: Peoria County Historical Society, n.d.); Orders, 16 December 1846, *Wren v. Moss et al., LPAL;* Aquilla Wren probate file. In October 1851 Wren's estate remained only partially settled. John T. Lindsay, the third administrator of the estate, petitioned the probate court to allow him to sell the remaining real property in the estate and distribute the proceeds among the estate's creditors.

53. In *Myers v. Myers* (1860–61) the defendant committed suicide after her husband refused to reconcile. The two cases in which the wife received alimony were *Brown v. Brown* (1841) ("upon the voluntary offer of the complainant," $500 in real estate in lieu of alimony) and *Rogers v. Rogers* (1838–39) ($126 and semiannual payments of $39). See *Myers v. Myers, Brown v. Brown,* and *Rogers v. Rogers, LPAL.*

54. Amaziah Hart probate file, #766, Peoria County Probate Case Files, Illinois Regional Archives Depository, Western Illinois University, Macomb, Ill.; Tazewell County Marriage Records, p. 147, Tazewell County Circuit Court, Pekin, Ill.; David C. Perkins, comp., *Tazewell County Illinois Marriage Records Index, 1827–October 1859* (Pekin, Ill.: Tazewell County Genealogical Society, 1982), 53. Clarissa Hart became the administratrix of Amaziah Hart's estate on October 23, 1847. When she remarried in the spring of 1848, her husband, Sanford H. White, became a coadministrator of Hart's estate.

55. Census Office, Seventh Census (1850), Peoria County. Most of this property was probably her dower from Aquilla Wren's estate, because Sanford and Clarissa White sold Amaziah Hart's real property on July 28, 1849, to pay the debts of his estate. Clarissa White received at least $822.55 from Amaziah Hart's estate, but most of it was personal property in the form of livestock ($245), provisions ($200), or household items ($118.50). She received $106.30 in cash but no real property. See *White & White, administrators of Hart v. Hart et al.,* May term 1849, Peoria County Circuit Court, Peoria, Ill.; Amaziah Hart probate file.

Contributors

MICHAEL GROSSBERG has a doctoral degree from Brandeis University and is a professor of history at Indiana University. He is the editor of the *American Historical Review* and the author of several books, including *Governing the Hearth: Law and Family in Nineteenth-Century America* (1985) and *A Judgment for Solomon: The D'Hauteville Case and Legal Experience in Antebellum America* (1996).

SUSAN KRAUSE has a master's degree in public history from the University of Illinois at Springfield and is an assistant editor with the Lincoln Legal Papers. She is the author of "Lincoln and Speed—Attorney and Client" in the *Illinois Historical Journal* (Spring 1996).

JOHN A. LUPTON has a master's degree in history from the University of Illinois at Springfield and is the assistant director of and an assistant editor with the Lincoln Legal Papers. He is the author of "'In View of the Uncertainty of Life': A Coles County Lynching" in the *Illinois Historical Journal* (Winter 1996) and "Basement Barrister: Abraham Lincoln's Practice before the United States Supreme Court" in the *Lincoln Herald* (Summer 1999), as well as other articles.

STACY PRATT MCDERMOTT has a master's degree in history from the University of Illinois at Springfield and is a doctoral student at the University of Illinois at Urbana-Champaign. She is an assistant editor with the Lincoln Legal Papers and the author of "A Lynching, a Woman, and a Movement: Ida B. Wells and the Anti-Lynching Struggle in Illinois" in the *Journal of Negro History* (Winter 1999).

CHRISTOPHER A. SCHNELL has a master's degree in American history from the University of Illinois at Springfield and is an assistant editor with the Lincoln Legal Papers. He has presented papers at various meetings on such topics as antebellum legal history, Lincoln's legal career, and research methods.

DANIEL W. STOWELL has a doctoral degree in American history from the University of Florida and is the director and editor of the Lincoln Legal Papers. He is the author or editor of three books, including *Rebuilding Zion: The Religious Reconstruction of the South, 1863–1877* (1998) and *Balancing Evils Judiciously: The Proslavery Writings of Zephaniah Kingsley* (2000), as well as several articles on southern history and American religious history.

DENNIS E. SUTTLES has a master's degree in history from the University of Illinois at Springfield and a master's degree in library and information science from the University of Illinois at Urbana-Champaign. He is an assistant editor with the Lincoln Legal Papers and the author of "Schism on the Prairie: The Case of the Free Portuguese Church of Jacksonville, Illinois" in the *Journal of Presbyterian History* (Winter 1997).

Index of Cases

General Index

Adams, James, 110
Adams, Johanns, 206
adultery, 22–25, 28–30, 59–61, 71, 77, 78, 80,
    82–86, 89–90, 190, 193, 204–6, 208–12,
    214, 216, 219–20, 223n.15
African Americans, 28–29, 41n.21, 152, 210
alcohol, 24, 27–28, 45n.63, 87–88, 113, 187–
    89. *See also* prohibition; temperance
Alexander, Augustus, 62
Alexander, Hiram, 26
Alexander, John, 62
Alexander, Mary, 62
alimony, 9, 56, 59–60, 78, 80–81, 85, 89–90,
    95–96, 204, 210, 213, 216–17, 219–20,
    223n.22
Ames, David, 51
Ames, Sophia Fields, 51
Anderson, Elias, 31
Anno, John, 109
Anno, Pollard, 109
Anno, Samuel, 109
Armstrong, Eunice A., 208, 223n.13
Armstrong, Sylvester, 208, 223n.13
Arnold, Charles, 32, 117
assault, 23–24, 36
Ater, Deborah, 36
Ater, Jacob, 36, 45n.63
Awl, Charles S., 213

Babbitt, Catharine, 24, 25
Baker, David J., 56
Baker, Elizabeth. *See* Pike, Elizabeth
Bardaglio, Peter W., 13n.11, 183, 190
Barnes, John, 115
Bartelme, Mary, 19
Basch, Norma, 3, 6, 75, 93, 128n.78
bastardy, 30–32, 42n.30, 190
Batterton, David, 110
Batterton, Nancy, 110
Beard, Mary, 22

Beck, Maria Barbara, 151
Beerup, Caroline, 17, 19, 23
Beerup, Stephen, 17, 23
Bell, Benjamin, 108
Bell, David, 108
Bell, Elizabeth, 108, 126n.26
Bell, James, 106–10
Bell, Jane, 106–10
Bennett, Ann, 110
Bennett, John, 110
Bennett, Maria, 59–60
Bennett, Richard, 110
Bennett, Richard E., 59–61
Berry, Elizabeth, 24
"best-interests-of-the-child" doctrine, 8,
    54, 56–57, 62, 65, 67nn.40, 52, 122, 221
Bevans, John, 113
Bevans, Margaret, 113
bigamy, 22, 77, 82–83, 89, 95, 120–22
Birchall, Caleb, 107
Birkby, Ann, 79
Birkby, John, 79
Bissell, William H., 196
Blackstone, William, 18, 28, 38n.1, 185, 198
Blakely, Phebe, 42n.31
Bloom, Henry, 186
Bobo, Sarah, 214–17
Bodenhamer, David J., 4–5
Braken, Sarah, 151
Brewer, John, 23
Brewer, Nancy, 23
Broeckel, Elizabeth, 25, 26
Broeckel, John, 25
Brooks, Albert I., 50
Brown, James, 89
Brown, John, 163–65, 167, 173, 178nn.9, 19
Brown, Maria, 89
Brundage, W. Fitzhugh, 189
Bryan, William F., 206, 210, 212, 215, 218,
    222n.10

Lincoln, Abraham, 6–8, 29–31, 38n.1, 51, 63,
83, 110, 113–15, 135–36, 172, 176, 193–95,
198, 202n.71, 204, 214–16, 218, 220–21;
attitudes toward children, 20, 190, 221;
attitudes toward women, 20, 94–96, 136–
37, 221; and law partners, 1, 27, 32, 33–34,
85, 94, 102n.95, 107, 115, 117, 142, 181n.56,
206, 215, 222n.10; law practice of, 1–2,
20–21, 48, 65, 94–95, 105, 119, 136, 169–70,
182, 190–91, 194, 219, 221; political career
of, 1, 169–70, 205
Lincoln, Mary (neé Todd), 20, 96
Lincoln, Sarah Johnston (neé Bush), 138–39
Lincoln, Thomas, 138
Lincoln Legal Papers, 1–2, 66n.14
Lindemann, Barbara S., 183
Linder, Usher, 37
Lindsay, John T., 226n.52
Locke, John, 46
Logan, David, 222n.10
Logan, Stephen T., 1, 85, 94, 107, 114, 117, 172,
181n.56, 206, 215, 222n.10
Logan County Circuit Court, 34, 62
Lucas, Caleb, 35
Lucas, John, 34, 110
Lucas, John A., 34
Lucas, Sarah. *See* Mann, Sarah Lucas
Lucas, Thomas K., 34, 44n.57

Macoupin County Circuit Court, 78–79
Mahlon Williams and Company, 109
Mann, Michael, 34
Mann, Sarah Lucas, 17, 34, 110
Manniere, George, 52
Margrave, Thomas, 31
Marietta, Jack D., 188
Mark, David, 184
Marquis, Abraham, 115
Marquis, Parmilla, 115
marriage, 20, 74, 83–84, 92–93, 120–21, 130,
134, 139; as a contract, 17, 22, 30–31,
43n.43, 63, 91; interracial, 29, 224n.24
Married Women's Property Act, 33, 130, 135,
153–54, 155n.20, 175, 221
Marshall, Samuel D., 10, 169–70, 172, 175–
76, 180n.44
Mason County Circuit Court, 28, 35
Matheny, James H., 108
Mathews, Elizabeth, 147–48
Matthews, Margaret, 87
Matthews, Robert, 87
Maus, Joseph S., 183–84
McCann, Jane, 151

McClernand, John A., 165, 179n.40
McConnell, Murray, 29
McCook, L. A., 184, 186
McCoy, Eliza A., 208–9, 223n.13
McCoy, John A., 223n.13
McDaniel, James, 111, 113–14
McDaniel, Joseph, 111, 113–14
McDaniel, Luanna. *See* Sparks, Luanna
McDaniel, Margaret, 111, 113–14
McDaniel, Martha. *See* McIntyre, Martha
McDaniel, Mary Ann. *See* Herrin, Mary Ann
McDaniel, Robert, 111
McDaniel, Rufus, 111
McDaniel, Sally. *See* Correll, Sally (Sarah)
McDaniel, William, 104, 111, 113–16, 118–19
McElvain, Jane. *See* Fletcher, Jane
McGarr, Catherine. *See* Glynn, Catherine
McHenry, Henry, 24–25
McIntyre, Aaron, 113
McIntyre, Martha (neé McDaniel), 104, 111,
113–16
McKean, Samuel T., 212–14, 225n.39
McNutt, Sarah, 141
Means, Joseph, 137
Menard County Circuit Court, 49, 60–61
Merriman, Halsey O., 215–16, 218
Metcalfe, George T., 205, 215, 218, 222n.6
Midwest. *See* law: regional variations in
Miner, Charlotte H., 56–59
Miner, Laura L., 56–59, 67n.52
Miner, Martin B., 56–59
Minier, Abraham, 205
Mischler, Catherine, 147
Moffett, Thomas, 106, 109, 118–19
Monroe, James, 150
Moor, Matilda, 137
Moore, Maria L. *See* Dutch, Maria L.
Morgan, Elizabeth, 147
Morgan County Circuit Court, 78
mortgages, 33, 43n.51
Moss, William S., 212–15, 217–18, 225nn.31, 39
Murphy, John, 37
Murphy, Lucy Eldersveld, 5
Murphy, Margaret, 32
Murray, Margaret Glynn, 120–21
Murray, Matthew, 120
Mycenhammer, Sally (neé Hinkle), 118–20

Neal, Leonora, 209–10
Neale, Harriet B., 137

orphans, 62
Overstreet, Jane, 42n.31

The University of Illinois Press
is a founding member of the
Association of American University Presses.

Composed in 10.5/13 Minion
with Minion display
by Jim Proefrock
at the University of Illinois Press
Designed by Paula Newcomb
Manufactured by Thomson-Shore, Inc.

University of Illinois Press
1325 South Oak Street
Champaign, IL 61820-6903
www.press.uillinois.edu